therapy, communication, and change

Human Communication
Volume 2

Edited by Don D. Jackson

SCIENCE AND BEHAVIOR BOOKS, INC.

Palo Alto, California

THERAPY, COMMUNICATION, AND CHANGE

Human Communication, Volume II

Fourth Printing, September 1973

Library of Congress card catalog number: 68-21577
ISBN 0-8314-0016-1

FOREWORD TO THE MRI VOLUMES

On a bleak January day in 1954, I gave the Frieda Fromm-Reichmann lecture at the Palo Alto Veterans Administration Hospital. In the audience was Gregory Bateson, and he approached me after the lecture. My topic was the question of family homeostasis, and Bateson felt the subject matter related to interests that he shared on a project with Jay Haley, John Weakland, and William Fry.

From that moment on, I became more closely related to the social sciences than to medical psychiatry, I have never regretted this decision.

Once the research bug bit, I felt for the first time the pressing need in the San Francisco Bay Area of a behavioral science research foundation. In November, 1958, with the help of some influential friends, the Mental Research Institute was born. Our first grant started in March, 1959, and the staff then consisted of myself, Jules Riskin, M.D., Virginia Satir, A.C.S.W., and an inexperienced, frightened secretary. The Bateson project maintained its autonomy, but we had a close working relationship. The MRI operated under the umbrella of the Palo Alto Medical Research Foundation (thanks to Dr. Marcus Krupp) and continued to grow until it split off as an autonomous research foundation with its own administrative staff and board of Directors.

The Bateson project was never formally under the MRI label, even though Jay Haley and John Weakland subsequently became fulltime principal investigators at the MRI. Gregory Bateson became a research associate and participated in teaching, as well as in generously acknowledging requests for his time from puzzled investigators.

Thus, in the first two volumes of the MRI papers, there is a mixture of pre-MRI papers, early MRI papers, papers from the Bateson project, and papers of Haley and Weakland after they were formally MRI research associates.

About the papers themselves, it is necessary to give a brief note about orientation context and selection. We did not select all the papers of all principal investigators, since some obviously had been hastily prepared for trivial occasions. In 1954 there was no conjoint family therapy or family research in the literature, and as far as we were concerned, the MRI investigators were pioneering because the then-extant family studies were of individual family members and dealt with quite different phenomena from those encountered when the family is seen together as a unit. Haley's brilliant laboratory research with intact families demonstrates how totally different the family as a unit is from the "family" created by amalgamating the results of studies of its individual members.

To the extent that the MRI has influenced psychiatry and the behavioral sciences, it has probably occurred because of our common conviction that group phenomena cannot be clearly depicted in the language of the individual's psyche. The grasp that psychoanalysis has had on the body politic in psychiatry and on the thinking of behavioral science academicians (many of whom are arriving on the scene ten years late) makes it difficult to transmit the simple message that individual and group at the present time are discontinuous phenomena. We haven't even the language to handle our insights, let alone a holistic theory.

It is my hope that the papers in these volumes will depict a course and a struggle. It is a further hope that papers even ten years old contain semblances of fresh information to some of the readers. It is also simple expediency to collect articles that stem from some well-known, some obscure sources and the finding of which presents the student with manifold logistical problems.

Finally, I must call attention to the fact that a research institute is not just a body of happy scholars and experimenters. Without the generous help of our Board of Directors, our administrative assistants, secretaries, research assistants, and receptionists, we would since have settled beneath the waters of obscurity.

These papers, then, representing my own early work, the efforts of the Bateson project and the MRI staff, are presented more as a challenge than a monument.

Don D. Jackson

November 1967

PREFACE TO VOLUME 2

This volume, like Volume 1 of this series, contains papers covering a considerable span of time, substantive focus, and levels of generality, but with unity in its manifest diversity. To orient the reader not already familiar with this body of work, we have attempted to indicate this unity by the arrangement of the papers, without adding undue commentaries to the presentation.

This arrangement derives from both logical and chronological considerations: The first two sections contain theoretical papers on behavior and its interactional contexts, focusing in Part I on psychotic behavior and in Part II on other phenomena, such as anxiety reactions, asthma, and hypnosis.

The last two sections proceed to considerations of therapy and change, focusing in Part III on some interactional views and reviews of psychotherapeutic training, theory, and technique, and in Part IV on some facets of conjoint family therapy embracing theoretical, technical, and research considerations.

CONTRIBUTORS

DON D. JACKSON, M.D., Director, Mental Research Institute, Palo Alto, California; Associate Clinical Professor of Psychiatry, Stanford University School of Medicine. *

GREGORY BATESON, currently working on a Research Career Grant under the auspices of the National Institute of Mental Health, at the Oceanic Foundation, Sea Life Park, Oahu, Hawaii.

WILLIAM F. FRY, M.D., Research Associate, Mental Research Institute; Clinical Staff Member, Psychiatry Department, Palo Alto—Stanford Medical Center.

JAY HALEY, Director, Philadelphia Child Guidance Clinic; Editor, Family Process; formerly Research Associate, Mental Research Institute.

VIRGINIA SATIR, A.C.S.W., Secretary-Treasurer, Esalen Institute, Big Sur, California; Consultant, Mental Research Institute.

PAUL WATZLAWICK, Ph.D., Research Associate, Mental Research Institute.

JOHN H. WEAKLAND, Research Associate, Mental Research Institute; Research Associate, Studies in International Conflict and Integration, Institute of Political Studies, Stanford University.

JOHN E. WEBLIN, M.D., Ch.B., D.P.M., in private psychiatric practice, Palmerston N.W., New Zealand; formerly Research Associate, Mental Research Institute.

IRVIN YALOM, M.D., Research Associate, Mental Research Institute; Assistant Professor of Psychiatry, Stanford University School of Medicine.

---

*Publisher's Note: Dr. Jackson died suddenly on January 29, 1968, just as this book was going to press.

TABLE OF CONTENTS

SCHIZOPHRENIC SYMPTOMS AND
FAMILY INTERACTION

Don D. Jackson
and John H. Weakland

A good deal of criticism has been leveled at speculations about the relationship between a schizophrenic's symptoms and his life experience, past or present, particularly when these speculations are made on the basis of intensive psychotherapy of a single patient. Before the intensive study of the families of schizophrenic patients was begun, relatively few years ago, only the patient's statements and the hunches of the therapist were available as data, because it was not considered proper for the therapist to see the family and the hospital was usually happier when they did not come around.

However, we now have available three sorts of data about the family that can be directly studied in relation to the patient's current symptomatic behavior, and which may or may not eventually be related to the etiology of schizophrenia.

1. Psychological, sociological, and anthropological information about families. The standard psychological tests, the Q-sort, child-rearing practice questionnaires, and the study of roles in families of different socioeconomic levels are examples of this category.

2. The collection and collation of data obtained by individual interview with family members. This approach is best exemplified by the studies of Lidz and Fleck.

3. The joint observation, and often treatment, of the family together with the patient. Papers by Bowen, Wynne, Bateson, and Jackson have reported on this type of data collection.

Reprinted from A.M.A. ARCHIVES OF GENERAL PSYCHIATRY, 1:618–621 (December 1959). Copyright, American Medical Association, Chicago; reproduced by permission.

We should like to describe a few specific examples of how connections between a patient's symptoms and his family's interaction can be seen during family interviews, and then to outline some points about the general nature of these relationships as they have appeared to us in a number of instances.

Family A. The patient is a 32-year-old divorced woman with an 18-month-old daughter. She was first hospitalized for schizophrenia, catatonic type, when she was 19 and has had five years of on-and-off residence in mental hospitals. Family therapy was instituted because she had left her husband after five months of hospitalization to live with her parents. Since it was expected that her child, who was in a foster home in a distant city, would eventually join them, individual therapy did not seem sufficient to cope with the complexities of their situation.

The symptoms most complained about by the parents was the patient's indecision. Every decision, however simple, was a problem. Deciding which dress to wear could occupy an entire morning. How could such irritating behavior be adaptive? In the family sessions it was noted that both parents sounded "too sure" of themselves, especially when responding to evidence of indecisiveness on the patient's part. When the therapist questioned their bland oversimplifications, they revealed great indecisiveness, and their past histories reeked of it. As an example, the family was asked to discuss how they would cooperate in rearing the baby when she arrived, while the therapist watched from a one-way glass. Neither parent spoke, but both looked at the patient. Finally, she expressed concern about how well all of them could handle a baby. She reminded them that she had never cared for a child and that it had been some years since her parents had. When was the child to be fed, bathed--evening or morning, etc.? As the mother leaped in to reassure her, she went too far. She stated, among other things, that "daddy will be glad to help out." At this a shadow passed over the father's face, but he kept quiet and later joined his wife in her happy picturing. The therapist returned to the room and aided father in admitting he had had nothing to do with the care of his own children and that the thought of starting now was less than appealing.

If the patient's symptom of indecision was an adaptation, then the loss of it should cause changes in the family. To support this hypothesis, the mother was describing her care of the patient, her nursing her son through a "nervous breakdown," and her mothering her husband through recurrent depressions and retreats from his profession. The therapist asked the mother whether she was ever allowed to break down, or whether she always had to be the strong one. She responded like a person choking on a fishbone; when finally able to speak, she dismissed the question by stating that it was over now and just a silly business in the past, but she never did specify what it was that was over. The patient, intensely alert during all this, stated she wanted to fly to her daughter and fetch her home. That afternoon she returned to the therapist's office to pick up a letter from him assuring the foster home that he felt she could bring the child home. The mother was trailing her daughter in the manner of a sheep dog, reflecting her helplessness. When she appealed to the therapist, "What are we going to do about the ticket? I don't have enough money on me," the patient reassured her that she had already called the travel service and they would accept a check. This decisiveness on the patient's part was immediately followed by three events unusual in this family: The father flirted at a party, had a violent argument with his wife, and that evening was impotent reportedly for the first time in their marriage.

Another reaction to a decision by the patient occurred when they were expecting a visitor labeled as "the patient's friend," although the mother had invited her. The patient expressed fears, which the parents pooh-poohed, that this visitor might report back to the husband her behavior with the child. This fear seemed sensible, since the patient had met this person through her husband originally, and there was a natural fear he might try to get the child back. The therapist suggested that this woman's visits be limited and that a room be obtained for her in a nearby motel so that the patient could see her only during her better moments. The parents fought this bitterly, calling it an inhospitable act. The therapist finally turned to the patient and asked what she preferred to do, since the mother had said they would do whatever she wanted. She said in a very quiet voice: "I think it would be simpler," then, looking at her parents, "but some people would think it was inhospitable." Immediately the father jumped in with, "You see, she agrees with me. She says it would be inhospitable," and the mother was vigorously nodding. The therapist protested that he had heard her say, "It would be simpler," and that she had looked at her parents and tried to modify it for their sake. Finally, he played back the tape, and it was necessary to run through the recording three times before the parents heard her actual statement. The father kept hearing only the second half, and the mother was so amazed by the sound of her own voice, "I sound like a witch; I sound like a man," that it took almost bodily force to get them to hear the patient say she had come to a decision.

There are many instances in this family in which the patient's indecision arises at those moments when the parents are oversimplifying complicated matters. She protects her parents by not arguing with them and not pointing out their fallacies in logic, and yet her very behavior confuses them at the same time. Only when she is acting psychotic and speaking "schizophrenese" does she accuse them in more direct fashion, and then she overdoes it, so that the parents say she is out of her mind.

Family B. The patient is an unmarried 25-year-old man, who has been hospitalized for schizophrenia for the past five years, except for four months at home on a trial visit in the midst of this period, during which he became worse and the family very upset. When family therapy was initiated after the parents expressed concern that the patient was getting nowhere with other treatment, which had included individual psychotherapy, the patient's most prominent symptom was withdrawal, expressed by silence or by a stock answer of "Uh--I don't know," when asked a question. His parents repeatedly expressed several kinds of concern about his withdrawn behavior: They would like him to participate more in family activities during his week-end visits home; they would like him to cooperate more with the family, and they felt he had things on his mind but they could not tell what, and he wouldn't say. All this was phrased as showing their love and concern rather than as criticism of the patient.

In the course of the family sessions, however, although there was a good deal of reemphasis on this picture of noncommittal withdrawal by the patient and parental concern over it, it also became noticeable that 1) the parents, as well as the patient, avoided personal communication, although the patient's uncommunicativeness rather screened theirs from view, and that 2) when the patient did speak up, the parents were disturbed and evasive.

In the first place, both parents actually said about as little about their own feelings and relationships in the family as the patient. The father talked at length, but mainly in a rambling, repetitive, and superficial way, although he recurrently demanded that the therapist get down to cases more. Often too, he appeared to be the spokesman, or "front man," for his wife. She usually talked rather little except for remarks at the level of polite social conversation. Later on, when some family conflicts were more out in the open, she made this attitude explicit, saying that she didn't like to discuss personal matters and thought it only disrupted family "harmony," which she tried hard to maintain. This context seems pertinent to the patient's silence, and to his occasional statements about it, such as the following episode: The patient had mentioned expecting his ward chief to renege on a promised pass. The therapist asked whether his parents had gone back on promises to him. At this the patient began to speak up more than usual, but said the therapist must be "crazy" to bring up such matters.

Another example showed not simply keeping away from the personal and interpersonal but positive cooperation in doing so. The parents frequently referred to subjects like heredity, shock treatment, surgery, and tranquilizers when mental illness was referred to, while the patient often closed off discussion approaching his personal feelings by saying, in a rather grand and general way, that "mental illness is all a matter of physics and chemistry." The significance of this was especially evident in one family session, in which the mother anxiously insisted that the patient did have thoughts and could speak up, until he burst out: "You keep pounding on me about mental illness." But then he subsided and shifted back to "mental illness is all a matter of physics." This tape-recorded interchange was replayed to them at the next session, and immediately thereafter the mother commented: "I agree with him; it's all a matter of physics." Asked just how she meant this, she became very vague.

These examples suggest that the patient's symptom of withdrawal and impersonality is largely shared by the parents, but that they ordinarily have better conventional covers for this. Therefore the patient's behavior can function as a cover for their fundamentally similar difficulties. This notion receives support from observations that the patient's silence and withdrawal occurred, or was intensified, in situations where the parents avoided their own problem by turning the focus, whether of concern, anger, or whatever, on their son. This focus was so routine at the start that a particular clear example is easier to find later on. After considerable therapy, in one session, the parents were expressing great concern that the patient was troubled by something, as they could see by his behavior on visits home, but that he wouldn't say what. The therapist suggested they discuss their own thoughts and feelings about this, but they insistently returned the focus to the patient, and he finally walked out of the session, angrily. Further discussion with the parents finally revealed that the son's behavior at home had changed from a mixture of dreamy withdrawal, and some superficial polite remarks, to a much more clearly angry avoidance, and that while the mother was very bothered by this, the father disagreed with her privately, seeing it as improvement, even if not pleasant. But they would not admit their disagreement before the son, speaking only of concern for him instead.

Finally, the valuation and functioning of the patient's silence and withdrawal in the family system is especially emphasized by the nature of parental responses when, exceptionally, he did speak up, or, after long restraint, burst out. Considerable light is thrown on this by the mother's remark, after insisting how much they wanted their son to talk to them, that of course he should talk nicely; she could tolerate anything from him but "rudeness." But an example of ostensibly quite "crazy" behavior points things up most clearly. At a certain period, the therapist had been pointing out that father-son conflict was often emphasized but mother-son relations were little discussed. The mother was not happy about this interpretation, and the patient had shown some suspicion and withdrawal. The parents were asked what might be occurring, and the father began to lecture his son on how he didn't appreciate all that was being done to help him. The patient got angry, at which the mother interceded in an obscuring way, claiming that the son was just protecting himself and currently was irritable if anyone got personal about anything. The therapist suggested that perhaps the patient also protected his mother. The patient angrily denied this, saying she had something coming to her. She gave out a shocked and angry "What?" and the father hurried to suggest that the patient was angry at them both. The mother then recovered her more usual style and claimed she didn't get what her son meant. At this point he went into a lengthy, angry harangue about death and destruction being visited on the area and how the family wouldn't escape. This was couched in terms of Russia, atom bombs, revolution in Iraq, and so on, yet the feeling involved and the immediate family reference seemed rather clear. The parental responses, however, avoided all this. The father responded quite literally: "You're talking about the present world situation?" The mother responded literally to some details but mainly claimed puzzlement: "It's too far-fetched; I don't understand." So the patient's speaking up led nowhere.

COMMENT

We can summarize our views, as illustrated concretely in these examples, in this way: In the past, the customary view of the symptomatic behavior of schizophrenics was that it was crazy or senseless. This implied one or both of two main characteristics separating it from "normal" behavior: that it was <u>unlike</u> the behavior of other people, and that it was pointless, purposeless, <u>unrelated</u> to the patient's life situation. It rather seems to us that schizophrenic behavior, when viewed in its family context, 1) resembles the behavior of other family members, though it may be exaggerated almost to a caricature (or possibly be an inverted form at times; this is not yet certain), and 2) appears to subserve important functions within the family. These may be seen either by directly considering how this behavior helps preserve the status quo or, a reverse approach, how change in the patient's behavior is disruptive and disturbing, at least in the short run.

It seems probable that these relationships have been hard to see in the past because there is a pervasive duality about schizophrenic behavior and its functioning in the family, which we may point out in closing.

1. The patient's symptom characteristics have a dual aspect.

(a) They obscure, interrupt, and <u>focus</u> <u>on</u> <u>him</u> the interaction occurring at that moment. An example would be the patient who threatened the therapist physically, calling him a spy and an FBI agent at that moment when the therapist was following up a lead that the mother may have had a psychotic episode when illegitimately pregnant with the patient.

(b) The patient's symptom communicates information which, if understood, can lead to new information about the family or about his relationship with one of the members or with the therapist. Thus, in the previous example, the word "spy" carries an opprobrious connotation, but "FBI agent" does not have this ring. Later it was discovered that, despite the patient's anxious concern for her mother, she wanted her mother's emotional illness to be revealed.

2. The fact that the patient's communication has a dual aspect is supported by the response of the parents, and sometimes of the siblings. The "crazy" aspect is supported by (a) laughter, ridicule, amusement, and the "leading-on" type of questions, or by (b) the family's refusal to take it personally, so that the possible meaning is ignored through silence or passing over it or by attempts to get the patient not to say such a ridiculous thing.

3. The message is thus lost, but if the patient is able to state the message more explicitly, several events may occur.

(a) If this is a single attempt on the patient's part, he may receive the sort of agreement that is like running into a brick wall;
or he may be organized against until he backs down or withdraws,
sometimes into silence, sometimes physically, and sometimes into more profound psychosis.

(b) If the more explicit statement represents a real change in
the patient which he can maintain over a significant time period,
we then find new coalitions and fresh disturbances in the family.

It is this sort of duality that simultaneously obscures and reveals the nature of schizophrenia and creates the possibilities and
difficulties of its psychotherapeutic treatment.

THE BIOSOCIAL INTEGRATION OF BEHAVIOR
IN THE SCHIZOPHRENIC FAMILY

Gregory Bateson

As a result of the growth of cybernetics especially and systems
theory in general, we can now guess what the words "biosocial integration" denote but we are still very far from being able to say
how any given biosocial system is integrated. We are at the stage
where no particular theory can be proposed, although we know
enough about what such theories should look like to be able to ask
many questions.

I shall assume that the words "biosocial integration" suggest
that we look at biosocial systems--individual organisms, families,
communities, or ecological systems--as entities that maintain stability by some combination of two processes: calibration and feedback. [1] And, in those cases that fail to maintain stability, I shall
assume that we have to look for the pathologies that may be expected in these two processes or in their combination.

FEEDBACK AND CALIBRATION
I shall first describe the processes separately. Feedback,
which today is the more familiar term, is applied to a system containing a sense organ (such as the thermometer in the thermostatic control of a househeating system) that collects information about
the value of some variable within the system. This information
(that is, some transform of events in the sense organ) is then
transmitted to some effector organ of the system, such as the furnace, and causes this organ to act in an appropriate sense to modify the value of the perceived variable. (When the temperature of

[1] Horst Mittelstaedt. Regelung in der Biologie, Regelungs-
technik:II, (No. 8) 177-181, 1954.

Reprinted from EXPLORING THE BASE FOR FAMILY THERAPY,
(Nathan W. Ackerman, M. D., Frances L. Beatman, and Sanford N.
Sherman, eds.) pages 116-122, 1961. Copyright, Family Service
Association of America, New York; reproduced by permission.

the house falls, the furnace is activated; or when the temperature rises, the furnace shuts off.) A similar system obtains in the aiming of a rifle. The rifleman looks along the sights and observes the error of his aim at Time 1. He then moves the rifle to correct this error and observes the new value of error at Time 2, and so on, until he decides to press the trigger. The essence of the matter is that a corrective process is activated by perceived error.

In contrast to the method of feedback is the method of calibration. A man firing a shotgun at a flying bird does not depend upon a process of successive self-correction. He receives a single slug of information at Time 1 (an estimate of the bird's position, the velocity and direction of its movement). He immediately raises the gun to a position which he computes will place the shot where the bird will be at Time 2, and fires. There is not "error activation" between the moment of initially observing the bird and the moment of pressing the trigger. It is as if the marksman were calibrated to rigid mechanisms that will predictably compute in a given way. It is only in _learning_ to handle a shotgun that feedback enters. The learner may observe that in a series of shots he has fired too high or too low or too soon and he may use this observed error to change his habitual calibrated response.

Note that _habit_ is, in general, an economical method of solving familiar problems by the substitution of calibration for feedback.[2] The first time we meet a new problem we solve it by feedback or trial and error. Later, habit will short-cut this process.

The first question to ask about any system characterized by feedback or calibration is: Is this system stable? But to attribute "stability" to a system is to make a statement about the ongoing truth of some statement about the system. More rigorously, we should ask what descriptive statements about this system have ongoing truth? Within what limitations?

An organism is a system for which many statements describing process inside the system continue to be true up to the limit of death and in spite of the gradual replacement of the material of which the system is made. A social system may show stability in spite of the death and replacement of the individuals of which it is composed.

---

[2]To rely upon feedback is a common "bad habit" of beginners with the shotgun; strictly, this is perhaps a meta-habit.

THE FAMILIES OF SCHIZOPHRENIC PATIENTS

We can now ask some first questions about the families containing schizophrenics. Are these systems stable? What descriptive statements about these systems have ongoing truth, despite what sorts of impact or disturbance?

1. Our observations show that these families, in a gross sense, continue as families. The statement, "This is a closely intercommunicating system," continues to be true in spite of the very considerable unhappiness of the members and even in spite of such external divisive forces as the military draft. [3]

2. These families seem to be stable with relation to the descriptive statement, "This family contains a schizophrenic." If the identified patient shows sudden improvement, the behavior of the others will change in such a way as to push him back into schizophrenic behavior. Or if the identified patient recovers, behavior in the family will change in such a way that some other family member starts to show psychological stress. He may almost invite the "normal" members of the family to treat him as the identified patient.

3. It has been noted that some of these families are stable in regard to the descriptive statements that the neighbors might make about them. In spite of gross cultural abnormality within the family circle, the family maintains stability in its external appearance and respectability. The identified patient may, and usually does, try to disrupt the external veneer, but the rest of the family will make strenuous efforts to defend the external appearances.

4. The families containing schizophrenics exhibit a stability that is, in general, not present in normal families. Many descriptive statements about the relationship between members remain true much longer than in usual families. Indeed, these statements may be said to be stable under the impact of the processes of maturation of the independent members. The growing up of the identified patient and the senescence of the parents scarcely seem to

---

[3] The families with which we have worked in the Palo Alto projects are, however, a specially selected sample. We insist upon the availability of both parents, and we take only families in which it is the offspring who is the identified patient. This descriptive imputation of family stability seems characteristic of this sample.

affect the patterns of behavior between parent and offspring. Over-protectiveness, if present, continues undiminished and the incessant inconsistencies of relationship that we have called "double binds" continue unabated.

Many other statements might be made about these families and we could profitably discuss the mechanisms that determine their ongoing truth. The statements made above, however, are enough to illustrate the method of study.

Next, we have to ask whether the on-going truth of these statements is maintained by feedback or by calibration or by some com-bination of these processes. This question must, however, be delayed until the combination patterns have been briefly discussed.

COMBINATIONAL PATTERNS

Characteristically, feedback and calibration seem to operate at alternate levels. By translating the word "stability" to mean an imputation of ongoing truth to a particular descriptive statement, I have implicitly suggested that there are levels of stability, just as there are levels of descriptive statement. In fact, these levels must necessarily be in a hierarchy of logical types and, as mentioned above, feedback and calibration seem rather commonly to be used alternately at alternate levels. For example, the thermostatic system of a house operates by feedback, but this feedback is controlled in turn by a calibrational device on the wall of the living room which can be set (calibrated) to a given temperature from which the actual temperature of the living room will vary only slightly. The dial on the wall in an inhabited house is controlled in turn by feedback mechanisms involving the sense organs of the inhabitants. Somebody says, "The house is always too cold." He is "error activated" to go and change the calibrational setting of the dial which in turn will change the feedback operations of the thermostatic system.

A similar alternating hierarchy can be observed in society's attempts to control culturally deviant behavior. When certain norms or thresholds are overpassed, this deviation activates po-licemen or psychiatrists to go and do something about it. But the setting of these norms is, at least in some societies, achieved by a calibrational system called "the law." The setting of this sys-tem determines what shall be regarded as deviance and how far an individual may go before either policemen or psychiatrists are ac-tivated. The law itself, however, is subject to change by complex feedback mechanisms involving debate, voting, and so on. The

Medes and Persians who boasted that their law "altereth not," were living under a relatively primitive system of law which antedated the luxuries and complexities of democratic automation.

We must expect that the ongoing truth of any given descriptive statement about a system will be maintained by a hierarchy of mechanisms--some of them feedback, some of them calibration. Let me recall again the fact that in human behavior there is a tendency for feedback mechanisms to be replaced gradually by the calibrational mechanisms of habit. This principle obtains even at the social level, where precedent lays a base for law; for example, cohabitation may ultimately constitute a common law marriage.

RE-EXAMINATION OF STATEMENTS

When re-examined in the light of these considerations, our statements about the family become classifiable as belonging to several levels, and at a higher level we have statements about the family in relation to the outside community. Statement 1, that the family continues as a closely intercommunicating system, contains mixed elements of both these levels. On the one hand the family is stable, in the sense of avoiding visible signs of disruption, such as divorce, scattering, and so on, but the statement also contains comments about closeness or interdependence as exemplified by behavior within the family constellation.

Statement 2, that the family contains "an identified patient," also seems to be valid on two levels. This is a statement about interpersonal behavior, but it also implies a degree of habit formation, that is, calibration, within the identified patient. To be a schizophrenic is more than merely acting schizophrenic when the occasion demands. The statement suggests that the identified individual is partly unable to drop his schizophrenic behavior in contexts where that behavior would be inappropriate; the behavior is no longer totally subject to feedback control.

Statement 3, that "external appearances" are maintained, may be seen as a statement of a calibrated law or rule for these families.

Statement 4 concerns only the interpersonal behavior and suggests certain impacts and pressures under which this behavior still remains constant--the changing stresses of maturation.

But what was said earlier about the alternating sequences of feedbacks and calibrations suggests that we ought to look for sequences of this kind as an over-all structure within which the statements to which we have imputed ongoing truth would have their place. Precisely at this point, our schizophrenic families begin to show very peculiar characteristics. The only calibrations that seem to be viable in these families are at the very low level of individual habit formation and at the highly superficial level of external appearances. Perhaps I am exaggerating, but I shall illustrate this statement by observations of one particular family.

I observed that this family regularly arrived for their family sessions between fifteen and twenty minutes late. I briefly investigated the mechanics of this regularity in the course of a conversation in which I was trying to find generalizations that could be regarded as "rules" for this family. It became evident that it was inconceivable for them to operate by a regular rule that would ensure their arrival for a family session at any specified time. The regularity of their lateness was, in fact, achieved by complex family interaction and interpersonal struggle which lasted about the same length of time every week. The father--an intermittently authoritarian character--claimed that he tried to lay down rules, but the mother acted on the premise that no rule that he laid down could have validity because she was sure he would not maintain his own rule.

There was also in this family no regular premise giving authority to any member and no regular premise governing how rules, if there were any, should be changed. The father's edicts fell to the ground not only because the mother would not let them stand, but also because he could admit no feedback correction or flexibility.

To propose a calibration in this family would be to commit an error that would immediately activate feedback processes. In sum, we have here a system that operates between the fixed points of individual habit (and no member dare change his habits) and certain premises regarding external behavior. The latter premises are under constant attack by the identified patient, who is likely to remark in a clear conversational tone in church, "We haven't had a nice crackling storm lately; have we, dad?" All between these points is feedback.

Perhaps a truly anarchic system might work with only feedback, and feedback controlling feedback, without intermediate calibration. This, at least, is the anarchist's ideal. The system described, however, is not anarchic. Habits are rigid; external appearances must be controlled, and the father continually tries to lay down inflexible rules. The result is a system which, while pathogenic, is yet stable. Many statements about it appear to have enduring truth.

You will note, however, that what I have been able to say is very inconclusive. I believe that we are today only on the threshold of being able to ask those questions about family organization that will be both answerable by research and incisive. These questions will transcend the unique episodic detail of what happens in a given family, by relating the details to our small formal knowledge of the processes of biosocial integration.

THE ACUTE PSYCHOSIS AS A MANIFESTATION
OF GROWTH EXPERIENCE

Don D. Jackson
and Paul Watzlawick

The argument over the etiology of the psychoses continues to flourish. This paper is not considered a contribution to the weighty problems that face any disputant in such arguments: rather it is an attempt to present data on a somewhat different facet of the problem of the acute schizophrenic psychosis.

In our opinion, an individual experiencing a psychotic episode is usually thought of as suffering from a defect--a weak ego or a thinking disorder. Perhaps because in traditional medical thinking a psychosis is regarded as an illness and necessarily a bad thing that must be gotten rid of, the psychotic experience as an important method of individuals achieving adjustment is frequently ignored. However, Erikson has recently pointed out: "... there are characteristic emotional disturbances in each stage of life which--although subject to differential diagnosis--are essentially determined by the life-tasks of that stage and are most easily ameliorated during the very period of their emergence. If studied and treated as circumscribed crises of inner growth, which are aggravated by discernible tension in the sufferer's social condition, these disturbances may be prevented from becoming chronic ailments reinforced by the fatalistic diagnoses which they evoked in the past. " (1)

French and Kasanin many years ago reported on two cases of acute psychotic episodes and stated that an acute psychosis may be a transitional episode in the process of emancipation from an old method of adjustment to learning a new one and further that during an acute psychosis, the mechanism of recovery may be indicated in advance by the content of some of the delusions. (2)

Reprinted from PSYCHIATRIC RESEARCH REPORTS 16, 83-94 (May 1963). Copyright, American Medical Association, Chicago; reproduced by permission.

It is possible to discern at least three classes of individuals within that group that encounter a psychiatrist for the first time and are labeled "schizophrenic":

Class I. Individuals, chronically handicapped, either organically, intellectually, or emotionally so that they cannot maintain a position in their particular ecological niche. They either seek rescue, for example via a suicide attempt, or are caught by a social sieve (police, psychiatric agencies, etc.) and removed to a custodial setting. At that moment, they become "psychotic" since they are now labeled. Such labels include "process schizophrenia" and "simple schizophrenia."

Class II. Individuals who are temporarily handicapped by acute forces of a severely stressful nature which are limited in duration and who achieve their former performance level when the stress has ceased. Stresses would include alcohol and various other toxins, wartime combat, medical illness, surgery, and sensory deprivation.

Class III. Individuals who are trapped in a social nexus which places limitations on their maturation at the same time that they are exposed to a new situation demanding an increase in their maturational level. The crippling elements of the new situation are not consciously known to the individual (for example, the nature of his family relationships), but should they become psychotic they may become known in striking relief. By being labeled as "ill," the individual may be offered maximum opportunity to influence his surroundings, for example to remove himself from certain situations, insert himself into others, or bring family members into treatment. The nature of his social field and the timing of the illness may be crucial in creating a new beginning following the psychotic episode.

Obviously, the therapeutic approach and treatment possibilities vary with each class. In the first class, the struggle will be over the question of whether the individual is to be cared for by society or is eventually willing to go on his own, and this question has many psychological and sociological ramifications. In the second instance, a temporary surcease from the stressful situation or the toxin may be all that is required. In the third class, the individual may be in an ideal situation to undergo rapid and successful therapeutic change which may be long-lasting.

The following brief case illustrates how taking the "sick role" brings to bear social instruments and privileges which may be more crucial than insight in achieving a better adjustment for the individual, and how important these forces are in shaping the outcome of a psychotic experience:

A young woman in her early thirties was referred as an emergency by her internist. She had had several teeth extracted under gas anaesthesia a few days prior to being seen by the psychiatrist and since that time had been feeling increasingly unreal, having bizarre thoughts, and becoming withdrawn and suspicious. At the time she was seen, she appeared frightened, suspicious, hostile, and hallucinating. On questioning, she was able to say that the voices had to do with derogatory remarks about herself on the one hand, and on the other hand, a distrust with what was going to happen to her in this new situation. She had never previously seen a psychiatrist and was poorly acquainted with what she could expect. The therapist told her that she was undergoing a personality reorganization and that this was outside of her awareness. He urged her to furnish information that would allow her and the therapist to accelerate this personality reorganization so that she could consciously make sense of it. She was told that the voices accusing her represented one side of the problem and the suspiciousness the other side. The suspiciousness was deemed proper since she did not know what to expect in the new situation and was in a very vulnerable position. She was told that she must bring the two sides of herself together and that perhaps the best place to begin was to focus on events that had happened to her recently and had to be of an unusual nature. It turned out that she had become involved with another man, although she had been married ten years, and thoughts of infidelity were abhorrent to her because of her religious upbringing. She had never loved her husband, but had married him as a way out of a difficult home situation and because he was extremely forceful. She had become torn with desire to leave her husband for the other man, and at the same time had doubts as to whether he would marry her. He was a quiet, sensitive person who made her feel very much loved, but was not one for taking positive stands. His concern about her illness made him much more positive, and he even volunteered to go to her husband. Her husband's concern about her illness produced an unusual solicitude in him, and she was finally able to speak to him about their marital difficulties. These events took place within a few days after initially seeing the psychiatrist, and following them she appeared mentally completely clear.

The patient finally went through a long, stormy, and difficult divorce proceeding with her husband without manifesting any signs of psychosis. In the last several years, her relationship to her children has changed as well. She has become much more interested in and attentive to them, and this is obvious in their response to her. She became quite realistic about the assets and liabilities of her lover, and has made a satisfactory adjustment with him. One of the most striking things about the whole experience to her has been the increase in her energy. Formerly, she was tired a great deal of the time whereas now, in addition to being a housewife, she is engaged in creative pursuits which are quite rewarding to her.

This brief example gives some support to the idea that psychosis may have its growth-promoting aspects, especially if it occurs in a situation where the individual appears to be problem-solving and help is at hand.

There is one particular situation that frequently seems to produce psychoses of the class three variety. This is the college student who lives away from home and has difficulty in adjustment. In the course of some ten years of examining students who have had psychotic episodes while at a university, a number of these situations have come to light. What these cases usually have in common is the fact that at home the patient has adjusted to a specific learning context involving a paradox which can only be dealt with by a shift in logical types. This paradox most frequently centers around a relabeling by a parent of feelings, perceptions, or contexts which is different from, or even contrary to, the child's own immediate experience. Faced by the dilemma of either doubting his own perceptions or incurring parental disapproval or punishment, the child sooner or later learns to behave in a way which both takes into account the way things are for him and at the same time denies that they appear so. In terms of logic, such behavior is of a different logical type. Once away from home, however, he is likely to experience a breakdown in communication in the extrafamilial world which neither imposes, nor is able to deal with, behavior based on the tacit assumption of such an all-pervading paradox. One such case involves a girl who was seen in individual psychotherapy by one of us (P.W.); at the same time she and the parents were seen for a number of conjoint family therapy sessions by the other author (D.D.J).

The patient, a 19-year-old college girl, had a psychotic break six weeks before completing her junior year in college in the Eastern part of the United States. She was flown back to her home in California after ten days of hospitalization during which she was diagnosed as suffering from an acute paranoid reaction. She was admitted to our local psychiatric ward, and, when seen by us, her hallucinations had apparently ceased, but psychotic ideation, especially ideas of reference, were very much in evidence. She appeared frightened and confused, but was intact enough to be difficult with the ward personnel. Her ideas of reference and their subsequent modification lend themselves quite well to illustrate the learning aspects present in a psychotic episode.

When first seen, the patient immediately declared that she had now discovered the real reason for her breakdown. It had to do with the fact that at the age of seven or eight, she was raped in the garage of her home by a Chinese gardener. She screamed for help, her mother came and watched the scene, giving the gardener certain suggestions as to how to proceed. In a subsequent interview, the patient declared that she had meanwhile spoken to her father about this incident in order to obtain more facts. He maintained that the gardener had attempted some kind of sex play with her, but was caught before anything happened, and fired. A few days later, the patient produced another memory: at the age of thirteen, during one of her mother's numerous hospitalizations for a variety of psychosomatic illnesses, the father had her sleep in his bed and had put his arms about her. She also remembered, or thought she remembered, that on the following morning, father fired the nurse, who was replacing mother during her stay in the hospital, for having criticized his intimacy with his daughter. The patient stressed the pathogenic nature of this incident during the next week or two while the original story about the Chinese gardener began to fade in importance; at the same time, she minimized the importance of similar incestuous material reported by herself in relation to incidents which occurred only two months before her hospitalization. While at home during the spring vacation, she would almost daily lie in bed between her parents and her father had a habit of entering her room at any time. She found this unimportant in comparison to the incident at the age of thirteen. Finally, during one of her first overnight leaves from the hospital, the father left the parental bedroom door ajar and the patient coming to the door observed him naked in the adjoining bathroom. This incident, which appears to have been seized upon by the patient since the father on other occasions behaved in an exactly similar manner, now enabled the patient to accuse her father openly of seductiveness. It led to a very heated discussion in the family session, during which the parents "jumped on" the daughter for constant interference with their privacy and the mother made the statement: "Jeanne, you have always tried to interfere between me and your father for the past twenty years." At this time, the patient was still nineteen years of age.

From the foregoing, it would appear that the incidents mentioned are highlights in the evolution from psychotic fantasy to actual facts in the patient's incest problem. To explain the steps of this development simply in relation to the patient's growing reality adaptation does not seem to cover the essence of the phenomenon. Admittedly, more absurd formulations of the problem were gradually abandoned in favor of more realistic ones; for instance, the shift from the Chinese gardener to father's behavior in the past, and from there to the present, as well as a shift from the actively abetting mother to the openly critical nurse and then to the passively resigning mother. But it seems to us that every phase of this evolution contained in itself the germ for its own reductio ad absurdum; that in each instance there was one element just a little "too good to be true" which then enabled the therapeutic function of doubt to arise in the patient's mind and compel her to look around and explore further until reality eventually broke through during a conjoint family session.

At this point, the family therapist intervened with a forcefully framed instruction for the father to abandon his passive, despairing attitude toward wife and daughter and adopt an active role of referee between them. The patient became panicky, and accused the therapist of betraying her and leaving her at the mercy of the person least suited for this role. By the following morning, however, she was calm and collected, and began to realize that her father's role was precisely the one which would enable her to establish a more healthy relationship with him. Only a week later, she announced that she was now ready to return home; until then, she had refused to leave the hospital on the grounds that she could not live with her father under the same roof. She was discharged on the following day, and has remained out of the hospital.

Another similarly structured change occurred during this patient's improvement, this time in relation to her mother. After her discharge from the hospital, much time and effort had to be spent in individual therapy as well as in the family therapy in working through the mother-daughter relationship. On the surface, the relationship was characterized by mutual tears, accusations, and attacks in anticipation of expected attacks, with the daughter caricaturing teenage defiance and the mother helplessness and self-pity. Underneath the surface, but outside both opponents' awareness, there was an almost continual interchange of double-level

messages which kept mother and daughter locked in bitter, hopeless struggle. One afternoon when this situation reached a cli-
max, they came to blows. After a brief fight, the mother managed to get a hold of the girl's wrists and to immobilize her while
repeating over and over again: "Go to your room, go to your room
immediately." At this point, the patient was struck by the absurdity of the situation, and was for the first time able to comment
on the inconsistency of the mother's injunctions saying, "How can
you expect me to go to my room if you're holding me here?"

Following this incident, the patient lost much of her intense
apparent hatred and fear of her mother, realizing that the mother's
helplessness and tears were not just a cloak for aggression but
also represented real helplessness in which she relied a good deal
on the father to help her control the daughter. In effect, the incident consisted of a resolution of a double-bind situation, and was
important because it came about in an actual two party interaction
rather than the previous change which had depended on the patient's
scrutiny of her own ideation.

Hamlet feigns insanity to be able to make his point in an environment which for good reasons denies the truth. In making his
point, he utilizes fantasy, i.e., the play that he directs the roam-
ing players to perform, recognizing that this is a more effective
tool than his direct accusations. In the case of the girl we have
described, her psychosis may have utilized similar mechanisms.
As far as she is concerned, she finds herself labeled wrong, whatever approach she may try. Had she been able to say openly what
she knew, she would not have gotten anywhere. In fact, she would
have only reinforced the parents' united front against her. To complain about the incestuous situation and the damage she felt it was
doing to her personality development (especially her relationship
with her mother) would have been as impossible as to try to defend herself at the age of thirteen against father's advances in
mother's absence. Her fears of attacking father directly at this
age would have been reinforced by the fate of the nurse, who she
believed was fired for criticizing father. However, at the age of
nineteen, at which time her problems in relation to her father
were revivified by her becoming seriously romantically involved
with a boy-friend, and at a time when her behavior had changed her
usual label from "wrong" or "bad" to "psychiatric illness," she
can afford to bring about a repetition of the incident as though she
were now able to say to father, "Now I have caught you--you are
still doing it to me," in a situation which has the additional advantage of having mother present as a witness. In fact, one might

speculate that if she does not work the situation out with her father, she at some level recognizes that her relationship to her boy-friend is doomed.

In this question of labels lies one of the important differences between neuroses and schizophrenia. The neurotic can complain about some kind of pain or unhappiness but the psychotic cannot. Since we have reason to think that, on the whole, the schizophrenic experiences terrible loneliness, self-doubt, and confusion, it may seem strange that he does not seek help long before social pressures or other social sieves bring him into the psychiatrist's office. The difference lies partially in the label attached to the two conditions. The neurotic and those around him recognize that something has occurred (stress, conflict, etc.), while the schizophrenic is living in a situation that is constantly labeled for him by his family as normal. This is nowhere more obvious than in initial interviews with the family of chronic schizophrenic patients wherein no one is unhappy about anything other than the fact that Jim or Mary happens to be sick. It is a superhuman task for the patient to point out that this is not the only problem in the family, and if this task is to be accomplished at all, it probably can only be done by resorting to a shift in logical types which to the observer appears "crazy." This patient, for instance, when invited by the therapist to sit down at the beginning of the first family session, looked at her parents who were sitting down to her left and right, respectively, and remarked, "Here we are--the eternal triangle"; a metaphor which at the time was completely lost on her parents. How difficult it is even for normal people to rely on their own perceptions and to defend them in the face of massive group disqualification is strikingly shown in Asch's experiments in which a normal subject finds himself a lone dissenter when he gives the correct answers to simple tasks involving visual perception. (3)

The patient's ability to utilize inconsistencies in his own psychotic productions as a learning experience is illustrated in two recently published books. One is "Perceval's Narrative," (4) the account by a British prime minister's schizophrenic son of his derangement and spontaneous remission, written in 1838, and recently reedited and given an introduction by Gregory Bateson. At the height of his psychotic involvement, Perceval does not dare to doubt the reality and truth of his voices, even though he finds himself unable to comply with their contradictory commands. "I perished," he writes, "from an habitual error of mine... that of fearing to doubt and of taking the guilt of doubt upon my conscience." As Bateson points out in his introduction,

Perceval writes here, as often, with hindsight wisdom as though it were only necessary to discover the uses of doubt in order to escape from a complex network of delusions. He ignores the facts of his own experience: that the courage to doubt his voices and his delusions grew in him slowly and painfully, and that the delusions themselves contributed to the process of this growth. Fearing to doubt, he falls into literal beliefs in his delusions and in what his voices tell him. But these messages are, after all, exaggerated caricatures of his own distorted Puritanism and guilt. By their very nature, his delusions contain, in an inverted or concealed form, the very doubts which he is afraid to entertain in a more conscious shape. These same delusions lead him to those experiences which are their reductio ad absurdum, and it is, among other things, these repeated experiences of the ridiculous that finally drive him sane.

Of this later period of his psychotic experiences, Perceval has this to say:

At another time, my spirits began singing to me in this strain: "You are in a lunatic asylum if you will—if not, you are in et cetera, et cetera." "That is Samuel Hobbs if you will—if not, it is Herminet Herbert, etc." But I had been so long deceived by my spirits that now I did not believe them when they spoke the truth.

However, by listening and finding that the patients called him Samuel Hobbs and by other accidents, I discovered at last I was yet here on earth, in natural, although very painful circumstances in a madhouse. My delusions being thus very much abolished, I soon got liberty of limb during the daytime.

The other book, Operators and Things, by Barbara O'Brien, (5) is the autobiography of the author's schizophrenic experiences. After having been at the complete mercy of the "operators," as she refers to her voices, for a considerable time, they begin to give her helpful hints. At one point, a voice called Hinton dictates to her a list of operators' terminology with definitions. And a little later:

"Go across the street to the drugstore, " Hinton said
in a tight voice. I looked up "psychologist" in the
classified directory, as he suggested, selected one,
phoned and made an appointment. That afternoon,
armed with my glossary of operators' terms, I went
to his office. "He is better than nothing. He can
provide an adjudication although God knows what kind
it will be. "

Hinton left me at the door of the building and I went
upstairs to the doctor's office. He was, I discovered,
not a psychiatrist but a psychoanalyst. The difference
meant nothing to me. I gave him the glossary. He
read it carefully, listening to my story, gave me a
list of phone numbers where I could reach him at all
times of the day and asked me to come back the following afternoon.

If the patient's own psychotic material and psychotic experiences provide the possibility of a useful learning experience,
then obviously there must be therapeutic possibilities inherent
in this situation. For example, Scheflen's report on John Rosen's
work at the Institute for Direct Analysis in Philadelphia (6) points
out that those patients who were able to acknowledge and respond
appropriately to the double-level messages and other logical inconsistencies which Rosen deliberately introduced into the treatment situation had by far the best prognosis. Those patients who
even after months of therapy reacted to such situations with anxiety and withdrawal into psychotic behavior had the poorest
prognosis.

One of us (D. D. J.) has deliberately attempted to make use of
the psychotic material the patient presents, in putting the patient
into a therapeutic double-bind. The most obvious example of this
technique is in teaching a paranoid schizophrenic patient to be
more suspicious. For example, a young Negro male was interviewed before the resident staff at a Veterans Administration
Hospital. The patient was tall and bearded, with a regal bearing.
He deliberately placed his chair some twenty feet from the interviewer, and stood staring at the audience, refusing to acknowledge
the presence of the interviewer or to answer his questions. The
interviewer told him that undoubtedly the patient thought he was
God, and indeed he might be. However, this was a very dangerous position to be in since if one were not really God, he would
allow himself to be lulled to omniscient and omnipotent fantasies

and not to keep guard and constantly check what was going on around him. The interviewer made it clear that if the patient wanted to take this kind of chance, that it was up to him, and if he wished to be treated as if he were God, the interviewer would go along with it. The patient became increasingly uneasy and yet interested in what was going on. The interview was climaxed by the interviewer's taking a large, hospital-type key from his pocket, getting on his knees, and presenting it to the patient, stating that since he was God, he had no need of a key, but, on the other hand, if he were God, he was more deserving of having a key than the interviewer. When the interviewer returned to his desk, the patient grabbed up his chair and pulled it over within two feet of the interviewer. Leaning forward, he said earnestly and with some uneasiness, "Man, one of the two of us is certainly crazy." A somewhat similar technique was used in the example of the married woman given above. She was told that her "crazy" experiences had meaning which she must discover.

What, then, seem to be the steps of growth in acute psychosis? Clinical experience suggests quite definitely that the first phase of schizophrenic involvement is characterized by a gradual or rapid build-up during which the patient is engaged in the hopeless task of maintaining, on the one hand, his shaky contact with reality, while, on the other hand, he eagerly and painstakingly collects evidence for the reality of his hunches and suspicions. This build-up of a full-grown delusionary system is frequently climaxed and completed by pseudo-insights like, "Now, all of a sudden, everything is clear to me."

At this point the person concerned is likely to acquire the "patient" label, and thus to enter into a very peculiar relationship with society. He exhibits what on the outside appears as the monolithic edifice of his delusionary system. This system, however, is by no means a stable one. In fact, it is our contention that to remain even relatively stable, this system requires a definite kind of feedback from the outside world, mainly the rejecting, censoring, or otherwise ridiculing or shaming attitude often adopted in good faith by relatives and therapists alike under the mistaken assumption that a "forceful confrontation with reality" is beneficial. While we are far from claiming to understand the phenomenon of spontaneous remission, we do believe that one of the contributing factors is the development of a run-away in the delusionary system and this, we hope to have shown by our examples, eventually permits the function of doubt to arise, first as part and parcel of the delusions themselves and later as a conscious attitude of the patient. It is interesting to note how in this second phase the patient turns from a passive victim into an active inquisitor, and how this can only come about after the psychotic experience has been allowed to develop to the point of stark absurdity. Once having become an active inquisitor, it is hoped that through therapy the patient can be made to maintain this role.

If this assumption is correct, it follows that the psychiatrist's attitude toward the patient's delusions should be one of acceptance tinged with doubt in order to be therapeutic. He should assist what we believe to be the natural course of the disease toward remission by promoting the reduction to absurdity rather than fighting absurdity with interpretations or other invocations of a reality which at this point is inaccessible to the patient. This attitude is somehow akin to that of a Judo fighter who utilizes his opponent's thrusts for the latter's ultimate defeat rather than meeting them head-on with counter-thrusts of at least equal force.

We do not claim that these ideas are new. In fact, they are reassuringly old, as proven by the following Zen story (7) which contains every single one of the points we have tried to make in this paper:

A young wife fell sick and was about to die. "I love you so much," she told her husband. "I do not want to leave you. Do not go from me to any other woman. If you do, I will return as a ghost and cause you endless trouble."

Soon the wife passed away. The husband respected her last wish for the first three months, but then he met another woman and fell in love with her. They became engaged to be married.

Immediately after the engagement, a ghost appeared every night to the man, blaming him for not keeping his promise. The ghost was clever, too. She told him exactly what had transpired between himself and his new sweetheart. Whenever he gave his fiancee a present, the ghost would describe it in detail. She would even repeat conversations, and it so annoyed the man that he could not sleep. Someone advised him to take his problem to a Zen master who lived close to the village. At length, in despair, the poor man went to him for help.

"Your former wife became a ghost and knows everything you do," commented the master. "Whatever you do or say, whatever you give your beloved, she knows. She must be a very wise ghost. Really, you should admire such a ghost. The next time she appears, bargain with her. Tell her she knows so much you can hide nothing from her, and that if she will answer you one question, you promise to break your engagement and remain single. "

"What is the question I must ask her?" inquired the man.

The master replied. "Take a large handful of soy beans and ask her exactly how many beans you hold in your hand. If she cannot tell you, you will know she is only a figment of your imagination and will trouble you no longer. "

The next night when the ghost appeared, the man flattered her and told her that she knew everything.

"Indeed, " replied the ghost, "and I know you went to see that Zen master today. "

"And since you know so much, " demanded the man, "tell me how many beans I hold in this hand. "

There was no longer any ghost to answer the question.

Admittedly, the problem remains if this isolated therapeutic experience would suffice to protect the man from a relapse into his delusions, or, in other words, whether his psychotic experience was in fact turned into an ego-enhancing one. But it may be assumed that the acceptance of a delusion conveys a nonverbal communication that the therapist values the patient. If this acceptance is not tinged with doubt, the patient may feel that the therapist is playing games. His self-esteem is thus sustained by this acceptance, and the delusion might not be so vital to him. To quote Perceval once more:

> Had my brother but said to himself, "There is some-
> thing strange here; I will try to understand it"--had he
> but pretended to give credit to what I said, and reasoned
> with me on the matter revealed to me (by the voices),
> acknowledging the possibility, but denying or question-
> ing the divine nature of my inspirations; I should, per-
> haps, have been rescued from my dreadful situation,
> and saved from ruin; but it was not so.

REFERENCES

1. Erikson, E. H. In Emotional Problems of the Student, G. H. Blaine, et al. p. xiii, Appleton-Century-Crofts, Inc., 1961.
2. French, T. M. and Kasanin, J. A psychodynamic study of the recovery of two schizophrenic cases. Psychoanalytic Quart., 10:1-22, 1941.
3. Asch, S. E. Studies of independence and submission to group pressures. Psych. Monographs, 70, No. 416., 1956.
4. Perceval's Narrative 1838. Ed. with an introduction by Gregory Bateson, Stanford University Press, 1961.
5. O'Brien, Barbara. Operators and Things, The Inner Life of a Schizophrenic, Cambridge, 1958.
6. Scheflen, A. E. A Psychotherapy of Schizophrenia: A Study of Direct Analysis, Thomas Books, 1961.
7. The World of Zen. Edited by Nancy Wilson Ross. Random House, New York, 1960.

COMMUNICATION AND SCHIZOPHRENIC BEHAVIOR

John E. Weblin

"I wave. I have a handkerchief, I wave. Bye Bye."
With these words a schizophrenic woman of 50 stood at
the door of my office and then entered for an interview.
What really was happening?
Her greeting was a farewell. Her face smiled, yet her
voice seemed wistful and sad.
She spoke and made gestures--she was heard and seen;
that is--communication took place.
That was the simple, basic and irreducible fact of those
few moments.

In this age the word communication evokes visions of ticker-
tape and television, Chevrolets and Caravelles, and even Mach-
5 mobilized beatniks in Sputniks.

Whether these splendours of civilization ultimately promote or
impair true communication is uncertain. What is certain is that
communication is, elementally, the means whereby one person relates to another.

When communication takes place a relationship is formed, and
this is built on the interaction that develops between the participants.

Communication is a basic condition of human life, and its work-
ings mould and shape the individual personality through its relationships with others. Indeed personality, that complex marriage
of "nature" and "nurture," may be described as the sum pattern
of a person's way of communicating--the total impression he makes
on others.

Reprinted from FAMILY PROCESS, 1, No. 1:5-14 (March 1962).
Copyright, The Mental Research Institute of the Palo Alto Medical
Research Foundation and the Family Institute. Reproduced by per-
mission.

One of the remarkable things about personality is its mutability. Perhaps one can do no better than quote the celebrated comments on personality structure of the greatest of Elizabethan psychiatrists--"All the world's a stage, and all the men and women merely players. And each one in his time plays many parts."

Or again, reviewing the works of a most familiar modern authority who is still producing monographs of the utmost erudition--Communication could be a term used to describe the moves of the Great Game of Life--GAMESLIFE. With singular astuteness he sees in communication a universal jockeying for position, by myriad maneuverings and subtle signallings, to achieve mastery and the "One-up" position.

The drab and colourless concept of "normality" in behaviour and personality, the essential meaninglessness of which they have seen with unique insight, is not for these observers.

Within our frame of reference of modern psychiatry, they would urge us to acknowledge that there are two great Groups of Players: --namely the "sane" who by being the majority, are sufficiently "one-up" to maintain the arbitrary divide between themselves and the minority, the "mentally ill" or "insane."

It is against this backdrop, and on this great playing field that we, as psychiatrists, at present members of the majority, must view the subject of communication.

It is logically inescapable that our judgment of the communication of members of the minority--that is, that classification of their behaviour that we call "psychiatric diagnosis"--depends in part on the communication pattern, the personalities, of ourselves.

This much of course is known. It is in fact often felt to be beneficial to embark on a short "know yourself" course for three or four years,--an ANALYSIS. Sometimes this widens one's range of stage-parts and enriches one's game of lifeman moves.

When we come to consider schizophrenia, we have--a priori-- a phenomenon of behavior--and relationship. The schizophrenic is known to us only through, in its widest sense, his communication, and similarly, only so, are we known to him through ours.

Thus, by definition we have an interaction between the schizophrenic and ourselves.

What is there about the communication of a schizophrenic that is so characteristic?

Is there any way of looking at his behaviour, his apparently disjointed repertoire of moves, such that they form a coherent whole, an ordered pattern of "lifemanship technique"? I believe there is.

I believe that it is possible to regard schizophrenic communication as a highly goal-directed activity towards avoiding almost any clearly defined relationships at all. This may be illustrated as follows:

A schizophrenic may come into our office for an interview. He may pause and then start gazing distractedly at the walls and pictures, at the curtains or out of the window, or start examining minutely a book on one's desk. He behaves as if he is alone. He will almost certainly say nothing unless spoken to. A friendly enquiry "Hello, how are you?" may evoke a response "All right thanks" from a pale, vacant face, or accompanied by a strangely out of place smile--in either case rather queering the pitch for a friendly chat.

Actually silence and withdrawal are the schizophrenic's commonest tactics, and indeed isolation is often his main long-term strategy.

Less often, he talks--at high pressure, often a very successful ploy as it forces the listener, in sheer desperation, to break off the subject. If used when having a session with the doctor, this seldom fails to herald the imminent closure of the interview.

Even at normal pressure, though, the talk of the schizophrenic has a unique property of "losing" the hearer. It is rich in metaphor and oblique associations which divert the listener's attention into a maze of by-ways.

But the classic, primal, schizophrenic gambit--retained, though in a softened form, long after recovery--is the "off-beat" response. I have yet to encounter a schizophrenic who is not superbly skilled here, with words which say one thing, and a tone of voice, facial expression or bodily gesture which means about the opposite. Alternatively he may follow a statement at once by another which implicitly contradicts it, or throws serious doubt on it. For example--I recently asked a young schizophrenic patient if she was depressed: "No" she said with a strange smile, "I have no problems in Hospital."

What she had not said is whether she has problems outside the hospital, or in her head, or whether she now understands her problems in a new light so that they no longer depress her as we in Hospital think they might, even though the difficulties themselves remain.

Thus, through incongruity both of gesture and manner and through statements which leave a lot unsaid, the schizophrenic commonly avoids truly relating to anyone.

He may even carry these verbal ploys to an extreme. He may mix his words at random, or more incredible, combine syllables of different words to form new ones. And so, while apparently talking, he is not really talking.

However, a schizophrenic is not always a man of mere words.

At times--he is a man of action.

He may start breaking up his house, or his mother, or even the windows of his ward.

This poses him a problem--for these actions are particularly positive kinds of communication, as he soon finds out. Retribution is likely to follow, and here his cavalier laugh and eloquent double-talk tend to fall on deaf ears.

But his ingenuity may now produce the schizophrenic trump cards --delusions and hallucinations.

For he is in fact not really Bill Snooks at all, but Hitler or Stalin, or even Christ or the Devil. He is unlikely to be believed but this sometimes succeeds in partially staying the hand of retribution. (I have yet to hear a schizophrenic claim to be Mr. MacMillan or Mr. Gaitskell--which suggests that the latter have not yet assumed sufficient authority from which mandate can be claimed for truly great--or terrible--deeds).

Alternatively, or in addition, the patient may top this, and imply with conviction that he was not the author of his own behavior at all, but that a voice--that of his Father or God--made him do it, or that he saw someone attacking him, and so struck the person-- perhaps a nurse or orderly--in self-defence. He may say that radio or television control his thoughts. This is an effective way of disowning authorship of thoughts and behaviour in a world which has not yet seen itself conditioned like Pavlov's dogs to mass media of communication.

In another direction, during an interview, the schizophrenic may imply that you have no right to be questioning him at all, because in fact he considers you to be a spy, or police-agent, masquerading as a doctor. He may allege that he has been brought to a police-station or prison, at a place many miles from where he actually is and that this isn't a hospital at all--so suggesting that the whole interview is a frame-up and fake, and should not be taking place at all.

Overall, the schizophrenic throws an intricate net of obscurity and uncertainty. On reviewing this array of techniques of the psychotic "life-man," it must be acknowledged that they indeed rank high in ingenuity. How have they been achieved? In what training school have they evolved?

His training has in fact started from the cradle, for he has entered a family which uses almost exclusively the same basic principles on which his own communication pattern is later so floridly developed.

The family is pervaded by anxiety, ambivalence, and inherent instability, and derives its total pattern of interaction from the parents. No one feels secure. Doubt of mutual love, and fear of mutual latent hostility together create an air of unreality, covert suspicion and indecision, or hollow unity, which stifles the straightforward expression of true emotion.

The schizophrenic is no violater of learning theory, though some observers suggest that his communication is the result of an insult from inheritance, a metabolic muddle in his brain! This is perhaps more in fun, than seriously--and who will deny that humour in such topics serves a useful and stimulating purpose?

In a minority of the families--about 10-15%, one or both parents may actually have resorted at times to the psychotic gambitfield, with a full range of schizophrenic "lifemanship."

Mostly though, the young pupil learns from the simpler, yet potent, elements of ambiguous parental emotions, words and action expressed within a more apparently normal setting.

What evidence is there for these things?

In the first place, one notices that the schizophrenic is surprisingly sensitive to questions about love, sympathy, trust and sincerity. If one asks him if he thinks most people usually say what they really feel, he often gives a knowing smile, or says with conviction that he doesn't think they do. This may be one of the few, or only, moments of appropriate response in a whole interview. Or again, if one meets his parents one feels they are ill at ease--as though they've "got something on their minds." How easily one hears oneself and others using such a concise psychiatric description about a parent as "old so and so's mum's a queer fish."

And that wider family circle too--Civilised Society--advancing affluently to the paradise of a Nuclear Nirvana, seems to be mighty sore about this tiny family affair in its midst, as though it too had something weighing on its collective mind. It will soon apprehend the young schizophrenic violator of the peace and incarcerate him behind walls, and surround his parents and siblings with obloquy and opprobrium.

However, in the rarefied air of adult psychiatry, the opportunity seldom if ever arises to study the young schizophrenic-to-be in his natural habitat, interacting in his relationships with his family, and they with him.

Nevertheless, a direct--though admittedly second-best--method of observation is available in our quest to understand the nature of schizophrenic communication, namely the family interview.

Here, the patient is seen jointly with parents, or spouse, depending on which is the immediate relevant family unit. These are interesting, sometimes electric, situations. Understandably, in front of a tape recorder, everyone including the interviewer, feels uncertain and ill-at-ease. However, the close relatives of the schizophrenic--as I have said, seem so anyway, without the presence of the symbolic mechanical father-figure.

They find it necessary to adopt attitudes like strong silent indifference, jocular, casual unconcern, or timid, yet intimate effusive gratitude. An indefinable atmosphere of unreality surrounds the situation.

There follows shortly excerpts from recordings of two parent-relative interviews. Both are young female schizophrenics, within first 7-10 days of their first admission.

In both, the interaction with parents has a remarkable effect on the patient, indeed in the second of which one could almost speak of the production of a model psychosis.

The first one features E. B. and her mother. The mother had become very anxious because of a letter E. had just written, declaring her intention to get engaged to a male patient. She had rung the Medical Superintendent in great concern. I saw her with E. the same afternoon, and anticipated she would be in a state of great anxiety. But this is not so clear, from what follows. Indeed, when it came to assessing what she really did mean, it was not only the patient who had difficulty. The interviewer was forced into some decidedly "off-beat" responses! The patient, however, had had much longer experience in learning how to reply to her mother. Nevertheless, eventually even she was put so far "one-down" that she had to switch the level of communication dramatically, in fact, by terminating it.

The important thing to note is an almost complete lack, in mother's and daughter's statements to each other and often in mother's statements to me, of clear straightforward, unambiguous responses. When this is not evident from the words alone, it was very clear from inappropriate tones of voice, captured on the tape-recordings but not on paper.

Doctor: What was it you actually wanted to see me about today, Mrs. B?
Mother: Well I hadn't met you--and I thought it was a good idea to meet you.
Doctor: Yes.
Mother: I haven't felt very happy about her.
Doctor: I see, --hmmm.
Mother: She doesn't look very happy herself, does she?
Doctor: At times.
Patient: At times.
Doctor: Hmmm. (longish pause) Have you been particularly worried today about her--over this little business of--hmm--E. saying she wanted to get married?
Mother: Well--er--it is a little startling.
Doctor: Yes.
Mother: Obviously she can't decide she's going to get married till she's well, can she?
Doctor: I think this is possibly true--what would you say about this? (turns to face E.)
Patient: I'm so rarely ill. I find it difficult to know what to say.

Doctor: Hmm—hmm.

Patient: At least, ill in my own estimation; I can quite see I may be ill in other people's estimation.

Doctor: What--hmm--did you hear Mrs. B. about E. asking if the bans could be read, what actually did you hear; what message did you get? I mean you were quite worried this morning when you rang up.

Mother: Oh, she wrote to me.

Doctor: Oh, I see.

Mother: Didn't you, darling? You wrote and told me you were --er--thinking of getting married?

Patient: What did I say in the letter? How did I put it?

Mother: Hmmmmm--"I think I'm going to marry Malcolm, so then I shall change my name from B. to W."

Patient: So I didn't mention anything about the bans?

Mother: No.

The same indirect, tangential, and oblique exchange of remarks and replies followed for several minutes. The interaction ended in a manner which took one completely by surprise:

Doctor: Have you--er--been worried about any of--er--E's boyfriends in the past at all?

Mother: No, not particularly--you haven't had a great many, have you, darling?

Patient: Not scores.

Doctor: Has E. been upset by her boy friendships as far as you know, Mrs. B?

Mother: Well, you were by R. weren't you? Did you tell the Doctor about that?

Doctor: I don't think I've heard about--er--R. no.

Patient: I went to America 5 years ago--

Doctor: Oh I'm sorry. I beg your pardon, I didn't remember the name, you have told me, yes.

Patient: I may not have told you the name.

Doctor: No, perhaps you didn't, or I didn't remember it.

Patient: I don't always remember it myself.

Mother: It seems to me that until she's sort of settled in her mind, she can't take decisions for life; I mean it isn't possible is it?

Doctor: Well--hmm--she--. No, I agree that it is--er-- very difficult--to--hmm--make decisions when one's not settled in one's mind. True enough.

Mother: I mean--you--you--must be cured of your trouble first, Darling.

Patient: What is my trouble?
Mother: Well, it was put down as a nervous disorder (sounds as though she is yawning).
Doctor: Hmm.
Patient: Whose nervous disorder?
Mother: Yours (with loud emphasis), Darling.
Patient: And mine alone?
Mother: Yours alone (softly).
Patient: Nothing to do with you?
Mother: No (very softly).
Patient: Or Granny?
Mother: No (virtually inaudibly).
Patient: Or D--(her brother)?
Mother: No (a visible, but completely inaudible articulation of this word). (Pause)

Patient then gets up and leaves the room and makes considerable noise moving her chair and banging the door.

There now follows the second family interview, in which only a motion film could have captured the full range and intensity of the extraordinary and explosive interaction.

It features a young 17 year old schizophrenic--S. R.--and her parents. All I will say as preface is that on admission she was mildly fatuous, girlish and immature in general manner. She became calmer and more at ease over the next few days, though she had been resorting to major schizophrenic ploys at home--for example by sitting in a corner for hours on end at the behest of her voices, she had managed to disrupt the usual family triangle of interaction completely. However, a week after admission she was quiet and fairly relaxed, she was able to converse with lucidity and spontaneity and was reading novels and participating rationally in the life of the Ward. Then her parents arrived and she was summoned into the office for the family interview, about which she had not been told. Within minutes her colour faded, and the Ward Sister commented "she looks ghastly." She sank into a chair as though it was her grave.

Initially there were the off-beat exchanges in Family Play, similar to the previous interview. Then I left the room and later on replayed the session recorded in my absence.

After a few very tense moments--reflected earlier so graphically by the expression on her face--the patient had seized the initiative. She produced some dazzling hebephrenic ripostes, that left, as it were, her parents merely standing on the side-line, laughing with a burst of monumentally incongruous admiration.

Patient: Do you really want me to stay in this place?
Mother & Father: (in unison) Yes.
Mother: Until you're better.
(pause)
Mother: Your nose is a little red dear, from your cold.
Patient: Yes it is a bit. (pause) Oh I'm tired.
Mother: Sleepy-tired, or just lazy?
Patient: Hmm? Sleepy tired (in a squeaking voice). I'm a very sleepy sort of child (in a stilted, extremely "childish" tone of voice). (Mother and father laughed heartily at that) (pause)
Patient: I suppose that thing is still going? (Presumably meaning the tape recorder whose microphone is fully visible, the machine itself working softly yet audibly behind a screen).
Father: I don't know.
Patient: Well he didn't switch it off when he went out.
Father: Didn't he?
Mother: Perhaps you'd like to sing a little song Susan--(then laughs).
Father: ... on the Joanna dear (first part of sentence obscured by incidental noise). (pause)

Patient strikes heavily on nearby piano keyboard a loud, slow, descending succession of notes recognisable as neither a melody or scale. This is accompanied by laughs from mother, and from the patient come some remarks obscured by the general noise).

Patient: I must try that again, --that was very nice (once more in a voice of extreme fatuity).
(She then repeats the "performance," the notes getting more violent as she descends the keyboard. As she ascends it again the notes soften and a brief almost melodic sequence of five or six notes follows before she stops.

(It should be noted that she has, in fact, sufficient experience of the piano to play some simple tunes).

With the echoes of that last study in grotesque humour ringing in our ears, we are brought back to another remark of the lady whose words opened this paper:

"Better to laugh than cry. "

"Better" perhaps because to cry is to arouse anxiety in those around one? Has she learned, and has S. R. learned, that her tears are unacceptable? Is only her "happy" self wanted?

Perhaps--as in this paper--to find humour in an approach to mental illness, is in itself an attempt to deny the conflict and mystery in life!

Certainly it seems possible to realise that in the tragedy of schizophrenia there is a "sanity" which attempts to live with this conflict. Then the "madness" of our sanity is our attempt often to deny its existence.

THE MARITAL CONTEXT OF
AN ANXIETY SYNDROME

William F. Fry, Jr.

Many clinicians, from Freud on (1, 2, 3), have described cases of neurotic anxiety with accompanying symptoms in the individual patient. It appears, however, that the relationship with the marriage partner is intimately related to the psychopathology of the patient. This paper will add a brief description of the marital context in which some patients develop these symptoms.

The syndrome of concern here is that of anxiety, phobias, and stereotyped avoidance behavior. The anxiety usually takes the form of intermittent, acute attacks of panic accompanied by the usual psychologic and physiologic phenomena. There is nothing obvious about the etiology of these attacks; they seem to occur in a variety of emotional and interpersonal situations with variable intensity and a fluctuating range of phenomena. This symptom generally conforms to classic descriptions of neurotic anxiety (4).

The phobias include fear of being afraid, fear of being alone, fear of open spaces, wandering, traveling, and sometimes claustrophobia and fear of crowds. These phobias, like the anxiety attacks, are not individually remarkable, or unlike, in any way, phobias described in classical psychiatric and psychoanalytic literature. It is interesting to note however, that as a group the phobias encountered in this syndrome concern concepts of space and area and distance. The single exception to this generalization is the fear of fear. The fear of being alone is no exception, since it is more a fear of the sensation of being physically isolated than of the emotion of loneliness. As a matter of fact, the emotion of loneliness, as we shall see, is rather constantly present and is relatively well tolerated, in contrast to these phobias.

Reprinted from FAMILY PROCESS, 1, No. 2:245-252 (September 1962). Copyright, The Mental Research Institute of the Palo Alto Medical Research Foundation and the Family Institute; reproduced by permission.

The avoidance behavior is related to the phobias by acts that are calculated to prevent the patient's contact with phobia-stimulating situations. For instance, a patient insists on remaining housebound to avoid stimulating her fear of wandering about. Another demands the continuous presence of another person-- preferably the marriage partner--to forestall any stimulation of her fear of being alone. These behavior symptoms frequently are so intense and so far-reaching that serious restrictions on the patient's activities are imposed. One couple with whom we have had contact was so restricted by behavior symptoms that neither husband nor wife was able to leave the house for a period of several years.

From the intrapsychic point of view, these patients are defending themselves against unconscious ideas. The conflict consists of a struggle within themselves. Granted such a point of view, the marital partners of these patients should be a heterogeneous group. Although the patients might be similar to each other since they have similar problems, the spouses need not be similar if they are not involved in the psychopathology.

It is the fact that the marital partners are similar to each other which is the point of this paper. Their similarity raised the question whether the anxiety syndrome described might not be described as a relationship conflict as well as an intrapsychic conflict.

It should be pointed out that different relationship conflicts may provoke a variety of other syndromes besides the anxiety syndrome described here. A quite different clinical outcome has been described in another paper (5), and others are familiar to clinicians. No simple system of dynamics can apply to all anxiety reactions because so many factors are involved in the determination of human behavior. Nor is it necessarily so that the anxiety syndrome described here will invariably occur in a particular type of conflictual relationship. However, we have observed this syndrome linked with this type of conflict in a sufficient number of instances to consider it a major psychiatric entity. When a couple is trapped together in a self-perpetuating, pathologic relationship there will be an intensification of symptomatology in both partners.

THE SPOUSES

Although the spouses of the patients in this group have many superficial differences, they are typically negativistic, anxious, compulsive, and show strong withdrawal tendencies. Their statements indicate doubt about their commitment to the marital union, indeed to deep involvement in any human relationships. The feelings of inadequacy and inferiority of the spouse affect his functioning as a marriage partner, parent, his job performance, sexual behavior, and his entire self-concept. In no case of a patient's suffering from this anxiety syndrome was there a successfully functioning spouse.

One wife was referred for psychiatric evaluation by her internist with a history of marked behavior restrictions associated with episodic acute anxiety and a state of chronic apprehension. For an eight-year period this woman had not been able to leave her home except in the company of others. She also suffered from phobias already described--a fear of being conspicuous, of being in the presence of bright lights, of being in crowds, and of standing in line. There were strong feelings of reference expressed. She spoke of marital strife.

The husband was interviewed and was found to conform to the spouse-personality pattern described above. Although of obviously superior intelligence, he was a minor city employee. He had declined numerous opportunities for promotion, despite direct encouragement by his superiors. His experience and capability were evidenced by the fact that he substituted for his superior on the latter's vacations, but he avoided any opportunity to make the advancement a permanent one. Working part-time as a bartender, he had many acquaintances but no close friends. He was very jealous of his attractive wife, feeling inadequate to meet any competition for her favor. He experienced infrequent episodes of impotence. He and his wife had built their own home some ten years before, but this was never considered completed because little details like doorknobs and bathroom hooks and window catches, etc., just never seemed to get put in--by the husband. The wife's symptoms first developed during a period when the house was largely completed but there was intense conflict between them over the husband's inability to put the finishing touches on the house.

Another couple was first contacted when the wife was seen because of intense anxiety attacks, chronic apprehension, and phobias with avoidance behavior. These symptoms had developed suddenly about six months prior to first contact. The fears were of being alone, of wandering, of traveling, of being afraid, and of crowds. The patient's activities were restricted to avoid these situations. She felt forced, by her symptoms, to have some adult

--preferably her husband--with her at all times. Marital dissatisfaction was described.

The husband was also interviewed and again conformed to the
pattern. He was a corporation lawyer, still in the lower ranks
despite obvious ability and good experience. He had passed over
opportunities for advancement. He had no close friends, spent
little time with his legal colleagues, read and slept most of the
time he was at home. He was occasionally impotent. Even before the development of his wife's symptoms, he avoided taking
trips away from home alone, usually had lunch at home--despite
the one-half hour drive from work, and phoned his wife at home
at least one or two times a day from his office. Furthermore, he
presented many subtle disinvolvement techniques in regard to his
relationship with his wife. He felt that he had asked her to marry
him because she liked him.

It is of special importance that the spouses reveal, upon careful study, a history of symptoms closely resembling, if not identical to, the symptoms of the patient. Usually they are reluctant
to reveal this history. For example, a wife was not only unable
to go out alone, but even in company she would panic if she entered a brightly lighted and/or crowded place or had to stand in
line. Her husband disclaimed any emotional problems of his own
at first, but then revealed he experienced occasional episodes of
anxiety and so avoided certain situations. The situations he avoided were: being in crowds, standing in line, and entering brightly
lighted public places. However, both marriage partners insisted
the wife should be considered the patient because she was more
afraid of these situations than he was.

In another case the wife was labeled the patient because she
was afraid of enclosed places and could not ride in elevators.
Therefore, the couple could not visit a cocktail lounge on the top
of a tall building. However, it was later revealed that the husband
had a fear of high places which he never needed to face because of
the marital agreement that they never went to the tops of buildings
because of the wife's fear of elevators. Often the patient's symptoms appear protective: as long as she has them, the spouse's
symptoms do not become pressing. A difficulty in the patient's
recovery rests upon the revelation of the spouse's problems as
her problems are solved.

One further characteristic of these marriage partners must be
described. They all evidence a tendency to over-react. This ten-

dency is of varying degree from one spouse to another, and is of varying degree at different times in the same individual. It is present in many areas of his life--such as overworking on the job or being overprotective with his children. This tendency is most frequently associated with demands being made upon him by others. It is most prominent in his relations with the so-called patient.

An example of this characteristic in operation is the husband who, in response to his wife's fear of being alone, spends every possible minute with her, to the exclusion of any personal activities. He phones her frequently when unavoidably away, stays near the phone at all times should she wish to phone him, rushes home immediately after work. If he can't be near the phone, he may take the wife on business appointments and have her wait in the car.

The relation of this over-reaction to the perpetuation of the so-called patient's symptoms is seen most obviously in the lengths to which the over-reaction often goes. Even if the patient does not ask the spouse to remain with her, he will volunteer to do so. Or he will arrange for a sitter to be with her when he cannot--this, without consulting her or asking her if she feels she needs one. At times, when she does not phone him, he may phone to ask if she is all right (raising the possibility that she might not be). Often when the patient considers defying her phobia--perhaps by planning to go out alone--the spouse reassures her and then adds, as an afterthought, the warning that she shouldn't venture too far alone (6). In one case of a wife who went alone to the store for the first time in eight years, the husband dragged himself from his sickbed to drive to the store and bring her home, "just to be sure she'd be all right."

ONSET OF SYMPTOMS CORRELATES
WITH CHANGE IN SPOUSE

During a period of four years, we have had contact with seven such marriages as these. Let us consider the implications and consequences of this pattern. It has been discovered that the patient's symptoms typically develop at the time that something out of the ordinary has occurred in the spouse's life which might arouse his anxiety. The lawyer, with a previously rather desultory employment history, was given a better position in another city. He uprooted his family and took the position, which was unusual self-assertion for him. At this time the couple also began to sleep in the same bedroom again after sleeping in different rooms for over a year. The wife developed severe anxiety attacks and was unable to venture forth from the new house.

The city employee, on a small salary, largely completed building a rather elaborate house by himself. His wife shortly developed anxiety attacks which kept her at home. Another husband finally received his graduate degree and obtained a job. His wife, who had previously been supporting him, collapsed with anxiety. Another husband began to make money as a member of a professional gambling group, instead of losing money as he had in the past. In another case where it was the husband who suffered anxiety attacks and could not function, the onset occurred when the wife decided to return to her chosen profession after many years of not working. In a case where a husband failed, the wife developed her anxiety when she discovered that her husband's business would ultimately fail and he would do nothing about it. After the bankruptcy, he began to write bad checks and her symptoms increased.

It is suggested that the onset of symptoms correlates with an important change in the life of the spouse and the symptoms are perpetuated by the ways in which they support the continued functioning of the spouse. The symptoms would seem to maintain the marriage at a time when it threatens to break up, but also they perpetuate a conflictual and difficult marital relationship. Although the patient may insist at the beginning of therapy that the spouse is perfect, deep dissatisfactions with the marriage soon become apparent.

DUAL CONTROL
The husband and wife find themselves participating in a peculiar problem of dual control (8). The patient's symptoms put her in the position, as the ailing member, to demand that the marriage partner always be at her beck and call and do what she says. The partner cannot make a move without consulting the patient and clearing it with her. Yet at the same time the patient is constantly supervised by the spouse. He may have to be near the telephone so she can contact him, but he is also checking upon all her activities. Both patient and spouse will often report that the other is always getting his or her own way.

The patient's difficulties function to permit the spouse to avoid many situations in which he might experience anxiety or other discomfort, without being confronted with the possibility of symptoms. She can be an elaborate excuse for him. He may avoid social life, ostensibly because the patient is uneasy. He may limit his work, ostensibly because he must attend the ailing patient. He may deal inadequately with his children because of his withdrawal and over-reaction tendencies. But he is spared self-confrontation by the suspicion that the children's problems are caused by the patient's symptoms. He may avoid sexual experiences with the patient ostensibly because she is ill and wouldn't be up to it. He may be uneasy about being alone but since the patient is afraid to be alone, he can always have her with him without it being emphasized that he has this symptom.

The discontented patient may indicate some desire for an extra-marital relationship, but her phobia symptoms prevent her association with other men. Because of his personality characteristics and his reaction to the patient's illness, an affair usually does not become a serious possibility for the spouse. Both the patient and spouse are relatively protected from this exigency by the patient's symptoms.

SYMPTOMS KEEP COUPLE UNITED

Usually the marriage is miserable and the couple distant and discontented, but the symptoms function to keep the couple united. This type of marriage might be called a compulsory marriage (7). With the onset of symptoms, the patient becomes unable to leave the home, far less the spouse. The spouse experiences the belief that the patient is not living with him because she wishes to, but because she must. She encourages this belief by saying sometimes that if she were able to go out alone she would leave him. The husband assumes she is staying with him only because of her illness, not because she loves him. He interprets her discontentment as resentment at being tied to him, and any affection she shows to him as bribery that he won't turn her out. He is, therefore, pleased with little she has to offer.

In turn, the spouse puts up with great demands on his time and energy by the patient. The more he puts up with, the more the patient comes to believe that he is putting up with her excessive demands because he is unable to leave her. She feels that he is with her by compulsion rather than by choice, and so any affection on his part seems a fraud.

As long as the symptoms persist, there is no way out of this dilemma. The patient, uneasy about whether her spouse wants her, demands more and more that he stay with her--because she is sick. He stays with her, but this does not reassure her, be-

48

cause he is apparently staying with her because of the illness, not because he wants to be with her. Since he feels compelled to associate with her for the sake of her illness, he can never reassure her or himself that he might voluntarily seek her company.

The spouse cannot resolve this problem. If he stays with the patient, it seems to be only because she is so ill. If he leaves her, he is a cad who does not care for her misfortune. Furthermore, if he left her or if she recovered, he would have to face his own anxiety and his symptoms. He cannot be openly sympathetic because of his resentment, nor openly unsympathetic. The patient, in turn, cannot be appreciative of the sacrifices the husband makes for her, nor can she be openly unappreciative of them.

The nature of the problem makes it self-perpetuating. Prior to therapy both husband and wife are compelled to live together in mutual distress, consoling themselves for all their difficulties with the mutual idea that this thing has been imposed upon them, beyond their control, and they can do nothing about it.

REFERENCES

1. Freud, S. Analysis of a Phobia in a Five-Year-Old Boy, Collected Papers, Vol. III, Hogarth Press, London, 1948.
2. Dixon, J.J., deMonchaux, C., and Sandler, J. Patterns of anxiety: The phobias. Brit. J. Med. Psy., 30:34-40, 1957.
3. Fenichel, O. The Psychoanalytic Theory of Neurosis, Kegan Paul, London, 1946.
4. Masserman, J. Principles of Dynamic Psychiatry, W.B. Saunders, Philadelphia, 1946.
5. Fry, W.F.,Jr. Destructive behavior on hospital wards. Psychiat. Quart. Suppl. 33 (part 2), 197-231, 1959.
6. Haley, J. The control of fear with hypnosis. Amer. J. Clin. Hyp., 2:3, 109-115, 1960.
7. Haley, J. The family of the schizophrenic: A model system. J. Nerv. and Ment. Dis., 129:357-374, 1959. Reprinted in Don D. Jackson (Ed.), Communication, Family, and Marriage (Vol. 1, Human Communication Series), Science and Behavior Books, Palo Alto, California, 1968.
8. Haley, J. Control in brief psychotherapy. Arch. Gen. Psy., 4:139-153, 1961.

PSYCHOGENESIS IN ASTHMA:

An Appraisal with a View to
Family Research

John E. Weblin

So long as asthma is ranked amongst diseases that are pecul-
iarly nervous, so long can we never hope to come to any correct
conclusions; the idea being so vague and the laws which govern the
nervous system for the most part so incomprehensible (1).

How the venerable physician of yesteryear explained the paradox of discerning comprehensibility using a mechanism--his own
nervous system--which works incomprehensibly is not clear. But
the illogic of both his remark, and my retaliation, underlines the
problem of knowledge--whether it be about asthma or anything
else, i.e., the knowledge is not the thing itself. The mirage...,
lest we forget...

But it is to be hoped that physicians, pathologists, endocrinol-
ogists and kindred brethren, will be not discouraged too readily
from making yet one more attempt to negotiate the seemingly un-
charted perils of psychiatric seas.

This paper attempts an assessment of our present understanding of the question of psychological factors in the genesis of bronchial asthma. It is based on a representative review of the literature, and whilst it essays some comment on the status of allergy
theory and attempts to harmonize this with the" psychological" side,
it is oriented more toward a research scheme for studying the
asthmatic patient and his family in an interactional setting.

It is difficult to adhere strictly to Koch's postulates in psychiatric nosology. In consequence, with relevant considerations
for pathogenesis being hopefully implicit, where they are not ex-

Reprinted from BRITISH JOURNAL OF MEDICAL PSYCHOLOGY,
36:211-225 (1963). Copyright, British Psychological Society,
London; reproduced by permission.

plicit, the deliberations presented here will be ordered around topics as follows:

<u>Part 1.</u>
   (A) Respiratory function as an indicator of emotion
   (B) Does asthmatic wheezing have a <u>meaning</u>?
   (C) The personality of the asthmatic patient
   (D) The early environment of the asthmatic patient

<u>Part 2.</u> Asthma as the "chosen" symptom
   (A) Allergy in asthma--some problems for theory
   (B) Requirements for a learning theory of asthma

<u>Part 3.</u> Discussion

<u>Part 4.</u> Conjoint family therapy (suggested avenue for research)

<u>Summary</u>

*   *   *   *   *

PART 1
(A) RESPIRATORY FUNCTION AS AN INDICATOR OF EMOTION

The word asthma comes from the Greek word meaning panting. In "common" English parlance, we "hold our breath" in surprise, and "sigh with relief" as the imprisoned breath escapes. Shock can even "take the breath away"; we can "choke" with emotion. Human situations can evoke a "stifling" atmosphere; parents can "smother" their children with affection. On the other hand, a person can be like a "breath of fresh air"; we can get trouble "off our chest", and can "explode" with mirth.

It seems that the human unconscious is deeply aware of the ebb and flow of the breath as a signal of the soul's true weal!

Sexual excitement, crying and laughter involve obvious alteration in respiratory activity.

Breath holding spells in children are regarded as a purely psychogenic upset, see Kanner (2), who also speaks of pseudo-asthmatic respiration in response to emotional stress, a phenomenon which closely resembles clinical asthma.

It is perhaps not too far-fetched to see in all this that anxiety-laden emotion can have an equivalence in retained or imprisoned

breath, and that from the mildest to severest extremes emotional
factors alone [1] appear able to generate respiratory activity with
some, or almost all, of the characters of asthmatic wheezing.

(B) DOES ASTHMATIC WHEEZING HAVE A MEANING?

Launched now into consideration of "true" asthmatic breathing,
can it be said, of itself, to have a meaning?

There has been a widely expressed view that it is equivalent to
repressed crying, and the work of Dunbar (3), Fenichel (4), Jessner
et al. (5), Long et al. (6), French and Alexander (7), Mohr et al.
(8), Alcock (9) and Barendreght (10) should be consulted for illustration of the various ways this idea has been developed. It suf-
fices here to say that these authors see the asthmatic person im-
bued by fear of separation from mother, or "mother-figure", with
a fear of the loss of love running centrally through his life. The
repressed cry is seen compounded of repressed grief, and anger,
over what these writers and others, particularly Miller and Baruch (11), see as parental rejection. Whilst the exact meaning of a
repressed cry is perhaps elusive, it is difficult not to be impressed
by certain evidence, viz. that in psychoanalysis some asthmatics
have shown a dramatic response--stopping wheezing in the process
--to early "confession" (of anger and guilt feelings, etc.) resulting
in profuse crying (see G. Wilson's contribution in French and Alexander (7)); also French and Alexander speak of dreams of fear and
hostility resulting in nocturnal attacks of asthma. Isolated, but
significant, case-history reports, as in one quoted by Knapp et al.
(12), speak of children being punished for crying. Very recently
Turnbull (13) has attempted to base, in part, a learning theory of
asthma on a concept similar to the repression of crying.

Some of these workers feel that a strong sexual conflict is involved in asthma, and see a marked erotic significance in attacks.
French and Alexander, the importance of whose monographs as a
fund of information and ideas can be scarcely overstressed, make
reference to sexual dreams which end in nocturnal attacks, and
they note the frequency and severity of attacks associated with love
affairs. Inasmuch as the latter imply a decisive, intrapsychic at
least if not always overt, separation from mother, then sexual and
grief-anger conflict can be seen as complementary themes.

---

[1] Ignoring for the moment the question of individual suscepti-
bility.

Homosexual, as well as heterosexual, doubts and fears are said to be common too.

Dunbar (3) also finds in asthmatic attacks, especially in children, an equivalence to a compulsion neurosis.

Inasmuch as several workers see a marked depressive underlay in the asthmatic personality, this point is not without interest in speculating about the repressed cry, for one recalls how difficult many depressives find it to cry.

Finally, in so far as asthma has been felt to correlate negatively with psychotic illness, and notice taken that psychotic phases and asthma alternate, but scarcely ever co-exist, it has been speculated that asthmatic attacks are equivalent to psychotic processes. The work of McAllister and Hecker (14), Leavitt (15), Sabbath and Luce (16), Funkenstein (17), Knapp et al. (12), and a recent review by Mandell and Younger (18), should be consulted. The concept is controversial, and is of uncertain value, because the meaning of psychosis still poses a problem.

(C) THE PERSONALITY OF THE ASTHMATIC PATIENT

If psychological stress is important in the development of asthma, there should be signs in the patient of personality disturbance, of whatever degree, resulting from this. The search for, and understanding of, such evidence has occupied many workers.

Knapp and Nemetz (19) found 83% of forty adult asthmatics subject to episodic depression of varying kinds between attacks--almost all are depressed during them--but seldom reaching psychotic intensity.

Dunbar (3) has reviewed the literature on asthma from the first 35 years of the century, and some later. She finds that writers like Fromm-Reichmann see a similarity in asthma to manic-depressive psychosis. It is interesting to note that whilst the latter is uncommon now in classical form, asthma continues unabated.

Brown and Goiten (20) also discover a cyclothymic disposition in asthma, coupled with paranoid features, but find a cross-section of other personality disturbances also.

Neuhaus (21), who considers that there is widespread agreement about the personality structure of asthmatic adults, sees over-anxiety, lack of self-confidence and dependancy as central features.

The interesting analytic case description of Lofgren (22), and of the various authors in the French and Alexander monograph Part II, appear to bear out most of the above impressions, though in anecdotal, unsystematized form.

Barendreght (10) in attempting to demonstrate a comparative specificity between the asthmatic and the peptic-ulcer personality, concludes that the former shows, inter alia, much more evidence of hostility and impulsive behaviour than the latter.

But it is on this question of specificity of the disturbances noted that important disagreement exists. Leigh (23), for example, can find no evidence for it, and Knapp et al. conclude that despite the incidence of depressive episodes, "no single personality profile" exists for asthma. Further, studies of personality in asthmatic children have led to just as much uncertainty.

Thus, while Alcock (9) in a controlled study with normals and chronically sick children finds tension, restraint, and paranoid ideation common, Rappaport (24) considers that asthmatic children's emotional problems are no different from those of any other chronically sick child, and regards them as purely secondary phenomena.

Harris (25), in a study based retrospectively on school-teachers' reports, finds no evidence to indicate that asthmatic children's behaviour is easily differentiable from that of non-asthmatic children.

Neuhaus (21)--in a swing back of the pendulum--obtains very different, and to him, even astonishing, results in a study using personality inventory and projective tests on asthmatic children with their sibs, "cardiac" children and their sibs, and normals, as controls. He discovers that all the first four groups show a significant and equally greater evidence of maladjustment and neurosis than the normals, but is uncertain of the meaning of the findings, and he even questions the sensitivity of the tests used. The results of a recent study by Block (26), using similar material, are awaited with interest.

Mohr et al. (8) have introduced a fresh concept in the view that asthmatic children tend to show marked pseudo-maturity, with striving towards an artificial independence.

Irrespective of the issues of specificity, and whether the problems precede or are consequent upon the asthma, Kanner (2) concludes that "... by no means all asthmatic children are 'insecure' or 'lacking in self-confidence' ". He quotes Gunnarson as finding psychological components in slightly more than half a series of fifty-eight children.

(D) THE EARLY ENVIRONMENT OF THE ASTHMATIC PATIENT

The sources of psychological stress are generally looked for primarily in childhood experiences; and questions of parent-child relationships, inter-parental harmony, personalities of sibs, etc., have received attention by a number of authors.

Some earlier analytic writings, notably of Deutsch (27) and also those of Dunbar, French and Alexander, and Fenichel--to which reference has been made--express conviction over the prevalence of conflictful early life experiences. Focus is put particularly upon the child's fear of separation from the mother, as mentioned previously. Detailed case reports, where given, almost invariably reveal homes marked by overt disturbances such as divorce, alcoholism, and early parental death, or permeated on the other hand by coldness or parental eccentricity. In others, homes have been overshadowed by chronic, severe parental illness. In a detailed recent study of ten cases, Wittkower & White (28) discovered that three of them had lost mothers, and four had lost fathers, during childhood. Some of these situations involved obvious physical separation from mother.

Where less gross forms of maternal deprivation are concerned various workers have described the nature of this in different ways. Miller & Baruch call it all rejection and find a rejecting attitude present in nearly 100% of mothers studied. Jessner et al. (5) feel that the mothers show a clinging dependence on the child, coupled, however, with a tendency to push them to premature independence, and see these as alternating, reciprocal facets of rejection. Rogerson et al. (29) in early work from a psychological viewpoint, saw the maternal attitude as one of overprotectiveness compensatory to inner feelings of rejection of the child. Abrahamson (30) has viewed the situation rather as one where the parents and child are locked in mutual engulfment, an evocative term doing some justice to the complexity of these emotionally charged predicaments.

Some psychometric studies, notably those of Fitzelle (31) with parents and Neuhaus with siblings, respectively, have been carried out with the immediate relatives of asthmatic children. Reference to the latter has already been made, and Fitzelle's study, similar in its way, used parents of chronically sick children for comparison. The results are much the same, namely, that parents of asthmatic children rate highly for maladjustment and neurosis and the "chronically sick" parents likewise.

These findings, if confirmable, suggest strongly that the asthmatic child is reared in a "sick" environment, but this does not deny the possibility that, given a precariously poised but functioning family, the arrival of an asthmatic child may eventually "rock the boat" seriously and permanently. I know of no long-term study where the personalities of family members have been investigated "before and after" the impact of an asthmatic child.

Two quite recent groups of work have contributed to a more dynamic understanding of the early milieu of the asthmatic child, namely that of Mohr et al. (8) and of Wenar et al. (32). Mohr's group, in psychoanalytic sessions with child and mother individually, and featuring some interviews with father, joins with some earlier viewpoints in seeing the mother as a dominating, controlling figure, with the father meek and dependent. This group contributes a challenging opinion about the timing of asthmatic attacks; namely, that they occur when inter-parental hostility comes into the open. The attack, they suggest, in uniting the parents in care of the child, restores a precarious peace and with it his tenuous supply of affection. The child, pushed to pseudo-maturity, thus has an important part to play in maintaining a guilt- and resent-laden symbiotic system. The value of this dynamic picture of the "asthmatic family" suffers a little in that it is based apparently on data unevenly drawn from the three members of the system, and one wonders how far a fuller contribution from the fathers would have modified the conclusions.

The studies of Wenar et al. (32) devoted to mother-child relationships included asthmatic children in a larger "psychosomatic" group studied. Using various interesting tests, their picture of the mothers is similar to that of Mohr and others; but of special interest to our present purposes is that Wenar's methodology included direct viewing of mother-child interaction from behind one-way viewing screens.

One further--as yet unpublished--study, that of Block mentioned briefly earlier, also has employed direct observation of parent-child and mother-father interaction. It seems likely, as the planning of our own project shows, that interactional observations will play a growing part in the investigation of psychopathology.

Finally, though tangential to our present direction, mention must be made of the very interesting work on the nature and intensity of the mother-child bond as it is reflected intra-psychically in the patient. Using various techniques such as dream interpretation, children's play fantasies, and TAT responses, French & Alexander, Jessner et al., Long et al., and others have become impressed with the prevalence of "claustral" or "intrauterine" themes in which a longing for, or fear of--perhaps both--enclosed spaces and water is prominent. There is room for speculation about what these notions mean, and how they have achieved reinforcement to survive extant into adult life. However, the intrauterine theme receives a little gloss in the observations of Jessner et al. and Mohr (in French & Alexander, Part II) that birth histories of asthmatic children often show an unusual incidence of delayed or difficult labours. Does mother reveal her clinging even at this early stage...?

PART 2. ASTHMA AS THE "CHOSEN" SYMPTOM

At this point it is clearly important to raise the issue of <u>allergy</u>, for the question of "choice" of respiratory symptoms would be widely regarded as meaningless without invoking the concept of allergic sensitivity in the bronchial tree.

It is accepted there that asthma attacks can occur in response to allergic stimuli, and the task as envisaged in a study of psychogenesis is to attempt to reconcile the basic fact of "allergic response" with processes more easily regarded as "psychological."

With respect to asthma some problems pertaining to allergy emerge, but in discussing them no pretence is made to an adequate coverage of the body of allergy theory as a whole.

(A) ALLERGY IN ASTHMA--SOME PROBLEMS FOR THEORY

(i) <u>Allergic</u> vs. <u>psychogenic</u> <u>asthma</u>. It is difficult nowadays to find much support for a distinction between these supposed "pure strains" of asthma. Occasionally an ingenious attempt, such as that of Bray (33), has been made to attribute everything, from irritability to enuresis that can go with asthma, to a pervading allergic disruption of mind and body.

An important study of Dekker et al. (34) has, however, recently demonstrated that comparable groups of asthmatics, labelled allergic and non-allergic according to their response to inhalational and skin tests, score equally highly with a typical neurotic group on a well-tried rating scale for neuroticism.

There is a line of evidence however in the study of Feingold et al. (35) which on a rather different basis of allergy sampling appears to diverge from this, though the significance of the difference is not easy to evaluate. Using a Personality Inventory (M. M. P. I.) on allergic--not only asthmatic--women, they find that weaker skin-test reactors tend to be more deviant on the test than strong reactors, who in fact claim a closer approximation to normal social interaction. An exception was that scoring tended to be reversed on the K scale, which may suggest that a dominating "conventionality" may mask a deeper meaning to the responses in the rest of the test than is apparent--though this is highly speculative.

The important question arises--of course--about the primary, or possible secondary nature, of psychological disturbances, both in the patient and his family. Could they be a response to the upheaval and restrictions of a chronic distressing illness in the family? It cannot always be shown that maladjustment occurred prior to the commencement of asthma, or--where it develops very early in life or is preceded by infantile eczema--that disturbed parental interaction preceded the child's birth. This is often perhaps because retrospective accounts from parents or patients are incomplete, but it cannot be assumed that this is invariably so.

(ii) Inconstancy of reaction to allergens. Whilst some patients have attacks with great regularity when exposed to their particular allergen(s), this is not always so, and it is doubtful whether this is adequately explainable on immunological grounds alone.

(iii) Alleviation of asthma by psychological intervention. Both Diamond (36) and Mason & Black (37) report on the apparent cure of intractable asthma by hypnosis--including on occasion even the abolition of positive skin tests. There are also numerous reports of success of psychoanalysis and of other simpler psychological therapies, though these results so far lack perhaps adequate collation and evaluation to satisfy critical scientific appraisal.

Certain aspects of the dilemma facing an attempt to rigidly separate allergic and psychogenic factors are well shown by the work of Long et al. (6), who like Peshkin & Tuft (38) in their description of "parentectomy, " have treated institutionalized, intractable, asthmatic children. Not only did the asthma attacks invariably cease within 2 days of admission, the children no longer had attacks when exposed to sprays of their own house dust, despite obvious sensitivity prior to hospitalization. Furthermore, the children commonly had attacks when notified of the parents' intention to visit, or during the visit.

(iv) Whence the allergic sensitivity? Prominence is given, clinically, to establishing the presence of a familial, inherited allergic disposition to asthma, eczema and hay fever. While the familial trend is often undeniable, it is perhaps doubtful whether --as it were--Johnny's asthma is proven as inherited, just because Aunt Sue had hay fever, and Grandma suffered from eczema as a little tot.

Moreover, it is rare to find a specific mode of transmission cited. Bray (33) has suggested a Mendelian dominant, but Wittkower (28) finds the evidence inadequate, and he goes on to point out that a tendency to other illnesses, especially serious respiratory illness in general, often preponderates over known allergic maladies in these families. He suggests that a "susceptible respiratory tract" should be the more general focus for genetic thinking. Asthma may of course arise without any allergic family history.

As a possible alternative to the problematic hereditary nature of asthmatic allergy, have any mechanisms for its development on an acquired basis, after birth, been suggested? This overall issue, which could raise deep immunological issues, is beyond my scope, but I wish later in this paper to set forth again a possible mechanism for allergic acquisition, hinted at by earlier writers, which by repetition in a family tree could mimic inherited transmission.

Thus, for present purposes one is perhaps justified in regarding the role of allergy at slightly less than face value. But in doing so one is obliged to try and propose an alternative interpretation as a basis for the simultaneous presence of allergic phenomena and emotional disturbances in the same patient.

(B) REQUIREMENTS FOR A LEARNING THEORY OF ASTHMA

(i) Emotional disturbance and asthmatic breathing. It is generally felt that any form of learning, including that of a neurotic symptom, requires two kinds of processes: (a) an initial association by chance, or by some "trial-and-error" process, of the par-

ticular behaviour with a state of high drive (fear, anxiety, etc.);
and (b) the subsequent repeated reinforcement of this association
through its success in relieving the state of drive. This is a very
scanty outline of the application of conditioning principles to the
learning of neurosis, but it is essentially that which is embodied
in many current writings, e.g., that of Turnbull, mentioned shortly.

In its simplest form a way is thus hinted at whereby, through
unconscious imitation of, or identification with an asthmatic member of one's household, a person might learn, or "catch"--liter-
ally "grasp at"--a habit of wheezing respiration. Should this then
be followed by adequate reinforcement in the form of an increase,
or restitution, of maternal attention in an otherwise deprived relationship, established asthma might result.

In seeking a mechanism for situations where there is no asthmatic progenitor, we find that Turnbull (13) has devoted considerable attention, among other things, to crying; noting that it is
a universal phenomenon in young children, he also regards it as
being essentially asthma-like in character. He suggests that an
infant's crying is a particularly severe source of conflict to the
mothers of asthmatics-to-be, and that the mother responds in
some kind of aberrant non-rewarding way, e.g., by punishment or
by ignoring it for a prolonged period. He holds that this situation
is one in which sighing, gasping, coughing or wheezing--being
common respiratory accompaniments of prolonged or disturbed
crying--would readily replace it if sufficiently rewarded by mother's renewed care and attention. The crying would then in fact
undergo extinction. If this is a basis upon which human asthma
could develop, there is very suggestive confirmatory evidence
from animal experiments, which Turnbull also discusses. Thus
the idea of the "repressed cry" is reborn in modern garb.

There is a theoretical problem here though, in that reduction
of a simple drive, anxiety, is perhaps an inadequate explanation
of this learning; for it is likely that the infant drive is a complex
one of anxiety and resentment, or frustration, and that the maternal response is similarly compounded. The problem this poses
for learning is hinted at by Turnbull, and it seems likely that the
concept of instrumental conditioning needs expansion in explaining
neurotic behaviour. But at present the model must serve our purposes.

In seeking how emotional conflict and respiratory symptoms become coupled, it is clear that respiratory illness in general could provide a focal meeting-point for anxiety and distorted breathing. We could speculate that, between the "imitating asthma" and "replacement of crying" models just outlined, a whole range of complex learning mechanisms is "available" to a child in a family situation where respiratory illness and serious emotional conflict are present together. The "requirements" could be met by respiratory illness in either a significant other family member, or in the pre-asthmatic himself, or both. Is there any suggestive evidence in support?

Departure into detailed references would serve no purpose, but Deutsch (27, 39) and Jessner et al. (5) have written along these lines, and more recently Wittkower & White (28). The detailed case histories in the French & Alexander monograph abound in close relatives suffering from tuberculosis, pneumonia, chronic bronchitis and congestive heart failure. Bray (33), quoting from his own and others' work, is impressed--though from a different viewpoint--with the high incidence of serious antecedent respiratory illness in asthmatic children. Knapp & Nemetz (19) note that half of their forty cases had ruminative fears about their nasal cavities out of all proportion to respiratory lesions they had themselves suffered, which again suggests a learning process in a family milieu.

To conclude this trend of thinking it is necessary only to add that other kinds of "assault" (actual or phantasied) upon the respiratory tree could, according to their severity, enhance the learning process. Whilst not necessarily regarding them in this light, the above authors refer to instances which can be mentioned here without comment: e. g. , a mother used to throw water over her child to stop breath-holding attacks; another child was smacked for the same behaviour; one case had her throat forcibly sprayed, and her limbs held, for repeated attacks of tonsillitis as a child; a boy received threats of drowning for not stopping his enuresis; inhalational anaesthesia, often for tonsillectomy, is common in early histories as also are fearful early experiences with water --to name only some of a wide range of situations quoted.

(ii) Allergy and learning processes. The possibly constitutional basis of allergic wheezing will be referred to again shortly, but the conditioning experiments of Dekker et al. (40) and of Ottenburg et al. (41) could be construed as paving the way for an alternative interpretation. A leap into conjecture could regard potentially allergenic substances, such as house-dust and pollens, as elements in the "inhalable environment" during the previously discussed asthma-learning situations. These substances (indeed, theoretically, any stimuli, like the colour of the wallpaper or a creaking floorboard) might, because of their association, become asthmogenic alone if selective reinforcement operated. Under what circumstances, through what mechanisms, might responses to inhalable substances--being those more usually involved--become reinforced?

Two hints that possible reinforcing circumstances might exist at the physiological level are implicit in the suggestion (a) of Bray (33) that previous infection traumatizes the mucosa of the bronchial tree and predisposes it to the allergic-type response, and (b) of Wittkower & White (28) who notes, in reference to Allergic Rhinitis, that in states of heightened or conflict-laden emotion there is oedema and congestion of the nasal mucosa which is sensitized thereby to allergens. As sinusitis, hay fever and polypi tend to be common in asthma, it could be conjectured that a similar mucosal mechanism might operate lower in the bronchial tree along with bronchospasm, the latter in itself might be "fear-induced" via an automatic mediation, or be a phenomenon or "voluntary" hyperventilation in stress, as suggested by the work of Dekker et al. (42).

This highly speculative proposal has two possible merits. First, it suggests the possibility of seeking experimental evidence in the constitution vs. environment controversy using asthma-prone animals. In these, asthma sensitivity could be traced in breeding experiments over several generations where the total environment (e.g., shape and colour of cage or box; "allergenic inhalants"; exposure to infection and to psychological stress, etc.) could be under constant control and be sensitively varied. Secondly, it might go some way to explaining inconstant and paradoxical responses to allergens in humans; i.e., if we could regard the psychological environment not only as a long-term determinant in the overall asthma-learning process, but as an important factor influencing allergic reactivity in the bronchial mucosa "here and now". An occasional case report lends itself better to a conditioning theory of allergy than to any other, as, for example, the case mentioned by French & Alexander (7) in which a patient, allergic to the vapour of creosote, recalled that creosote was the fuel of a lamp used to treat his croup as a small child.

However, it is clear from the foregoing that a "constitutional" theory for asthmatic allergy is at least as feasible as any suggested alternative. It is clear also, that as an unconditioned response wheezing might itself initiate learning situations. Being a frightening experience it could lead to fear becoming associated with disturbed breathing of any origin--be it emotional hyperventilation, crying, coughing, etc., or the hyperpnoea of infection or of violent exercise. The mutual reinforcement of events associated with these various factors could lead, via stimulus generalization and mediating agents, to complex patterns of causation whose origins might well become considerably obscured. Thus even though the "psychogenic vs. allergic" dichotomy is difficult to sustain in its extremes, we might perhaps have a reasonable theoretical basis for "mixed" cases where there was a relative predominance of one component or the other. Lofgren's astonishing case, in which an adult asthmatic woman had, as a child, been nearly strangled to death and had watched a relative's gasping death agony, to name only two of her bizarre experiences, suggest that many cases are over-determined, irrespective of the original mechanism.

PART 3. DISCUSSION

> The times are out of joint, o cursed spite
> That ever I was born to set them right.

Hamlet can serve as no model for an attempt to evaluate the foregoing. So vast, and at times so speculative, is the scope of asthma research that I must limit my comments to two controversial areas--namely the study of personality, maladjustment, etc., in the asthmatic patient and the description of his early environment--these areas being particularly relevant to the approach of family research about to be advocated here.

Furthermore, I am concerned more with how such differing conclusions in these areas can, and have, come about, and with some almost "built-in" problems of the research rather than with a detailed evaluation of the merits of individual conclusions. My "sub-topics" here will be:

(a) The influence of the observer (investigator, researcher, etc.).
(b) The search for meaningful data.
(c) The nature of "sickness", "normality" and "health".

(a) The influence of the observer. Despite the considerable variety of conclusions reached about both the personality of the asthmatic, and about his early environment, it is important to realize that these apparent "differences in opinion" are better regarded as different "viewpoints", or more correctly aspects of behaviour looked at from different "viewpoints". If this seems rather self-evident, this cannot be said of the implications attached to the fact that the many "different opinions" are often based on research or testing methods dissimilar in scope, "depth" and certainty of interpretation; which brings us to the first point, i.e., the selection of a method of investigation involves an inescapable value-judgement on the nature of the phenomena "asthma" and the "person-with-asthma". This, like any other value-judgement, has its origins in the whole life and experience--by no means limited to the fragment we call "professional"--of the observer up to that moment; the decision is not automatically relevant to the subject(s) or patient(s) about to enter the scene. These people do not experience, as it were, their lives or personalities divisible into the categories of "Rorschach responses" or items on a "personality inventory", helpful though this divisibility may be to that aspect of the scientist's personality which we may call "professional".

This aspect of research--ignored as often by their critics as by investigators themselves--leads logically to the allied problem of the interpretation of data, be it about similar or conflicting findings. Sapir (43) has expressed it thus: "...he (referring to 'the genuine psychiatrist") best realizes that the same types of behaviour, judged externally, may have entirely distinct, even contradictory, meanings for different individuals." While certainly applicable to the question of the asthmatic personality, this problem of the level of description or interpretation of behaviour is perhaps best exemplified by three studies of the asthmatic's early environment, namely, those which conclude that the child is subjected to:

(i) Maternal rejection (Miller & Baruch).
(ii) Alternating parental attitudes of clinging dependence and pushing to premature independence (Rogerson et al.).
(iii) Engulfment (Abrahamson).

Given adequate comparability of the groups studied, it is difficult to conclude other than that these descriptions represent varying penetrations of view between the authors, again a factor largely independent of the subjects under investigation.

Finally, in considering the influence of the observer, we have to realize the flaws in assuming that one and the same investigation or test procedure can be administered uniformly from occa-

sion to occasion. Even with apparently well-standardized psychometric methods, the effects of unplanned "verbal conditioning" and
"non-verbal" stimuli from the observer, either before or during
the investigation, may well be very important; understanding of
these phenomena belongs to a branch of communication study in
its early, but stimulating, stages of development.

(b) The search for meaningful data. Partly consequent upon
awareness of the above issues, we can see how inevitable it is that
a considerable variety of methods have been utilized to increase
"scientific" understanding of asthma. Looked at differently, this
array of techniques can be seen to polarize into two general kinds
of approach, and so pose a real dilemma in planning research:

(i) Methods of limited scope designed to illustrate certain aspects of asthma--like those alluded to above--and which are often
capable of definition in the form of concise psychometric tests.
These generally yield data "easy to handle" but difficult to integrate
into an over-all picture of the illness.

(ii) Laborious "depth" methods such as prolonged psychotherapy or psychoanalysis, whence--as seen in the French & Alexander
monograph--the data is rich and abundant but difficult to abstract
for scientific purposes. Here again the observer-influence is
marked, and even though it be claimed as "inert" or of a "blank-
screen" nature, its effect is still very difficult to evaluate.

(c) The nature of "sickness" and "health". There are two
groups of work, at least, in the research here reviewed which
raise this matter prominently. To refer the reader back they are:

(i) The studies of Dekker et al. (34) and of Feingold et al. (35)
concerning the question of relative psychological health in asthmatics with (a) weak and (b) strong, allergic reactivity, and (c) in
those without allergy.

(ii) The studies of Alcock (9), and Fitzelle (31), and Neuhaus
(21) in which the mental health of chronically sick children, and
their parents and sibs, is contrasted with that of asthmatic children and their families' members.

Close examination of these studies does not remove doubt that
serious conceptual problems may be involved. In fact what emer-
ges as a possible implication is that inadequate awareness of the
nature of "sickness" in contrasted groups is involved; also that

"health", if viewed as a statistical "norm"--as in many psychological tests--among "average populations", may be very misleading. These issues are of central importance to a holistic or "psychosomatic" approach to medicine, and the two main questions which this has to pose are:

(a) Does psychological conflict play a far more important part in the production of all disease than hitherto realized?

(b) Can this conflict be so "concealed" in social functioning which, though widely regarded as "normal"--even laudable--is in fact far from healthy, or may it be "manifested" in a wide range of somatic disease, or both?

It would be absurd to claim that the methodology becoming known as conjoint family therapy, being the particular approach in family research here favoured, could remove the three major problem areas discussed above or supplant the techniques involved. Nothing is likely to do so. It is seriously contended, though, that it reduces the "observer influence" problem markedly, bids fair to soften the "methodology selection" dilemma, and may help illuminate current concepts of sickness, health and normality. The paper will now conclude with a further few words on these points and with suggestions how the conjoint family method might be expected to contribute to understanding in the overall picture of asthma.

PART 4. CONJOINT FAMILY THERAPY (A SUGGESTED
         AVENUE OF RESEARCH)

It is unnecessary here to trace the origins and development of the conjoint family approach, be it used as a diagnostic or as a therapeutic technique. The interested reader is referred to the volume Exploring the Base for Family Therapy (44), and to the publications of Bowen (45), Wynne et al. (46), Ackerman (47), Bateson et al. (48), Jackson (49, 50) and Jackson & Weakland (51), and Laing (52), principally though not entirely in the field of schizophrenia. Further contributions have come from Bell (53), Mac Gregor (54), Sonne et al. (55), Boszormenyi-Nagy (56), Haley(57), and Weakland (58).

An attempt must now be made to illustrate its relevance to the problems in asthma research just discussed:

(i) Dilution of "observer influence". Experience of the conjoint approach with families having a schizophrenic or delinquent member shows a radically different interview situation from that of individual therapy. Family interaction patterns, though initially stilted by the strangeness of the situation, usually rapidly assert themselves. Typical family relationships are soon revealed, and in a diagnostic setting, where the observer is either behind a viewing screen, or if present is not striving strenuously to intervene qua therapist, the mutual "arousal" and interpersonal monitoring that goes on yields extremely rich verbal and non-verbal "material". The interactional contribution from the observer is diluted greatly; his presence is not irrelevant but it can be reasonably portrayed as contributing to an interactional situation which is a paradigm of the complex relationship of the family with the outside world--a world which can be charitable, is more often felt to be hostile, and because of this ambiguity is inevitably confusing and therefore a constant challenge. This clinical setting cannot be the natural family state, if by this is meant a sense in which it can be self-contained in isolation. But it is very doubtful whether such a conception has any real validity. In any case it is here claimed that the family interview, [2] observed and recorded, is the only way we have of putting the understanding of family interaction on a scientific footing. With the above qualifications the setting provides, as suggested in a recent paper of mine (59), a more or less direct view of the family interactional basis of his personality structure (and maladjustment, etc.) as also that of his sibs, and of the parents as far as parent-child interaction reveals this. The setting encourages the giving of historically accurate data also, so that the picture of the development of the family environment has a welcome reliability. The effect of social "input" gauged from the families' discussions of wider communal contacts can be discerned too.

In short, a considerable range of each individual's capacity for interaction is quite rapidly seen, which includes unexpected positive and creative potential in the "patient", as well as sick aspects of the "healthy" members.

Given a satisfactory technique for data collection to enable ready comparison amongst a series of patients and their families, the conjoint family approach would seem clearly appropriate to the study of the asthmatic child or adolescent.

---

[2] Home interviews perhaps closer approximate to the natural state, but the interviewer is still a factor, and the situation is less amenable to observation and recording.

(ii) The search for meaningful data. Particularly helpful here have been the writings of Haley (60, 61) on the nature of symptomatic behaviour. On the basis of some earlier ideas elaborated jointly with the other members of the Bateson group (48) he has shown how understanding of the multi-levelled nature of messages allows systematic description of relatively brief sequences of communication. Further, he has shown in what may loosely be termed "control theory", how "sick" messages (e.g., of a double-bind nature) denote "sick" relationships.

Subsequently Jackson, Riskin & Satir (62), using these and other concepts, have demonstrated considerable accuracy in identifying pathology from "blind" study of short excerpts of unfamiliar tape-recorded family therapy sessions.

Hope is held by these workers that a "typology" of families can be worked out, based on the classification of their communication patterns, which will add a new dimension to present orthodox categories of psychopathology. The cl ose study of interaction is a source of data as compact as that utilized by current psychometric tests and, in a sense, ontologically more directly meaningful. At the same time the data comes from the very soil in which psychoanalysis is grounded--whether or not this is openly acknowledged --i.e., family events and their significance for the communications of the individual.

(iii) The nature of "sickness" and "health". Little further can be said on this question. It is unlikely that philosophic and cultural obstacles to agreement in this area will ever be fully overcome. However, just as psychoanalysis has significantly increased our understanding of human behaviour, so the fresh approach of family therapy may add new insights still. It could, for example, be important if personality assessments of "asthma family" members using psychometric tests clashed consistently with those gained in family therapy situations. The basic presuppositions and "norms" of the former would be one of the variables requiring serious re-examination.

Bearing in mind now the material considered throughout this paper, it remains merely necessary to enumerate the general ways in which research employing the conjoint family approach might eventually be found to fulfill a useful function with respect to bronchial asthma. Clearly a variety of research programmes would be needed to survey these topics at all adequately.

(1) Shed fresh light on the question of personality disturbances in the patient and family members; furnish material for comparison with assessments using accepted psychometric techniques. Should this comparison yield obvious discrepancies, a need will be shown to check the basic assumptions of both the family approach and of the psychometric procedure (its "norms", etc.).

(2) Provide opportunity for a dynamic formulation of the family milieu, especially with respect to the role of the asthmatic attacks in family interaction and in the maintenance of family homeostasis. For example, would the onset of an attack be predictable in certain conflictful situations?

(3) Provide historical evidence whether or not disturbances in family interaction antedated, in some degree, the patient's asthma; enhance understanding of how the asthma further exacerbates these problems.

(4) Provide a cross-check on the significance of differences discovered hitherto between "asthmatic families" with a heavy, slight, or non-existent loading of allergy.

(5) Lend evidence to help support, or refute, a "learning process" mechanism for asthma; specifically this would involve tracing historical situations in which conditioning processes, either for emotional or allergic factors, might have been initiated and subsequently reinforced.

(6) Provide an evaluation of the method as a treatment adjunct for the patient's asthma, and as a more definitive therapy for psychological problems in all the family members. Experience with other conditions shows that where therapy is being successful, this is inseparable from a general movement toward health in the family as a whole.

Some of these aims are currently being incorporated into the planning of a pilot study on asthmatic children and their families. This hopefully will lead to the construction of more organized and sophisticated propositions for comprehensive research later.

The field of psychogenesis in asthma is seen here to be a large and formidable one, especially now as widening "psychosomatic" horizons and new methodologies exceed in many cases the experience of any individual worker and tax his conceptual abilities to (or beyond!) their limits. Furthermore, humility is clearly a

good companion when one notes the arresting and sobering reflexion that: "All of us in science are at the mercy of our prejudices.
If you happen to have the right prejudices they call it insight. If
you have the wrong prejudices you're likely to be called a crackpot" (63).

SUMMARY

This paper investigates the present status of theory and research into psychological factors in the production of bronchial
asthma. It describes how respiratory function is a sensitive indicator of emotion, and discusses the "meanings" that have been
attributed to asthmatic wheezing. Theories of the asthmatic "personality" are mentioned, and the various attempts to study his
"early environment" are described. With respect to the "choice"
of asthma as a symptom, the unlikelihood of two different kinds--
"allergic" and "psychological"--is discussed and the need for a
unified theory of allergic and emotional factors recognized. Possibilities for a "learning process" are suggested, with tentative
mechanisms being outlined to link together emotional conflict, allergic reactivity and disturbed respiration. Central to the theoretical problems of asthma are the diverging views about "personality" and "early environment". It is contended that inadequate
recognition of the influence of the investigator in planning, performing and interpreting research is partly responsible, together
with the lack of satisfactory ways of collecting meaningful data.
Over-simple conceptions of "sickness", based on inadequate understanding of "health" are also possibly contributory. Conjoint
family therapy is suggested as a new approach which might help
shed light on several of the areas involved in an over-all understanding of psychogenesis in asthma.

REFERENCES

1. Pridham, T. L. Brit. Med. J. i., 1860.
2. Kanner, L. Child Psychiatry, 3rd Ed., Thomas, Springfield,
   Ill., 1957.
3. Dunbar, F. Emotions and Bodily Changes, 4th Ed. Columbia
   University Press, 1954.
4. Fenichel, O. Psychoanalytic Theory of Neurosis, Norton &
   Co., New York, 1945.
5. Jessner, L. et al. Emotional impact of nearness and separation for the asthmatic child and his mother. Psychoanal.
   Study Child, 10:355, 1955.

6. Long, R. T. et al. A psychosomatic study of allergic and emotional factors in children with asthma. Amer. J. Psychiat., 114 (10): 890, 1958.

7. French, T. M. and Alexander, F. Psychogenic factors in bronchial asthma. In Psychosomatic Medicine Monograph 4, Parts I and II. Washington, D. C., National Research Council, 1941.

8. Mohr, G. J. et al. Department of Child Psychiatry, Mount Sinai Hospital, Los Angeles, California. Personal communication, 1962.

9. Alcock, T. Some personality characteristics of asthmatic children. Brit. J. Psychol., 33:133, 1960.

10. Barendreght, J. T. Cross-validation study of the hypothesis of psychosomatic specificity, with special reference to bronchial asthma. J. Psychosom. Res. 2:109, 1957.

11. Miller, H. and Baruch, D. W. Emotional problems of childhood and their relation to asthma. A. M. A. Jrn. Dis. Child, 93:242, 1957.

12. Knapp, P. H. et al. Personality variations in bronchial asthma. Psychosom. Med., 19:443, 1957.

13. Turnbull, J. W. Asthma conceived as a learned response. J. Psychosom. Res., 6:59, 1962.

14. McAllister, R. M. and Hecker, A. O. The incidence of allergy in psychotic reactions. Amer. J. Psychiat., 105:843, 1949.

15. Leavitt, H. C. Bronchial asthma in functional psychoses. Psychosom. Med., 5:39, 1943.

16. Sabbath, J. C. and Luce, R. A. Psychosis and bronchial asthma. Psychiat. Quart., 26:562, 1952.

17. Funkenstein, D. H. Psycho-physiological relations of asthma and urticaria to mental illness. Psychosom. Med., 12:377, 1950.

18. Mandell, A. J. and Younger, C. B. Asthma alternating with psychiatric symptomatology. Calif. Med., 96(4):251, 1962.

19. Knapp. P. H. and Nemetz, S. J. Sources of tension in bronchial asthma. Psychosom. Med., 19 (6):466, 1957.

20. Brown, E. A. and Goiten, B. L. Some aspects of mind in asthma and allergy. J. Nerv. Ment. Dis., 98:638, 1943.

21. Neuhaus, E. C. A personality study of asthmatic and cardiac children. Psychosomat. Med., 20 (3):181, 1958.

22. Lofgren, L. B. A case of bronchial asthma with unusual dynamic factors, treated by psychotherapy and psychoanalysis. Int. J. Psychoanal., 42:414, 1961.

23. Leigh, D. Asthma and the psychiatrist--a critical review. Int. Arch. Allergy, N. Y., 4:227, 1953.

24. Rappaport, H. G. Psychosomatic aspects of allergy in childhood. J. Amer. Med. Assn., 812, 1957.
25. Harris, M. C. and Shure, N. Study of behaviour patterns in asthmatic children. J. Allergy, 27 (4): 312, 1956.
26. Block, J. Children's Hospital of the East Bay, Oakland, California. Personal communication, 1962.
27. Deutsch, F. Production of somatic disease by emotional disturbance. In The Inter-relationship of Mind and Body. The Association for Research in Nervous and Mental Disease Processes, 19:271. Baltimore, Md, The Williams and Wilkins Co., 1939.
28. Wittkower, E. D. and White, K. L. Psychophysiological aspects of respiratory disorders. In American Handbook of Psychiatry, p. 690, Basic Books, New York, 1959.
29. Rogerson, C. H. et al. A psychological approach to the problem of asthma and the asthma-eczema-prurigo syndrome. Guy's Hosp. Rep., 85:289, 1935.
30. Abrahamson, H. A. Evaluation of maternal rejection theory in allergy. Ann. Allergy, 12, 1954.
31. Fitzelle, G. T. Personality factors and certain attitudes towards child rearing among parents of asthmatic children. Psychosom. Med., 21, (3), 208, 1959.
32. Wenar, C. et al. Origins of psychosomatic and emotional disturbances. Psychosom. Med. Monog., Hoeber, Inc., New York, 1962.
33. Bray, G. W. The asthmatic child. Arch. Dis. Child., 5:237, 1930.
34. Dekker, E. et al. Allergy and neurosis in asthma. In Advances in Psychosomatic Medicine, p. 235. Symposium of the Fourth European Conference on Psychosomatic Research. Robert Brunner, Inc., New York, 1961.
35. Feingold, B. F. et al. Psychological studies of allergic women; the relation between skin reactivity and personality. Psychosom. Med., 24 (2): 195, 1962.
36. Diamond, H. H. Hypnosis in children: the complete cure of 40 cases of asthma. Amer. J. Clin. Hypn., 3:124, 1959.
37. Mason, A. A. and Black, S. Allergic skin responses abolished under treatment of asthma and hay fever by hypnosis. Lancet, i, 877, 1959.
38. Peshkin, M. M. and Tuft, H. S. Rehabilitation of intractable asthmatic children by the institutional approach. Quart. Rev. Pediat., 11:7, 1956.
39. Deutsch, F. Thus speaks the body. Acta Med. Orient., 10: 67, 1951.

72

40. Dekker, E. et al. Conditioning as a cause of asthmatic attacks. J. Psychosom. Res. 2:97, 1957.
41. Ottenburg, P. et al. Learned asthma in the guinea pig. Psychosom. Med., 20:395, 1958.
42. Dekker, E. et al. Further experiments on the origin of asthmatic wheezing. In Advances in Psychosomatic Medicine, p. 240. Symposium of Fourth European Conference on Psychosomatic Research. Robert Brunner, Inc., New York, 1961.
43. Sapir, E. Culture, Language and Personality, p. 160. University of California Press, Berkeley and Los Angeles, 1960.
44. Exploring the Base for Family Therapy. Papers from the M. Robert Gomberg Memorial Conference, Family Service Assoc. of America, New York, 1961.
45. Bowen, M. A family concept of schizophrenia. In The Etiology of Schizophrenia, p. 346., Basic Books, New York, 1960.
46. Wynne, L. C. et al. Pseudo-mutuality in the family relationships of schizophrenics. Psychiatry, 21 (2):205, 1958.
47. Ackerman, N. W. The Psychodynamics of Family Life. Basic Books, New York, 1958.
48. Bateson, G. et al. Toward a theory of schizophrenia. Behavioral Sci., 1 (4): 251, 1956.
49. Jackson, D. D. The question of family homeostasis. Psychiat. Quart. Suppl., 31 (1):79, 1957. Reprinted in Don D. Jackson (Ed.), Communication, Family, and Marriage, (Vol. 1, Human Communication Series), Science and Behavior Books, Palo Alto, California, 1968.
50. Jackson, D. D. Family interaction, family homeostasis and some implications for conjoint family psychotherapy. In Individual and Family Dynamics, p. 122. Grune & Stratton, New York, 1959. Reprinted on pp. 185-203 of this volume.
51. Jackson, D. D. and Weakland, J. H. Conjoint family therapy. Psychiatry, 24, Suppl. to No. 2, 1961. Reprinted on pp. 222-48 of this volume.
52. Laing, R. D. The Self and Others. Tavistock, London, 1961.
53. Bell, J. E. Family group therapy. Publ. Hlth. Monogr. No.64, U. S. Dept. of Health, Education and Welfare, 1961.
54. MacGregor, R. Multiple impact psychotherapy with families. Fam. Proc. 1 (1):15, 1962.
55. Sonne, J. C. et al. The absent member maneuver as a resistance in family therapy of schizophrenia. Fam. Proc. 1 (1): 44, 1962.

56. Boszormenyi-Nagy, I. The concept of schizophrenia from the perspective of family treatment. Fam. Proc. 1 (1):103, 1962.
57. Haley, J. Wither family therapy? Fam. Proc. 1 (1):69, 1962.
58. Weakland, J. H. Family therapy as a research arena. Fam. Proc. 1 (1):63, 1962. Reprinted on pp. 271-76 of this volume.
59. Weblin, J. E. Communication and schizophrenic behavior. Fam. Proc. 1 (1):5, 1962. Reprinted on pp. 30-40 of this volume.
60. Haley, J. Control in psychoanalytic psychotherapy. Progr. Psychother. IV. Grune & Stratton, New York, 1959.
61. Haley, J. An interactional description of schizophrenia. Psychiatry, 22 (4):321, 1959. Reprinted in Don D. Jackson (Ed.), Communication, Family, and Marriage (Vol. 1, Human Communication Series), Science and Behavior Books, Palo Alto, California, 1968.
62. Jackson, D. D., Riskin, J. and Satir, V. A method of analysis of a family interview. Arch. Gen. Psychiatry, 5:321, 1961. Reprinted in Don D. Jackson (Ed.), Communication, Family, and Marriage (Vol. 1, Human Communication Series), Science and Behavior Books, Palo Alto, California, 1968.
63. Crick, F. H. C. Biophysicist, Cambridge University, Article in San Francisco Examiner, Tues. 10 April, 1962.

AN INTERACTIONAL EXPLANATION OF HYPNOSIS

Jay Haley

The only reasonable excuse for adding another theory of hypnosis to the many which have been proposed is an entirely new approach to the problem. Previous theoreticians have conjectured about the perceptual or physiological nature of hypnotic trance and the result is a literature on hypnosis consisting of conflicting ideas and insoluble paradoxes. The various theoreticians have proposed at least the following descriptions of hypnotic trance. The trance is sleep, but it isn't sleep. It is a conditioned reflex, but it occurs without conditioning. It is a transference relationship involving libidinal and submissive instinctual strivings, but this is because of aggressive and sadistic instinctual strivings. It is a state in which the person is hypersuggestible to another's suggestions, but one where only auto-suggestion is effective since compliance from the subject is required. It is a state of concentrated attention, but it is achieved by dissociation. It is a process of role playing, but the role is subjectively real. It is a neurological change based upon psychological suggestions, but the neurological changes have yet to be measured and the psychological suggestions have yet to be defined. Finally, there is a trance state which exists separately from trance phenomena, such as catalepsy, hallucinations, and so on, but these phenomena are essential to a true trance state.

One can wonder if a rigorous answer is possible to the question: Is there a state called "trance" which is different from the normal state of being "awake"? The "trance" state is by definition a subjective experience. It can be investigated only if the investigator examines his subjective experiences when supposedly in such a state. This is a most unreliable method of research, particularly when one is dealing with the slippery perceptive experiences of hypnotic trance. Whether or not another person is in a trance state

Reprinted from THE AMERICAN JOURNAL OF CLINICAL HYPNOSIS, 1, No. 2:41-57 (October 1958). Copyright, American Society of Clinical Hypnosis, Phoenix, Arizona; reproduced by permission.

cannot really be known any more than what another person is thinking can be known--or even if he is thinking. We can observe the communicative behavior of a person, but we can only conjecture about his subjective experiences. A rigorous investigation of hypnosis must center on the communicative behavior of hypnotist and trance subject with, at most, careful conjective about the internal processes which provoke that behavior. The theory, or descriptive explanation, of hypnosis offered here will not add to the current confusion about the trance state but will deal only with the interaction between hypnotist and trance subject.

Although most attempts to be "objective" about psychological processes tend to ignore the most significant problems involved, there is decided merit in analyzing the manifestations of a subjective state instead of making inferences about the state itself. Debate about hypnosis has always centered around the question of whether a subject is really experiencing a phenomenon or only behaving as if he is. Such a debate is essentially unresolvable. The few crude instruments available, such as the GSR and the EEG, indicate slight physiological changes, but no instrument can tell us whether a subject is really hallucinating or really experiencing an anesthesia. At most we can only poke him with a sharp instrument in the supposedly anesthetized area or amputate a limb, as Esdaile did, and observe his communicative behavior. Our only data are the communications of the subject, the rest is inevitably conjecture. It would seem practical to begin an investigation of hypnosis with an analysis of what can be seen and recorded on film in the hypnotic situation and thereby limit what needs to be inferred from the subject's behavior.

If an investigation centers on the process of communication between a hypnotist and subject, then answerable questions about hypnosis can be posed: Is the communicative behavior of a supposedly hypnotized subject significantly different from the communicative behavior of that person when not hypnotized? What sequences of communication between hypnotist and trance subject produce the communicative behavior characteristic of a person in trance? Answers to these questions will explain what is unique to the hypnotic relationship and differentiates it from all others. To answer such questions a system for describing communicative behavior is needed. An approach to such a system will be offered here with the argument that human interaction can be dissected and labeled and that a particular kind of communication sequence is characteristic of the hypnotic relationship.

ACCEPTED GENERALIZATIONS ABOUT HYPNOSIS

In the literature on hypnosis there is a sufficient repetition of ideas so that a few generalizations can be made about the hypnotic situation which would be agreed upon by most hypnotists. It is now generally accepted that hypnotic trance has something to do with a relationship between the hypnotist and subject. In the past it was assumed that trance was the result of the influence of the planets or merely something happening inside the subject independently of the hypnotist. Currently it is assumed that hypnotic phenomena result from an interpersonal relationship as hypnotist and trance subject communicate with one another by verbal and non-verbal behavior. It is also generally agreed that "trance" involves a focusing of attention. The subject does not while in trance report about activities outside the task defined by the hypnotist and his reports about the hypnotic task are in agreement with the hypnotist's reports. In addition, it is assumed that the relationship between hypnotist and subject is such that the hypnotist initiates what happens in the situation. He initiates a sequence of messages, and the subject responds. The common assumption that the hypnotist must have "prestige" with the subject seems to be an agreement that the subject must accept the hypnotist as the person who will initiate ideas and suggestions. Although the subject may respond to the hypnotist's messages in his own unique way, still by definition he is responding and thereby acknowledging the hypnotist to be the one who has the initiative in the situation. In those instances where the subject decides the task, it is implicitly agreed that the hypnotist is letting this happen. It is also accepted that in every induction the hypnotist at some point "challenges" the subject either explicitly or implicitly to try to do something he has been told he cannot do.

These few generalizations are about all the statements which would be acceptable to a hypnotic investigator. When more specific statements are made, debate and dissension arise. However, there is one further generalization which makes explicit what is implicit in most techniques and theories of trance induction, and some consideration should make it acceptable to most hypnotists. Hypnotic interaction progresses from "voluntary" responses by the subject to "involuntary" responses. "Voluntary" responses are those which hypnotist and subject agree can be deliberately accomplished, such as placing the hands in the lap or looking at a light. "Involuntary" responses are those which hypnotist and subject agree are not volitional, such as a feeling of tiredness, levitating a hand without deliberately lifting it, or manifesting an hallucination. Involuntary responses in general consist of changes at the autonomic level, perceptual changes, and certain motor behavior. The motor aspects of trance are particularly obvious during a challenge when a subject tries to bend an arm and cannot because of the opposition of muscles.

Every trance induction method known to this writer progresses either rapidly or slowly from requests for voluntary responses to requests for involuntary ones. This alternating sequence continues even into the deepest stages of trance. When the sequence occurs rapidly, as in a theatrical induction, the hypnotist quickly asks the subject to sit down, put his hands on his knees, lean his head forward, and so on. Following these requests for voluntary behavior, he states that the subject cannot open his eyes, or move a hand, or bend an arm, or he requests similar involuntary behavior. In a relaxation induction the sequence occurs more slowly as the hypnotist endlessly repeats phrases about deliberately relaxing the various muscles of the body and follows these suggestions with others suggesting a feeling of tiredness in his body or some other involuntary response. The most typical hypnotic induction, the eye fixation, involves a request that the subject voluntarily assume a certain position and look at a spot or at a light. This is followed by a request for an involuntarily heaviness of the eyelids. A "conversational" trance induction proceeds from requests that the subject think about something, or notice a feeling, or look here and there, to suggestions that require a shift in the subject's perceptions or sensations. The trance state is usually defined as that moment of shift when the subject begins to follow suggestions involuntarily. Either the subject struggles to move a hand and cannot because of an involuntary opposition of muscles, or he reports a perception or feeling which he presumably could not voluntarily produce.

Before dealing with hypnosis in more interactional terms the hypnotic situation can be summarized according to these general statements of agreement. In the hypnotic situation the hypnotist initiates ideas or suggestions which are responded to by the trance subject. The hypnotist persuades the subject to follow voluntarily his suggestions and concentrate upon what he assigns. When this is done, the hypnotist requests involuntary responses from the subject. The progress of the hypnotic interaction progressively defines the relationship as one in which the hypnotist is in control of, or initiating, what happens and the subject is responding more and initiating less.

DEFINING A TYPE OF RELATIONSHIP

As hypnotist and subject, or any two people, interact, they work out what sort of relationship they have with each other. If the relationship stabilizes, the two people work out a mutual agreement about what sort of behavior is to take place between them and therefore what sort of relationship it is. This agreement is achieved "implicitly" by what they say and how they say it as they respond to each other rather than by explicit discussion of what sort of relationship it is. To describe the working out of a particular relationship it is necessary to differentiate it from others and label it.

If one took all the possible kinds of communicative behavior which might be exchanged between two people, it could be roughly classified into behavior which defines a relationship as symmetrical and behavior which defines the relationship as complementary. A symmetrical relationship is one between two people who exchange the same sort of behavior. Each person initiates action, criticizes the other, offers advice, and so on. This type of relationship tends to be competitive; if one person mentions that he has succeeded in some endeavor, the other person mentions that he has succeeded in some equally important endeavor. The people in such a relationship constantly emphasize their equality to, or symmetry with, the other person.

A complementary relationship consists of one person giving and the other receiving rather than the two competing as in a symmetrical relationship. In a complementary relationship the two people are of unequal status, one is in a superior position and the other is in a secondary position. A "superior" position means that the person initiates action and the other follows that action; he offers criticism and the other accepts it, he offers advice and the other assumes he should, and so on. In such a relationship the two people tend to fit together or complement each other.

This simple division of relationships into two types applies to all two-person systems. No relationship between any two people will consistently be of one type in all circumstances; usually there are areas of the relationship worked out as one type or another. Also a relationship may shift from basically one type to basically another. Such a shift may occur rapidly back and forth or it may consistently tend in one direction. When a child grows up he progressively shifts from a complementary towards a symmetrical relationship with his parents as he becomes an adult.

Each person in a relationship defines the relationship by what he says to the other and the way he qualifies what he says. Although every message interchanged between two people will, in a sense, define the relationship--if only by expressing the idea "this is the kind of relationship where this sort of thing is said,"--still there are certain kinds of messages which make more of an issue of the sort of relationship than other kinds. A professor may lecture and one of his students may ask questions to clarify various points, but then the student may ask a question in such a way that he is implying, "I know as much about this as you do." The professor must then re-define the relationship as complementary--one between teacher and student. The professor does this either by showing that the student doesn't know as much as he does or by indicating that he doesn't appreciate the tone of that question. At certain moments, in response to certain kinds of messages, the type of relationship is put in question. The kind of message that puts the relationship in question will be termed here a "maneuver". In the example cited, the student made a symmetrical maneuver-- a maneuver defining the relationship as one between two equals. The professor's reply when he puts the student in his place would be a complementary maneuver--a maneuver designed to define the relationship as complementary. Such maneuvers are constantly being interchanged in any human relationship and tend to be most often used in an unstable relationship where the two people are groping towards a common definition of their relationship.

Maneuvers, or "relationship messages," tend to put the type of relationship in question and by their nature demand a maneuver in response. If two people, A and B, talk about the weather they may be defining the relationship as neutral and no particular issue is made of what sort of relationship it is. But when one or the other makes a maneuver, the nature of the relationship is immediately an issue. Maneuvers consist of 1) requests, commands, or suggestions, that another person do, say, think, or feel something, and 2) comments on the other person's communicative behavior. Should A ask B to do something, then B is immediately posed the problem of whether this is the sort of relationship where A has the right to make that request. B is also affected by whether the request was made tentatively or apologetically, or whether it was a rude command. Since the relationship is in question, B must either do what A says and accepts A's definition of the relationship, or refuse to do it and thereby counter with a maneuver to define the relationship differently. He may as a third possibility, do what A says but qualify his doing it with a statement that he is "permitting" A to get by with this and therefore he is doing it but not agreeing with A's definition of the relationship.

As an example, if one employee asks another employee of equal status to empty the wastebasket, this could be interpreted by the other as a maneuver to define the relationship as complementary or one between unequals. If the other raises his eyebrow, this is describable as a counter-maneuver to define the relationship as symmetrical. The first employee may respond to that raised eyebrow by saying, "Well, I don't mind doing it myself if you don't want to." In this way he indicates that his original request was not a complementary maneuver but really a symmetrical one, since it was something one equal would ask of another equal. The issue was raised because the first employee used that class of message termed here a maneuver--he requested that the other person do something. Similarly if a person comments on another person's behavior, the issue is immediately raised whether this is the sort of relationship where such a comment is appropriate. If one person suggests that another dresses rather sloppily, the counter maneuver may be, "Who the devil are you to tell me how to dress?" Such a comment indicates the relationship is symmetrical rather than complementary.

A complication must be added to this simple schema of relationships. There are times when one person lets another person successfully use a particular kind of maneuver. For example, A may act helpless and force B to take care of him. Ostensibly A is in a secondary position in a complementary relationship since he is being taken care of. Yet he arranged the situation, and therefore he is actually on the superior end of a complementary relationship. In the same way one person may encourage another to do something which implies that they are two equals. If A lets B use symmetrical maneuvers, then A is initiating the behavior and is in a complementary relationship with B. Whenever one person lets, or forces, the other to define the relationship in a certain way, he is at a higher level defining the relationship as complementary.

Therefore a third type of relationship must be added to the other two and will be termed a meta-complementary relationship. The person who establishes a meta-complementary relationship with another is controlling the maneuvers of the other. He is permitting, or forcing, another person to make maneuvers which define the relationship in a certain way. He may let someone else appear in charge of the behavior in the relationship, but since he is labeling what happens as happening with his permission then he is in the superior position of a meta-complementary relationship.

In summary, relationships can be simply divided into complementary and symmetrical with the type of relationship an ongoing

subject of definition between any two people. The type of relationship becomes a particular issue when one of the two peoples makes
a maneuver, defined as a request, command, or suggestion that
the other person do, say, think, feel, or notice something, or a
comment on the other person's behavior. A maneuver provokes a
series of maneuvers by both participants until a mutually agreed-
upon definition of the relationship is worked out between them.
These maneuvers involve not only what is said, but the meta-com-
munication of the two people or the way they qualify what they say
to each other. A third type of relationship is proposed, a meta-
complementary relationship, to describe that interaction where one
person permits or forces the other to use maneuvers which define
the relationship in a certain way. The person who acts helpless in
order to force someone to take charge of him is actually in charge
at a meta-complementary level.

THE HYPNOTIC RELATIONSHIP
    With these types of relationship as background, hypnotic inter-
action can be described as apparently taking place in a complementary relationship. The hypnotist suggests, and the subject follows
his suggestions so that each person's communicative behavior is
complementary. The act of making a suggestion is a maneuver to
define the relationship as complementary, and the act of following
the suggestion is an acceptance of that definition of the relationship.

    In hypnotic literature a suggestion is defined as "the presenta-
tion of an idea" as if a suggestion is an isolated unit unrelated to
the relationship between the two people. Actually the act of making
a suggestion and the act of responding to one is a process which has
been going on between the two people and will continue. It is a class
of messages rather than a single message and is more usefully defined in that way. A "suggestion" is defined here as a maneuver:
that class of messages which make an issue of what type of relationship exists between the person who offers and the person who responds to the suggestion. A suggestible person is one who is willing to accept the interpersonal implications of doing what he is told.
This idea is stated implicitly in such comments as "He willingly
follows suggestions." It is possible to follow suggestions unwill-
ingly, as well as not to follow them at all, but when a person willingly follows suggestions he is accepting a complementary relationship with the person who is telling him what to do. There are several crucial points about the hypnotic interaction which differentiates it from other relationships.

    1. It has been said that certain kinds of messages exchanged
between two people make an issue of what kind of relationship they

have. The hypnotic relationship consists entirely of the interchange of this class of messages. The hypnotist tells the subject what to do with his suggestions and comments on the subject's behavior. There are no other kinds of messages involved; talk about the weather is not interchanged.

2. When the hypnotist tells the subject what to do, he is defining the relationship as complementary. The subject must either accept this definition by responding and doing what he is told or respond in such a way that he defines the relationship as symmetrical. Some subjects are resistant, and every subject is resistant to some degree, and the central problem in hypnotic induction is overcoming the resistance of the subject. In communications terms "resistance" consists of countermaneuvers by the subject to define the relationship as symmetrical. No person will immediately and completely accept the secondary position in a complementary relationship. The hypnotist must encourage or enforce a complementary relationship by countering the subject's countermaneuvers. Whereas in ordinary relationships between people both persons may initiate or respond with either symmetrical or complementary maneuvers, in the hypnotic situation the hypnotist concentrates entirely on initiating complementary maneuvers and insisting that the subject respond in agreement with that definition of the relationship. When the subject is "awake," or when the two people are maneuvering differently, the hypnotist may behave symmetrically with the subject, but during the hypnotic relationship his efforts are devoted entirely to defining the relationship as complementary. A complication will be added to this description later, but for the moment let us describe the hypnotist-subject relationship as complementary.

When he meets with particular kinds of resistance, a hypnotist may explicitly put himself in a secondary position with a subject while implicitly taking control at the meta-complementary level. That is, if the subject insists on defining the relationship as symmetrical, the hypnotist may appear to hand control of the relationship over to the subject by saying that he is only guiding the subject into trance and must follow the subject's lead with whatever he wishes to do. Having placed himself in the secondary position of a complementary relationship, the hypnotist then proceeds to give the subject suggestions and expect him to follow them, thus defining the relationship as complementary with himself in the superior position. Whenever the hypnotist behaves in a symmetrical or secondary way, it is to take control at the meta-complementary level.

3. When a subject accepts a complementary relationship, whether he likes it or not, it becomes possible for him to misinterpret messages from the environment, from another person, or from inside himself. This statement is conjecture, since it describes the internal processes of an individual, yet such an inference seems supportable on the basis of the subject's communicative behavior. When the hypnotist suggests an hallucination, the subject will misinterpret the messages from the environment which contradict the hallucinatory image. The same is true of bodily sensations, emotions, and memories. The more the subject is unable to counter the meta-complementary maneuvers of the hypnotist, the more trance manifestations he is capable of experiencing. To describe his behavior from an interactional point of view, it is necessary to discuss what the evidence is for "involuntary" behavior.

THE INVOLUNTARY IN TERMS OF BEHAVIOR
An attempt to bring rigor into the investigation of hypnosis requires us to deal with observable behavior rather than to conjecture about the internal processes of a subject. When it is said above that the trance subject experiences involuntary phenomena, this statement is unverifiable. We cannot know whether or not a subject is experiencing an hallucination or various bodily sensations and emotions. For example, when a subject's arm begins to levitate we might say that this is an involuntary phenomenon and therefore a manifestation of trance. As a hypnotic subject, we might ourselves experience that hand levitation and feel that the hand was lifting up and we were not lifting it, thus we would subjectively know that this was involuntary. However, as investigators of hypnosis we cannot rely on our subjective experiences. Ideally we should be able to describe the processes of trance induction and trance phenomena while observing a film of hypnotist and subject interacting. Confined to our observations of the film we would not observe "involuntary" activities by the subject. We could only observe behavior which we inferred was involuntary. Our problem is to describe the communicative behavior of a subject at that moment when we draw the inference that he is experiencing an involuntary trance phenomenon.

To describe communicative behavior one must take into account the fact that people not only communicate a message but qualify or label that message to indicate how the message is to be received. A message may be qualified by another which affirms it, or it may be qualified by one which denies it. Thus a person can step on another person's foot and qualify it with a statement that this was accidental or involuntary. Or the person may step on the other person's foot and qualify this message with a "vicious" expression which indicates "I'm doing this on purpose." Thus a qualifying message may either deny or be incongruent with another message, or it may affirm or be congruent with the other message. When we observe a film of two people interacting and we conclude that something one of them does is "involuntary", we draw that conclusion from the way the person qualifies what he does. If we see a trance subject levitating an arm and hear him say in a surprised way, "Why, my arm is lifting up," we conclude that he is experiencing an involuntary phenomena. Our conclusion is drawn from the fact that the subject is doing something and denying that he is doing it. He may make this denial with a verbal comment, with a surprised expression, by the way he lifts the arm, by commenting on it later after he was awake, and so on. He may also say, "Why, my arm is lifting up," and thereby deny that he is lifting it, but say this in an "insincere" tone of voice. That is, he qualifies the arm lifting with two statements: one says "I'm not doing it," the other says, "I'm doing it." When we observe this incongruence between his tone of voice and his statement we conclude that the subject is simulating an arm levitation and that it isn't really involuntary. Our conclusion is based on the fact that two incongruences are apparent in the ways he qualifies his messages: 1) He lifts his hand and says he didn't, 2) he says he didn't in a tone of voice which indicates he did. If he should express astonishment that his hand lifted in words, in his tone of voice, and in his postural communication so that all of his messages are congruent with a denial that he is lifting his arm, then we say it is really an involuntary movement.

Besides the fact that we detect simulation of hypnotic behavior by noting two incongruences in the ways the subject qualifies some activity, it seems clear that the goal of hypnotic induction from the behavioral point of view is to persuade the subject to deny fully and completely that he is carrying out the activity. That is, the hypnotist pushes the subject towards qualifying his behavior with messages congruent with each other and which as a totality deny that the subject is doing what he is doing. When the subject behaves in this way, an observer reports that the subject is experiencing an involuntary phenomenon.

As an illustration, let us suppose that a hypnotist wishes to induce a hallucination in a subject. After a series of interactional procedures from hand levitation through challenges, the hypnotist suggests that the subject look up at a bare wall and see that painting of an elephant there. He may do this abruptly, or he may suggest that the subject watch the painting develop there and later press for an acknowledgment that the painting is there. The subject can respond in one of several ways. He can look at the wall and say, "There is no painting there." He can say, "Yes, I see the painting," but qualify this statement in such a way, perhaps by his tone of voice, so that he negates his statement. In this way he indicates he is saying this to please the hypnotist. Or the subject can say there is a painting on the wall and qualify this statement congruently with his tone of voice, posture, and a contextual statement such as, "Naturally there's a painting there, so what," or "Our hostess has always liked elephants." This latter kind of behavior would be considered evidence of trance.

Characteristic of a person in trance is (a) a statement which is (b) incongruent with, or denies, some other statement, but which is (c) qualified by all other statements congruently. The subject in trance (a) reports a picture (b) on a bare wall, thus making a statement incongruent with the context, and (c) he affirms his statement that there is a picture on the wall with other verbal messages, his tone of voice, and body movement. As another example, the subject lifts his hand during a hand levitation and indicates that he isn't lifting it. This statement, which is incongruent with the lifting hand, is supported or affirmed by the ways he says it. If a subject is experiencing an anesthesia, he responds passively to a poke with a pin, thereby responding incongruently, and he affirms his response with congruent words and tone of voice.

The behavior of a subject in trance is differentiable from the behavior of the subject awake by this single incongruence. A person in normal discourse may manifest incongruences when he communicates his multiple messages, or all of his messages may be congruent or affirm each other. The single incongruence is characterized of trance behavior. Even though several hypnotic tasks may be assigned a subject simultaneously, each is characterized by a single incongruence.

The single incongruence of trance has another characteristic which differentiates it from incongruences in normal communication. This incongruence consists of a denial that he is responding to the hypnotist. The subject is doing what the hypnotist suggests while denying that he is doing what the hypnotist suggests. If a subject levitates a hand, he qualifies this with a denial that he is lifting it. When he does this he is indicating that he is merely reporting an occurrence, he does not qualify the lifting hand with an indication that it is a response to the hypnotist even though at that moment the hypnotist is suggesting that the hand lift. Should the subject act like a person awake and lift the hand while indicating that he is lifting it, he would be acknowledging the hand lifting as a message to the hypnotist. By qualifying the hand lifting with a denial that he is doing it, he manifests an incongruence which indicates that he is merely making a report. In the same way the subject merely reports the existence of a painting on the wall instead of indicating that his seeing the painting there is a statement to the hypnotist.

To formalize the behavior of the trance subject, it can be said that any communicative behavior offered by one person to another can be described in terms of four elements: a sender, a message, a receiver, and a context in which the communication takes place. In other words, any message can be translated into this statement:

"I   am communicating something
(a)   (b)

to you   in this situation."
(c)   (d)

Since communicative behavior is always qualified, any element in this message will be qualified by an affirmation or a denial. In a hypnotic trance, the subject denies these elements and does not affirm them. Trance behavior denying each element can be briefly listed.

(a) Whenever he requests an "involuntary" response, the hypnotist is urging the subject to deny that he is responding or communicating something. The first element of the statement above, "I am communicating," is qualified with a denial and therefore changed to "It is just happening."

(b) The hypnotist not only urges the subject to deny that he is originating a message, such as an arm levitation, he may also urge the subject to deny that anything is happening, i.e., being communicated. The subject may appear to be unaware that his hand is lifting, thus qualifying the lifting hand with a statement that it isn't lifting. Or he may manifest a similar denial by manifesting amnesia. If he qualifies his behavior with a denial that it happened then nothing was communicated. He can not only say "I didn't lift my hand," but he can say, "My hand didn't lift," and thereby manifest an incongruence between his statement and his lifting hand. When a subject's tone of voice and body movement is congruent with the statement that he doesn't recall something, or congruent with the absence of a report of some activity during trance, then observers report that he is experiencing amnesia.

(c, d) It is also possible for the subject to deny the final elements in the essential message above. He may indicate that what he is doing is not a communication to the hypnotist in this situation but qualifying, or labeling, the hypnotist as someone else and/or the situation as some other. Hypnotic regression is manifested behaviorally by the subject qualifying his statements as not to the hypnotist but another person (after all if he is regressed he hasn't met the hypnotist yet), perhaps a teacher, and the context as not the present one but perhaps a past schoolroom. When all of his communicative behavior is congruent with one of these incongruent qualifications, then an observer will report that the subject is experiencing regression.

In summary, a subject in trance as well as a person awake exhibits behavior toward another person which is describable as the statement "I am communicating something to you in this situation." The trance subject qualifies one or all the elements of this statement incongruently so that the statement is changed to "It is just happening," or "Nothing happened," or "I am communicating to someone else in some other place and time."

The problem posed by hypnotic induction is this: how does one person influence another to manifest a single incongruence in his communicative behavior so that he denies that he is communicating something, that something is being communicated, or that it is being communicated to the hypnotist in this situation? More simply, how is a person influenced to do what he is told and simultaneously deny that he is doing anything.

TRANCE INDUCTION IN TERMS OF BEHAVIOR
When hypnotic trance is seen as an interaction consisting of one person persuading another to do something and deny he is doing it, then it would seem to follow that trance induction must consist of requests for just that behavior from a subject. The hypnotist must ask the subject to do something and at the same time tell him not to do it. The nature of human communication makes it possible for the subject to satisfy these conflicting demands. He can do what the hypnotist asks, and at the same time qualify this activity with statements denying that he is doing it or that it is being done. Thus he does it, but he doesn't do it.

To simplify the rich and complex interchange which takes place between a hypnotist and subject, let us describe a hand levitation induction. The hypnotist sits down with the subject and tells him to put his hand on the arm of the chair. He then says something like, "I don't want you to move that hand, I just want you to notice the feelings in it." After a while the hypnotist says, "In a moment the hand is going to begin to lift. Lifting, lifting, lifting." If we would divest ourselves of theories and naively observe this inter-action between hypnotist and subject, it would be obvious to us that the hypnotist is saying to the subject, "Don't lift your hand," and then he is saying, "Lift your hand." Since our observation is biased by theories of human behavior, we see this behavior in terms of the unconscious and conscious or in terms of autonomic processes, and so the obvious incongruence between the requests of the hypnotist is not so obvious. Yet we are faced with the in-evitable fact that if the subject's hand lifts, he lifted it. He may deny it, but no one else lifted that hand.

There are only two possible responses by a subject to a request that he lift his hand and not lift it. He can refuse to do anything and thereby antagonize the hypnotist and end the trance session. He can lift his hand and simultaneously deny that he is lifting it, or conceivably that it is lifting. [1] A third possibility would be for him to lift it and say he did, and then the hypnotist would say, "But I told you not to lift it," and the procedure would begin again.

Every trance induction method involves this kind of contradictory request. Indeed whenever one requests "involuntary" behavior from another person he is inevitably requesting that the subject do something and simultaneously requesting that he not do it. This is what "involuntary" means.

Not only is the double-level request apparent in trance induction, but during the process of deepening the trance it becomes even more obvious. At some time or other in hypnotic interaction the hypno-tist tests or challenges the subject. These challenges are all for-mally the same: the hypnotist asks the subject to do something and simultaneously asks him not to do it. The most common is the eye closure challenge. The hypnotist asks the subject to squeeze his

---

[1] The use of the term "denial" here does not imply that the sub-ject is calculatedly denying that he is lifting his hand. He may sub-jectively be certain that the hand is lifting itself. The emphasis here is on his behavior.

eyes tightly closed during a count of three, and at the count of three the subject is asked to try to open his eyes. He is told that the harder he tries to open them the more tightly they will remain closed. Once again the request "Open your eyes" is qualified by the statement "Keep your eyes closed." Essentially the subject is told, "Obey this suggestion," and then he is told, "Don't obey my suggestions." When the test is successful and the subject keeps his eyes closed, he is said to be "involuntarily" unable to open them. Observing his behavior we would say he is keeping his eyes closed and qualifying this behavior with the statement that he is not keeping them closed.

THE DOUBLE BIND

This double level request which the hypnotist poses can be labeled a "double bind" and its characteristics can be described. A "double bind" is present when one person communicates a message and qualifies that message with an incongruent message in a situation where the other person must respond to these contradictory messages, cannot leave the field, and cannot comment on the contradiction (1). The hypnotic situation not only contains double-level requests by the hypnotist, but also the other two elements; the subject cannot comment on the contradiction or leave the field. It is difficult for the subject to leave the field because he has usually requested a trance to begin with. Most hypnosis is done with voluntary subjects. It is also difficult for the subject to comment on the incongruence in the hypnotist's suggestions because of the hypnotist's approach. If a subject is asked to concentrate on his hand and comments on this suggestion by asking why he should, he is usually informed that he does not need to inquire why but should merely follow suggestions. The behavior of the hypnotist rather effectively prevents the subject from engaging in conversation about the hypnotist's behavior.

As an illustration of an obvious double bind during a hypnotic induction, a resistant subject once said to Milton Erickson, "You may be able to hypnotize other people, but you can't hypnotize me!" Erickson invited the subject to the lecture platform, asked him to sit down, and then said to him, "I want you to stay awake, wider and wider awake, wider and wider awake." The subject promptly went into a deep trance. The subject was faced with a double level message: "Come up here and go into a trance," and "Stay awake." He knew that if he followed Erickson's suggestions, he would go into a trance. Therefore he was determined not to follow his suggestions. Yet if he refused to follow the suggestion to stay awake, he would go into a trance. Thus he was caught in a double bind.

Note that these were not merely two contradictory messages, they were two contradictory <u>levels</u> of message. The statement "Stay awake" was <u>qualified</u> by, or framed by, the message "Come up here and go into a trance." Since one message was qualified by another they were of different <u>levels</u> of message. Such conflicting levels of message may occur when verbal statement, tone of voice, body movement, or the contextual situation, qualify each other incongruently. A double level message may occur in a single statement. For example, if one person says to another, "Disobey me," the other person is faced with an incongruent set of messages and can neither obey nor disobey. If he obeys, he is disobeying, and if he disobeys, he is obeying. The statement, "Disobey me" contains a qualification of itself and can be translated into "Don't obey my commands," and the simultaneous qualifying statement, "Don't obey my command to not obey my commands." A hypnotic challenge consists of this type of request.

When the hypnotist presents incongruent messages to the subject, the subject can only respond satisfactorily with incongruent messages. The peculiar kinds of behavior exhibited by a hypnotic subject are reciprocals to the hypnotist's requests. As an illustration, we can diagram hypnotic interaction in this way.

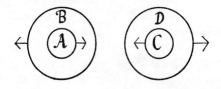

The letter A represents the hypnotist's statement, "Keep your eyes open and stare at this point." This statement is qualified by B, "Your eyelids will close." The subject cannot respond satisfactorily if he responds to A and keeps his eyes open. Nor can he respond satisfactorily by responding to B and closing them. He can only respond with incongruent messages when asked to close his eyes and not close them. He must close them, C, and qualify this closing with a denial that <u>he</u> did it, D.

Should the subject respond to only A or B, and thereby respond congruently, the hypnotist is likely to point out to him that he isn't cooperating and begin again. More clever hypnotists will handle a congruent response in other ways. For example, if a subject should stubbornly keep his eyes open, thus responding only to A, the hypnotist might suggest that he hold them open as long as he can, no matter how much of an effort this is. In this way he ultimately produces the eye closure and accepts the weariness as an "involuntary" response.

Essentially the hypnotist is saying to the subject, "Do as I say, but don't do as I say, " and the subject is responding with, "I'm doing what you say, but I'm not doing what you say. " Since human beings can communicate at two levels, this type of interaction becomes possible.

THE HYPNOTIC RELATIONSHIP

The relationship between hypnotist and subject was previously described as the enforcement of a complementary relationship by the hypnotist. When the subject responds to the hypnotist's messages rather than initiating his own, he is joining the hypnotist in a mutual definition of the relationship as complementary. When the subject "resists", he is opposing the hypnotist's complementary maneuvers with countermaneuvers. Characteristically these define the relationship with the hypnotist as symmetrical--one between equals--rather than complementary. The hypnotist counters these maneuvers with maneuvers of his own which define the relationship as complementary. He may, for example, ask the subject to resist him. In this way a symmetrical maneuver is re-defined as complementary. It becomes behavior requested, and therefore to respond symmetrically is to do as the hypnotist says and so behave as one does in a complementary relationship. This "topping" or countering the maneuvers of the subject was described as essentially an attempt by the hypnotist to win control of what sort of relationship he and the subject are in.

The particular maneuver of the hypnotist, the double bind, makes it impossible for the subject to counter with a maneuver which defines the relationship as symmetrical. If one is asked to do something and simultaneously asked not to do it, one cannot refuse to follow suggestions. If the subject responds or if he does not respond he is doing what the hypnotist requests and when one does what another requests, he is in a complementary relationship. The subject can only behave symmetrically by commenting on the contradiction or leaving the field and ending the relationship. If he leaves the field, the relationship is ended. If he comments on the hypnotist's statements and thereby behaves in a symmetrical way, he is likely to meet a countermaneuver which enforces a complementary relationship. The hypnotist may, for example, suggest that he comment on his behavior, thereby stepping to the meta-complementary level and defining the comments as responses to his suggestions.

Then, if the subject comments, he is doing what he is told and there-fore defining the relationship as complementary.

A complication must be added to this description of hypnosis. To say that the hypnotist imposes a complementary relationship and the subject in trance is agreeing to this definition is to leave hypnosis undifferentiated from other types of relationship. Conceivably there are many other situations in which one person tells another what to do and the other willingly does what he is told so that they mutually define the relationship as complementary. Yet in these other situations trance behavior is not apparent. The person doing what he is told does not manifest denials that he is doing so. It seems apparent that trance behavior is not explained by saying that the subject and hypnotist behave in those ways which define their relationship as complementary. The complication is this: the hypnotist not only prevents the subject from behaving in symmetrical ways, thus forcing him to behave in complementary ways, but he prevents the subject from behaving in complementary ways as well.

If the subject resists the hypnotist, thus behaving in a symmetrical way, the hypnotist may ask him to resist, thus forcing him to behave in a complementary way. However, if the subject behaves in a complementary way and follows suggestions willingly, the hypnotist then asks him to behave symmetrically. He asks the subject to refuse to follow his suggestions. Essentially a challenge is a request that the subject resist the hypnotist, since the subject is asked to do something the hypnotist has told him not to do. Actually the double bind prevents both complementary and symmetrical behavior. Just as one cannot refuse to respond to a double bind and is thereby prevented from behaving symmetrically, one cannot behave in a complementary way by responding because he is also being told not to respond. The subject is also prevented from achieving the third type of relationship, the meta-complementary. Conceivably he could let the hypnotist tell him what to do and in this sense be labeling what the hypnotist does as done with his permission. However, when he behaves in this way, the hypnotist requests that he try to prevent himself from doing what the hypnotist asks and acknowledge that he can't. The challenge forces him to abandon meta-complementary behavior. Whichever way the subject tries to define his relationship with the hypnotist, he finds the hypnotist refusing to accept that type of relationship.

The hypothesis offered here seems to have reached an impasse at this point. It was said earlier that all behavior of a person defines his type of relationship with another and it was then said that

all relationships can be classified as either symmetrical, complementary, or meta-complementary. Now it is said that the trance
subject's behavior does not define the relationship in any of these
ways. A way out of this impasse is possible when it is seen that
the subject is not behaving. All of his behavior is labeled as not
his behavior, and so he cannot be indicating what sort of relationship he is in. The goal of the hypnotist is precisely this: to prevent
the subject from controlling what sort of relationship they have. He
prevents the subject from defining the relationship as symmetrical,
complementary, or meta-complementary by inducing him to negate
or deny that behavior which would define the relationship. If Mr.
A is responding to Mr. B, the very existence of that response defines the relationship as complementary. However, if Mr. A responds to Mr. B and denies that he is responding, then his response
is not defining his relationship. The behavior of the subject in
trance does not define a particular kind of relationship but indicates
that the subject is not defining the relationship at all. The control
of what sort of relationship it is rests with the hypnotist, and this
differentiates the hypnotic relationship from all others.

To clarify and differentiate the hypnotic relationship from others,
a diagram can be drawn which represents any relationship. When
any two people meet for the first time and begin to interact with
each other all sorts of messages are potentially possible between
them. They may interchange insults, compliments, sexual passes,
rejecting statements, violent blows, and so on. All of these potential kinds of interaction are represented in Figure 1 by X's. As the
two people interact, they work out between them what sort of behavior, or what sort of messages, are to take place between them.
They agree that certain messages are not to occur in this relationship and that other kinds are to be included. Thus they draw a line
differentiating what is to take place in this particular relationship
and what is not. This is represented by the line in the diagram
which includes some X's and excludes others. For example, if
Mr. A criticizes Mr. B, thereby placing criticism from him within
the frame of the relationship, Mr. B may say, "I won't take criticism
from you," thereby excluding it from the relationship. If Mr. A
agrees to this, then criticism by him is outside the line rather than
in it. Human interaction consists of mutual behavior which indicates where this line is to be drawn.

All the items of behavior, or messages, interchanges by two
people can be classified as behavior which defines the relationship
as symmetrical or behavior which defines it as complementary.
Thus an X in Figure 1 becomes a member of the class "complemen-

tary" or the class "symmetrical." A criticism by Mr. A indicates a complementary relationship, and Mr. B's refusal to accept it indicates a symmetrical relationship. In this way the two people work out what sort of relationship it is, complementary or symmetrical, by what sort of behavior they agree shall be included within the relationship. Figure 2 represents a hypothetically extreme complementary relationship.

Any two people interacting are constantly working out what sort of behavior is to take place in the relationship. However, they are working out a higher level problem: who is to decide, or control, what sort of behavior is to take place. As they behave with each other, each message by the fact of its existence implies that it belongs in the relationship. At the same time each message is qualified by other messages which indicate such ideas as "This message belongs in our relationship," or "Does this message belong in our relationship?" or "This message belongs in our relationship whether you like it or not." Implicit in these qualifying messages is an attempt to work out who is to decide what message, or type of behavior, is to take place in this relationship. In a normal relationship this deciding is shared. A offers a message, B counters with one of his own, and each indicates that he is deciding what behavior is to take place and therefore what sort of relationship it is.

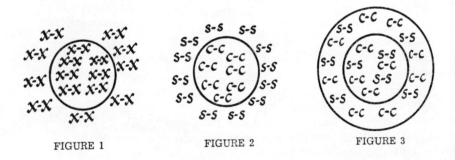

FIGURE 1   FIGURE 2   FIGURE 3

What differentiates the hypnotic relationship from others is the mutual agreement which is worked out that the hypnotist is to control what sort of behavior is to take place. All behavior from the subject is either initiated by the hypnotist, or if the subject does initiate some behavior it is labeled as not being initiated by him. To avoid controlling what sort of behavior is to take place, the subject must qualify what he does with denials that he is doing it, that it is being done, or that it is being done in this place and time. Thus at the qualifying level he is behaving in those ways which avoid defining the relationship by avoiding the implication that his behavior is done in relationship to the hypnotist. The hypnotist takes control not only of the behavior which takes place but of the qualifications of that behavior. A diagram of the hypnotic relationship would look like Figure 3.

By placing whatever happens in the relationship within a meta-complementary frame, the outer circle in the diagram, the hypnotist completely controls what sort of behavior is to take place and therefore where the relationship line is to be drawn. The trance is successful when the subject communicates the messages requested by the hypnotist, qualifies those messages with denials that he is communicating them and therefore denies that he is defining the relationship, and thereby acknowledges that the hypnotist is in control of the definition of the relationship. This is, of course, a statement about a hypothetically ideal hypnotic relationship. In practice no subject will let a hypnotist take complete control of the relationship.

When the hypnotic subject avoids defining his relationship with the hypnotist, he appears to experience a variety of subjective experiences at the perceptual and somatic level. His perception of himself, the world, time and space, and the behavior of other people undergoes distortions which seem to occur outside of his control and often outside of his awareness. This paper has not dealt with the nature or extent of these presumed distortions but rather an attempt has been made to describe the interpersonal context in which they occur. Such an attempt has relevance outside the field of hypnosis. Many types of psychopathology are characterized by intrapsychic distortions so similar to those which occur in hypnotic trance that hypnotic subjects are often used to demonstrate psychiatric symptoms. If less emphasis is put upon the intrapsychic processes of patients and more on their behavior within a relationship, it is conceivable that a descriptive system can be developed which will classify the interpersonal situations which provoke many clinical symptoms. Although the hypnotic relationship is a unique type, the peculiar kinds of communication sequences which occur between hypnotist and subject may be found outside the hypnotic situation in the personal relationships of individuals. Presumably when more exact descriptions of human interaction are developed, the interpersonal situations which provoke intrapsychic disturbances will be better understood.

SUMMARY
An interactional description of the hypnotic situation has been presented with special emphasis on the relationship between hyp-

notist and subject as they communicate with one another. The communicative behavior of hypnotist and subject was described in terms of the ways they behave and the ways they qualify that behavior. These two levels of communication function together to define the sort of relationship they have with each other. It was suggested that the hypnotist communicates two contradictory levels of message to the subject in a situation where the subject must respond, cannot comment on the contradictory requests, and cannot leave the field. This double level communication of the hypnotist was termed a "double bind." Induction techniques and "challenges" were described as requests that the subject do something and simultaneous requests that he not do them. The response of the subject is to do them and deny he is doing them and thereby manifest "involuntary" or trance behavior. The "involuntary" was defined as actions by the subject qualified by statements that the subject did not make those actions. His qualifying statements consists of statements that he did not do something, that something was not done, that it was not done for the hypnotist, or that it was not done in this time and place. The hypnotic relationship was classified as meta-complementary within a framework of three possible types of relationship. It was argued that trance behavior takes place when the hypnotist controls what sort of relationship he has with the subject and the subject cannot indicate what sort of relationship it is. The perceptual and somatic experiences of the hypnotic subject were considered a product of this kind of relationship with the emphasis on the interaction, which is observable, rather than on the subjective experiences of the subject, which are conjecture.

REFERENCE

1. Bateson, G. , Jackson, D. D. , Haley, J. and Weakland, J. H. Towards a theory of schizophrenia. Behavioral Sc. , 1:251-264, 1956. Reprinted in Don D. Jackson (Ed.), Communication, Family, and Marriage (Vol. 1, Human Communication Series), Science and Behavior Books, Palo Alto, California, 1968.

PSYCHOANALYTIC EDUCATION IN THE
COMMUNICATION PROCESSES

Don D. Jackson

Why should a term like "communication processes" even be juxtaposed with a broad term like "psychoanalytic training, " since communication between analyst and patient is essential to the analytic process? As a matter of fact, one could claim that our understanding of neurotic and psychotic communication came into being when Freud explained the nature of the beast and taught us to look for meaning within meaning. But two general assumptions are implied in my topic:

1. The rubric "communication processes" must differ in quantity or quality from the usual psychoanalytic view of the communication between patient and analyst.

2. That behavior subsumed under the term "communication processes" is not part of the usual curricula of psychoanalytic institutes.

Let me list some of the areas and assumptions involving communication processes that might be different in degree or kind from the usual emphasis given in psychoanalytic training and might be, some time in the future, a more usual part of such training:

1. Communication processes imply an interaction within at least a two person system.

2. Communication terminology is more suitable for the description of a wide range of human behavior than analytic terminology which is strictly oriented to the individual and his implied intrapsychic processes.

Reprinted from SCIENCE AND PSYCHOANALYSIS, 5:129-145 (1962). Copyright, Grune & Stratton, Inc. , New York; reproduced by permission.

I use terms like "communication processes" rather than "communication theory" because the latter does not yet exist. There is gradually being built up a body of knowledge about human communication and at present these data occupy a spectrum from mathematics to purely clinical observation. However, this embryo collection of ideas and data has enough cohesiveness to have been attacked in certain analytic quarters and thus has been bestowed with a respectability that it perhaps does not deserve. Such articles contend that:

1. "Communication processes" represent a point of view already covered by psychoanalytic concepts.

2. These two points of view, i. e., the communication and the psychoanalytic, are necessarily antithetical.

Mortimer Ostow, in discussing a paper of Arieti's on various theories of schizophrenia, states:

"Let me now turn to the double bind theory, a non-psychologic approach to schizophrenia. During the past decade and a half, mathematical theories of some eloquence have been devised to deal with problems of measuring and communicating information, extending logical thinking beyond the capacity of the human mind, predicting the probable outcome of dreams. These theories have proved themselves in application to the specific area to which they were directed. Together they constitute a general systems theory. In the journal, Behavior, (I think that here Dr. Ostow must be referring to Behavioral Science) one can find many attempts to apply this general systems theory to psychologic and psychiatric problems. I have yet to see such an attempt which has made a real contribution to our understanding. The reason for this failure is not that the theory is incorrect, or even that it is essentially inapplicable to human behavior. In my opinion, the reason is that those who try to apply the theory, in general, refuse to deal with the ultimate variables of human behavior as expressed in psychoanalytic metapsychology and postulate their own variables based solely on naive, a priori, and invalid assumptions. Such assumptions, no matter how elegant the theory applied to them, can yield only naive and invalid conclusions. The double bind theory is an example of this mathematico-logical-pseudopsychologizing. It is no novelty to any psychoanalyst that signals are communicated from one person to another by routes other than verbal. In psychoanalytic clinical reports of half a century ago, one will find reference to facial expressions, posture, vocal intonation, and even silence as modes of communication more faithful than speech. It is also no novelty to the psychoanalyst that a single situation may trigger more than one, often conflicting, response in the observer. It was a discovery of unverbalized and indeed unconscious intrapsychic conflict that marked the beginning of Freud's study of the neuroses."[1]

It can hardly be made more clear, short of pistols and bloodshed, how strongly this opinion would differ from my own. For clarifying this difference, I am grateful to Dr. Ostow. His statements serve as a model of the need to clarify the relationship between psychoanalysis and communication processes. For example, there is the statement that the double bind theory which is based on a communications framework in a "non-psychologic approach." The psychiatric dictionary of Hinsie and Campbell defines psychology as, "The science which deals with the mind and mental processes—consciousness, sensation, ideation, memory, etc." According to this definition, much communication work is non-psychologic. But it is a simple fact that in our field there is no other way to measure the patient than by using oneself as a measuring stick. As to Ostow's comment that our observations are based on naive, a priori and invalid assumptions, I can only say that the patient is the source of our data, just as he is in psychoanalysis proper. I will refrain from telling the story of the blind men and the elephant.

Perhaps the most troublesome comment in his discussion, and the most important for this paper, is the statement that it is no novelty to analysts that signals are communicated from one person to another by routes other than verbal. In any simple sense, to agree with this statement is like equating love of country with ability and diligence at saluting the flag. I am quite aware that psychoanalysts believe in non-verbal behavior, but the fact is that to date this belief has not become an important part of psychoanalytic theory. David Rappaport stated three years ago that the most serious weakness in psychoanalysis was its lack of a learning theory.[2] Researchers in communication are particularly interested in learning contexts, but formal psychoanalysis, to date, has not been.

---

[1] Arieti, S. Recent conceptions and misconceptions of schizophrenia. _Am. J. Psychother._, 14:320, 1960.

[2] In a speech at the Center for Advanced Study in the Behavioral Sciences, Stanford, Calif.

There is not only the problem of the "dynamics" of our patients but the learning situation in which these dynamics developed.

In the usual psychoanalytic view, movement goes from inside the patient's head to the outside. Whether this concept is expressed by neurophysiological and energic models or by terms like "free association," "transference," "topographic," "economic" and "structural," the primary focus is on how output reflects the intrapsychic situation rather than on what has been fed into the machine. The psychoanalytic situation itself is created in order to minimize input. This situation has many desirable features, as its long history will attest, but it would be fatuous to assume that the purest form of human communication--beamed direct from the "mind"-- is occurring because the analyst and patient are obeying a very specific set of rules. On the contrary, a recognition that communication is at least dyadic implies that one could never hope to have really "free" associations, but rather a flow of words appropriate to the psychoanalytic situation which is labeled "free associations." If the analyst and the patient had never met and the therapy was conducted through a one-way glass window, and the analyst's voice was mechanically modulated to remove its distinctive characteristics, even then there would be a dyadic system, since the patient cannot help having expectations of "analysts" and in particular his analyst, and would be reacting to that kind of individual who would study him in such a situation.

It is usual in my experience to encounter enthusiastic residents who speak of the "id" as if they were observing from a seat on the fifty yard line. Conversely, patients' expectations about psychoanalysts and the manner in which the analyst interacts with these expectations becomes a communication problem the moment the two participants meet. Occasionally, one has the opportunity to watch such an encounter and it can be rather disquieting. For example, a young man I was examining for the psychiatric boards tested a patient on the Benjamin proverbs. Unfortunately, he was not aware that his manner toward the patient was patronizing and that he was covertly rewarding every literal statement she made. Although this patient was a recovered psychoneurotic who had come back to the clinic for the examinations in order to pay a debt of gratitude, the young man diagnosed her as schizophrenic. Later in the same day, I witnessed another candidate examine this same patient with totally different results. The first young man was not stupid. Indeed, he was in his third year of candidacy at a psychoanalytic institute where competition for selection is very keen. Under the pressure of the examination, he oversold himself on the possibilities of the pure pipeline to the mind just as some analysts will oversell themselves on the meaning of a slip of the tongue even at a cocktail party (as long as they are not the ones to make it.) When the first rule of communication theory is ignored and the analyst behaves as if the patient could carry on a private conversation in his presence, then blind bias dilutes the utility of the data collected.

A second assumption I would like to make about communication concepts in comparison to analytic theory is that the former is more suitable for handling a wide range of human interaction and endeavor. Analytic terminology, when correctly used, has specific meaning within a well delineated context, but even Freud himself ran into difficulty in restricting his terminology to the original meaning he gave it. For example, Freud in "Analysis, Terminable and Interminable," describes his treatment of a young Russian (The Wolf Man) with whom he felt he had made good progress and then had come to an impasse. He told the patient that the coming year would be the last of his analysis, regardless of progress, and reports in this paper that in the last months of treatment, the patient produced all the memories and connecting links which were necessary for understanding his childhood neurosis. Freud then reports that following the war, the patient returned to Vienna in a severely neurotic state and required further psychoanalysis. Freud says, "There can be only one verdict about the value of this blackmailing device. The measure is effective provided that one hits the right time in which to employ it. But it cannot be held to guarantee perfect accomplishment of the task of psychoanalysis. On the contrary, we may be quite sure that while the force of the threat will have the effect of bringing part of the material to light, another part will be held back, become buried as it were, and will be lost to our therapeutic efforts." He further states that the analyst must not extend the time once the date for discontinuing treatment has been fixed, or the patient will lose all his faith in the analyst. I mention this particular case because, in discussing the patient's subsequent breakdown, Freud mentions, and I quote, "Some of these relapses were caused by still unresolved residues of the transference; shortlived though the attacks were, they were distinctly paranoic in character." In other places in this article, Freud uses the term "transference" in a similar fashion, even when he is describing a real life interaction between him and the patient.

You may remember that later in this same paper, Freud discusses whether it is advisable to stir up for purposes of prophy-

laxis a conflict which is not at the moment manifest. He rejects
this idea from several angles especially because "we have not the
plenary powers which such intervention would demand and most
certainly the object of this therapeutic experiment would refuse to
cooperate with it." Freud further states that any deliberate procedure of the kind mentioned would necessitate "unkind behavior on
the part of the analyst toward the patient... This would have an in-
jurious effect upon his affectionate attitude toward the analyst, i.e.,
upon the positive transference which is the patient's strongest mo-
tive for cooperating in the work of analysis." If one refers back to
the examples Freud gave of his intervention with the young Russian,
he states that the analysis came to an impasse before his setting a
deadline because the patient was enjoying the luxurious, undemand-
ing, Viennese life that he was leading. There is the implication that
the patient was something of a spoiled child. Surely Freud's setting a time limit must have seemed unkind to the patient, and yet
he attempted to keep the analysis going by providing Freud with the
material for which he was seeking. It is misleading to assume
that the patient's transference and the nature of his verbal productions were not markedly influenced by his special situation with
Freud, and Freud almost but not quite grapples with this point.

These observations of Freud's can now be matched against the
"Memoirs of the Wolf Man," translated by Felix Augenfeld and
Muriel Gardiner. In describing the period of 1914 to 1919, The
Wolf Man describes his leaving Vienna and states: "During my
treatment by Professor Freud, I had had the opportunity of hearing
from the very mouth of the founder of psychoanalysis, from the
original spring, the fundamental principles of this completely new
science of the deeper layers of the human psyche. Since we often
discussed all manner of things, I became familiar also with Freud's
views on literature, art, and various other matters.* Shortly before the end of my treatment, Therese, my future wife, came to
Vienna and together we visited Professor Freud. I had not expected that Therese would make such a favorable impression upon him.
Not only was he obviously impressed by her appearance (he had
evidently doubted whether Therese was really such a beautiful woman as I had described), but he was also pleased by her reserved
and serious nature. So my intention to marry Therese met with
his full approval." (In Bull. Phila. A. Psychoanal., 1961.)

These examples from Freud's paper and from the Wolf Man's
Memoirs illustrate that if one focuses on the intrapsychic mechan-

---

*Emphasis mine.

isms of the patient, he is very apt to overlook what is occurring in the two party interaction and he may be further aided in this overlooking by the very language of psychoanalysis. In this sense, the inadequacy of the word "transference" is obvious since it is used unwittingly by Freud to cover both the reactions of the patient to Freud himself and manifestations of the patient's childhood neurosis. This can be noted by the Wolf Man's observations of his attitude toward Freud which certainly consist of more than what is ordinarily meant by the word "transference;" and by Freud's willingness to participate with him in "real interaction." This view is strongly supported by the final section of Freud's paper in which he states: "It is too much to expect that the patient should have a firm conviction of the curative power of analysis, but he may have come to the analyst with a certain amount of confidence and this, reinforced by the various factors in the positive transference which it is our business to evoke* makes him capable of doing his share." Here we have a double use of the word transference. In one sense, it is used to mean the laying over of the patient's past onto the present, and in another sense, it is meant to describe a reaction to the analyst's attempts to gain the patient's confidence. When Freud put the pressure on, results were forthcoming. [3]

Others have also questioned the concept of transference as it is defined in psychoanalysis. For example, in an important paper, Ackerman asks among other things the question: "Why do we prize the irrationality of transference neurosis?" He goes on to state: "The weakest aspect of the Freudian conceptual model seems to be in the crucial question of reality testing and new social learning."[4] Destructive and hostile critics of psychoanalysis have raised questions about the therapeutic value of transference neurosis but usually with the almost moral implication that it is better to let sleeping dogs lie. Ackerman seems to be raising the question in order to ask: "Are we too busy digging the mine to process the ore?" If psychoanalysts were more interested in the actual nature of the exchange of messages between themselves and their patients, they

---

[3] Some years ago I suggested the term "palintropy" or "palintropic process" to describe the back-and-forth interaction in therapy which is more than implied by the concept transference. See Jackson, D. D. Counter-transference and psychotherapy. In Masserman, J. H. (Ed.). Progress in Psychotherapy. Grune & Stratton, Inc., New York, 1956.

[4] Ackerman, N.W. Transference and countertransference. Psychoanal. & Psychoanalyt. Rev., 46:3, 1959.

might be more cautious about equating the irrationality of the transference neurosis with "depth" (and thus potential insight), and would look at the elements in the psychoanalytic situation that are then labeled as evidence of transference neurosis. For example, I would hypothesize that, within certain limits, the more passive the analyst, the more irrational the transference neurosis. The "certain limits" refers to the kind of patient and to the fact that a completely passive analyst would probably lose the patient before treatment progressed far enough for a transference neurosis to occur.

I do differ with Ackerman slightly in regard to his stress on the fact that the analyst's anonymity does not provide the architecture for a true social experience. Even though I have just stated that the more passive the analyst, the more irrational the transference neurosis, I am using "irrational" not in an absolute sense but in terms of how the material would be labeled by analysts. In communication terms, the analytic situation, no matter how passive or anonymous the analyst, is as real a situation for two person communication as any other. The analyst's anonymity does not create an unreal situation; it simply provides a different kind of context from the one the patient usually experiences, and hence the kind of communication differs from that in ordinary social intercourse.

For example, analysts have labeled one type of communication, "Primary process material." This kind of communication can be thought of as the language of the unconscious, or it can be thought of as a partial outgrowth of the psychoanalytic situation. By utilizing this kind of communication, the patient can do several things at the same time:

1. He is obeying the rules of the game, and therefore furthering his own wish to get something out of the analysis and to please the analyst.

2. He is making the analyst work, and thus proves to himself that he is indeed complicated and requires the services of an expert for whom he is giving up time, money and energy.

3. By being somewhat obscure, he can indicate many things about his feelings toward the analyst without shouldering the responsibility for having said them. This is, he can deny that his symbolism has any meaning or that it has the meaning the analyst attaches to it, or he can deny that he said it even though his "unconscious" did. He can state "it was only a dream" just as in a social situation, a person might claim: "I was only kidding."

4. He can frame his comments to the analyst in terms of the past and hence implicitly deny that they have any reference for the present situation between him and the psychoanalyst.

To those acquainted with the work of our research group on communication processes in schizophrenia, much of the above has a familiar ring. This is not surprising because schizophrenics have been described as utilizing more primary process material in their comments than ordinary individuals, and the analytic situation has many of the covert contextual messages that exist in the schizophrenic's family. As one example: If the analyst is silent, the patient usually assumes that he is withholding for specific reasons, not that the analyst hasn't anything to say. On the other hand, the patient is in the process of saying more and more about himself which implies a relative ignorance on the analyst's part. Further, to the extent the patient uses symbolic communication, including dreams, to that extent he is vulnerable to having the meaning of his utterances explained to him. The schizophrenic gets himself exactly in the same spot, and then feels suspicious and victimized by other people. Let me hasten to make it clear that I am not accusing formal psychoanalysis of the propagation of schizophrenia. I am simply illustrating how one may look at the context in which communication is occurring and hypothesize the relationship between the communication and the implicit messages that arise in such a context.

Ackerman concludes the paper mentioned above by stating that when we know more about family interactions, we will learn more about the nature of transference and countertransference. You will not be surprised to know that I am in complete accord with this statement. However, I have very little to offer at this moment as to the language needed to make these relationships clear, observable, and measurable. Let me give you an example of an approach I can imagine being useful but one that barely scratches the surface at the present time. I have mentioned that context is an important tool in judging the analytic situation. Context can be thought of as a spatial temporal envelope which serves as a frame within which messages are uttered. The context in which a message occurs can carry very broad implications, including cultural and subgroup definitions and expectations, private rules of the family, and even what currently is being "done" or is "chic" or "gauche." Context, on the other hand, can impose as specific limitations as one's behavior in the process of being given a traffic ticket. In our family work, we have felt that a frequent way in which one family member attempts to define the nature of his relationship to another member is to change the context from that assumed by one of the other persons involved in the communication. The extent to which contexts are switched can be related to the extent of social pathology in the children, i.e., there are more and less harmful ways of switching contexts. Some of the methods utilized include:

1. Implying that this message was all right at one time but is not now appropriate--a method I have labeled "past-present switches." The mother might say to the child, "I want you to be frank, but you shouldn't have chosen this moment because I have a headache."

2. Implying that the individual has misinterpreted the context in which the message was uttered. This is a mechanism frequently used by parents to put a halt to certain behavior. For example, if they and the child are teasing each other, the teasing can be broken off by the parents' suddenly taking the situation seriously.

3. Implying that only this individual would send such a message, and that he differs from others in his family, his group, etc. in his selection of messages.

4. Implying that when other individuals utter similar messages, they don't mean them in the same way as this individual does. That is, the parent might say to the child, "Yes, but when I said that to you, I was only kidding."

It is possible to characterize certain methods of changing contexts as being more typical for a particular family than other possible choices. For example, some families regularly use tangentialization. This refers to the selection of one element of the sender's statement or message which is not necessarily the most relevant for understanding at that moment. The new element which is connected with, but not identical to, the most meaningful aspect of the sender's message is thus developed until the focus becomes more and more removed from the starting point. A husband might ask his wife to please use stretchers whenever she washes his socks. Instead of replying, "Yes, I will," or "No, I won't," the wife who uses tangentialization would reply that the husband must be buying a different brand of socks lately or else his feet were getting bigger. Further, she can't understand why a manufacturer cannot guarantee against shrinking when he charges $5.95 for a pair of socks. This method differs from and, in our opinion, is less pathological than, the complete change of context which would occur if the wife replied: "Incidentally, if I am going to have time to do all that's expected of me lately, I'm going to have some help from the doctor. I'm just tired out all the time." Such a statement does not merely say to the husband, "You have no right to criticize me;" it states: "You have no right to ask anything of me at all." Further, if the husband were to challenge the statement on the ground that she was refusing to use stretchers on his socks, she could deny this and ask him if he wasn't interested in her state of health.

The relevance for the analytic situation of having an intimate knowledge of contextual matters in communication is obvious. An individual from a family which uses a particular method of handling contexts will obviously try to adapt the analytic situation to his previously learned technique and vice versa both because he will tend to repeat his experience and because he expects to be communicated to in the old-fashioned way, and the best defense is a good offense. The analyst who can imagine the kind of family situation that would produce the patient's way of switching contexts may be more able to help this patient for two reasons:

1. His emphatic understanding will increase and he will be alert to the material which the patient hasn't mentioned but which has to be there.

2. He not only can try to avoid putting the patient in his old spot, but may devise techniques which will point out to the patient his limited patterns of communication, or actually teach him new ways of communicating. Education can occur only if the learning contexts are different from the patient's previous experience.

Much of the above is now done implicitly in a psychoanalytic situation by skilled analysts. I am merely pointing out that terms like "transference" make it difficult to define explicitly the interaction between patient and analyst and to select those techniques which might be most useful in maximizing the leverage in this relationship.

I have made two points about the communication versus the analytic framework. One, that the communication viewpoint assumes at least a two person system and thus introduces a different way of viewing or describing analytic situations; and two, the language of communication covers a broader descriptive range of human behavior and can implement classic terminology. Given these two assumptions, what about their immediate relevance to analytic training?

COMMUNICATION AND TRAINING

Obviously, the kind of training a psychoanalyst should have depends on how his task is defined and the qualifications needed to carry it out.

Thomas Szasz has stated:[5]

"There is no widely accepted definition of the psychoanalyst's exact task. Unfortunately, this problem itself is somewhat controversial, reflecting disagreements concerning the nature of psychoanalytic therapy. In general, the qualifications demanded of an expert will depend upon, and will reflect, the observer's conceptions of the expert's tasks and the mode of operation. We may consider the example of medical practice as an illustrative analogy. Our model of a qualified medical practitioner depends upon and reflects our image of the nature of medical illness and cure. If we think along scientific, physico-chemical lines, we shall require qualifications such as are asked of physicians. If, however, our image of illness and cure happens to be essentially mystico-religious, for instance along the lines of Christian Science, then we shall demand qualifications that in fact are asked of Christian Science practitioners. So much for the dependence of the therapist's qualifications on our conceptions of his task."

The task of the psychoanalyst could be defined as that of understanding his patient and the nature of the psychoanalytic process within the framework of classical psychoanalysis. However, it appears that candidates and members of psychoanalytic institutes are increasingly being called upon to exhibit a wide range of psychiatric competency. As medical school professors, consultants, researchers, advisers to social agencies, they often have first call because analytic training has high status with the public and with the majority of psychiatrists. It would appear that institutes will have to take such development into account as they devise new curricula, and indeed, a glance at some of the electives in various institute curricula convinces me that such changes are already under way.

The training of the psychoanalyst depends not only on how his task is defined, but what range of professional function is open to

---

[5]Szasz, T. S. The Myth of Mental Illness. Paul B. Hoeber, Inc., New York, 1961.

him. "Good" psychoanalytic patients are getting harder to find and most of the younger analysts conduct a grab bag sort of practice with a wide variety of patients, techniques, and results. Frequency of visits must be varied, some patients do and some do not use the couch, and it appears that relatives are getting harder to avoid and that the psychotherapy of married couples is definitely on the rise. Further, there is widespread interest in conjoint family psychotherapy and a number of analysts are in the vanguard of this movement.

Interest in communication processes can augment the dynamic formulations that the psychoanalyst uses in his psychotherapeutic work. For example, each spouse of a married couple can be understood by a psychodynamic formulation. However, an interest in the communication patterns between the two individuals will supplement the impression that the analyst has of each.

For example, if we label the wife a castrative female and the husband a passive masochist, we will be describing an apparent dominance-submission pattern. If we watch these two individuals interact, it becomes clear that neither is truly dominant or submissive, but that both are frustrated and unhappy. We might further learn that these individuals engage in a series of interlocking ploys to keep each other involved in a hopeless impasse. This impasse can be blamed on sadism or masochism or it can be regarded as the outcome of how each member is defining the nature of the relationship. The rigidity of the system can be attributed to the need of each member to systematize change and their inability to foresee what kind of change might take place. As you can see this is a very different way of describing couple interaction than if one were to use psychoanalytic terminology. Such conceptualization may influence the nature of the therapeutic intervention as I can illustrate with the following example:

I have been treating a young executive who was referred because of recurring panic states. We came to know something of these attacks, their relation to his past and so on and yet it seemed to me, but not to the patient, that a weekend at home was a frequent prerequisite for a panic on Monday--although it could be claimed, as the patient did, that Monday signalled his return to the pressures of work. One day this gentleman called me from a distant city with the news that he was falling part to the extent he doubted he could return to Palo Alto. I suggested a few ounces of man's best friend and a quick return. He called the next day for an immediate appointment and I suggested he bring his wife with him. He was obviously disgruntled but agreed. When they were seated opposite me, the patient immediately began an account of the horrors of this trip almost as if he were in one of his usual sessions with me alone, and I interrupted him to suggest to his wife that she must have had a pretty good week. There was some struggle in getting them to accept the relevance of this remark, but fortunately the wife was able to confirm my suspicion and the patient began to learn a new view of his difficulties. Among other things, we were able to nail down that both members used rather stereotyped messages that they would not desert one another. As a consequence, they were constantly arousing fear of desertion in each other. Neither was consciously aware of these messages and yet there were many standardized interactional patterns, i.e. ways of communicating with each other, that could be elucidated in a few hours of seeing them together.

Obviously this gentleman's symptoms could have improved during the course of analysis. He would have changed without the analyst's even knowing the kind of data described above. The patient would have changed the nature of his communication with his wife because of the analytic experience, and since it takes two to tango, she would be affected by receiving a different kind of feedback from him and could not engage in their characteristic transactions. This kind of example also raises questions of economy, efficiency, and whether couple therapy effects changes as deepseated as psychoanalysis, but these matters are all apart from the purpose of the paper.

What place, then, has training in communication in the psychoanalytic curriculum? I think it can be simply stated that no formal courses need be offered to introduce the communication point of view, for it is just that, a point of view--a matter of emphasis. Candidates could be encouraged to examine psychoanalytic concepts in different frames of reference and some candidates might then become curious and add to our meager knowledge.

Along with this "point of view" approach, I think an exposure to certain materials would be appropriate. Here I would think of the book, Communication, by Bateson and Ruesch, the recent book by Scheflen analyzing Rosen's technique, a very brief exposure, to slow motion or frame by frame movies with reference to Birdwhistell's "microkinesics," a smatter of information theory perhaps via a paper by James G. Miller, and some notice of linguistics, especially micro-linguistic analysis. These materials would occupy only a few hours, but would help to alert the student to one of the scientific dangers in the study of psychoanalysis; namely, that the very attractiveness of psychoanalytic theory can render one a convert rather than a seeker after light. Freud was an excellent clinician and a beautiful writer. Only careful attention to his writings reveals his cautionary statements about buying the whole package, and his occasional forgetting to take his own advice.

Education in communication theory would impel the student to examine constantly the arena in which he works because then he could never ignore the influence of himself as an observer. Even the most convincing consistency in his experience with certain patients would not be taken as the scientific proof of psychoanalytic concepts but would be examined at least from the standpoint of shared labels between him and his patient. Similarity in experience, interests and even in psychopathology between analyst and patient can create an illusion of "getting somewhere." Communication which is indicative of ego, superego, or id can create the illusion of neuroanatomic structures and Freud's statement "our psychoanalytic mythology"* is all too easily forgotten.

Currently, the majority of critics of psychoanalytic theories are those hostile to the whole system rather than those devoted to the movement yet discontented with the nature of the proof of its validity. The enormous popularity of psychoanalysis puts a great burden on those who would wear the critic's mantle. Indoctrination of the student begins early and is apt to last a lifetime. Typically the experience of the tyro therapist is to glean from psychoanalytic teachings a language that enables him to interpret to himself the actions, words, or dreams of the patient, and this becomes an exciting and convincing experience that sends him back to the books to learn more, and eventually produces yearnings for the nearest psychoanalytic institute.

The delight one experiences in learning a foreign language and conversing with the natives should not be mistaken for "understanding them." The student who foresees great victories in the consultation room because of his grasp of psychoanalytic principles will either suffer severe disappointment or decide he just doesn't see the right kind of patients. To attempt another kind of analogy, it is quite possible for anthropologists to learn and understand the symbols, rituals, and social structure of a community and to make shrewd speculations as to their probable origin and function. How-

---

*Emphasis mine.

ever, this knowledge in no way guarantees that the anthropologist could become a well-adjusted efficient member of this community, or even that his suggestions as to how this community might improve itself would be any better than chance. Furthermore, the "understanding" of a patient or, if one is an anthropologist, of a culture, belongs to the natural history or descriptive phase of scientific endeavor and does not imply action information any more than the ability to classify rocks helps one to build a bridge. While it is true that it is necessary to distinguish granite from clay in order to build a sound bridge, the geological information will not overcome the engineering problems.

Our use in psychoanalysis of "interpretation" does not include the pressure on the patient from his environment to stay the same. The student needs help in understanding that interpretations are not Dr. Ehrlich's Magic Bullet, otherwise he is apt to find resistant patients wherever he goes.

I think it would be useful for candidates to be taught that all interpretations are, in some sense, inexact. If we assume that event A inside the patient's head produces behavior B, we must assume the analyst experiences this behavior as B^1 since he is not identical to the patient. The analyst then comments on this behavior in terms of B^2 since his own psychic apparatus has selective functions, time lags, and so on. This situation would not be too bad, but unfortunately, the patient doesn't even hear B^2 as the interpretation because he also reacts to the analyst's having said B^2. Hence when textbooks on psychoanalytic technique refer to the timing of interpretations solely in terms of the relation of the interpretation to the equilibrium between the patient's id, ego, and superego, it may mislead the student into thinking of an interpretation as a scalpel rather than as a fairly blunt instrument (occasionally the blunter the better!).

The difference between psychoanalytic terminology and a communication framework can be vividly seen in relation to this question of interpretations. In the psychoanalytic sense, the interpretation, or intervention: "Every time you mention your father, I notice you close your fist," is not a deep interpretation and may be accepted by the patient and even repeated by him through carrying out the gesture again for his own verification. On the other hand, the statement that the patient's voyeurism relates to his futile attempt to confirm his wish that women have a penis is a deep interpretation not only in the sense that the patient is unconscious of this linkage, but also because the material referred to has an origin in the patient's very early years. The patient's inability or unwillingness to benefit from this interpretation can be ascribed to resistance and/or incorrect timing on the part of the analyst. However, from the standpoint of communication theory, one could not use the term "deep interpretation" in the same sense as in psychoanalysis. Rather, one would view these two statements on the analyst's part from the standpoint of a transaction between two individuals occurring in a particular context. When the analyst mentions the closed fist, he is instructing the patient in a fashion that is appropriate to the analytic context and which is appropriate also to the patient's prior knowledge. That is, the patient has previously learned from his culture that closing one's fist can connote anger; thus, the analyst's observation may form a bridge to the patient's awareness and his own repetition of the act will be further convincing to the patient as to the correctness of the analyst's labeling. However, connecting voyeurism with the fact that male and female anatomy is different and becomes a perplexing problem to some children is the kind of information that is usually out of the patient's prior conscious experience. In this sense, the analyst is not merely lancing a psychodynamic pus pocket, he is imparting a new system of labeling to the patient. To the extent the patient repeats this system back to the analyst, he can be considered to have been instructed. Furthermore, in the interpretation, there are actually at least two instructions: One, the imparting of a new method of symbolizing or labeling or teaching; and two, the implicit instruction, "As a psychoanalyst, this is the sort of data I am interested in relabeling for you in this way." The patient is learning a new way to communicate and hence to regard his own communications, and he is also learning to learn this new system; or if you will, he programs himself under the analyst's direction and learning to program himself in this fashion facilitates further programming of the same sort. Note again that the essential difference between these two ways of describing the function of an interpretation is that the communication view assumes at least a two party interaction that is specific for these individuals in this particular context. This is a very different view from a classical analytic one, which would regard the analyst as having caused an energy shift in the analysis and that allowed a piece of data that he had already known but repressed become conscious once again. The analytic view would assume that if the interpretation produces a useful change in the patient, it is because it was exact and properly timed. However, the peculiar problem of those patients who don't improve despite insight and self-understanding tells us that our present conceptual tools are not enough. A communication view of this problem might add something: For example, the kind of learning context that the patient experiences in psychoanalysis may influence his response to interpretations, however correct. This latter point is the subject of a paper in itself, but for the slightly far-out in the audience, I offer a bit of Zen that states it clearly:

"To think that I am not going
To think of you any more
Is still thinking of you.
Let me then try not to think
That I am not going to think of you."

TRANSFERENCE REVISITED

Don D. Jackson
and Jay Haley

Among the key concepts in psychoanalytic theory are the assumptions that therapeutic change is caused by an increase in the patient's self-understanding and the assumption that transference is necessary if that self-understanding is to be sufficiently effective or "deep." Intimately related, these two assumptions are the bedrock of the theory of psychoanalytic therapy. In this paper we will attempt to review the concept of transference from a somewhat different point of view. We will suggest a partially different way of looking at transference and the phenomena associated with it; a view that does not refute previous conceptions but simply adds a possible new dimension.

The concept of "transference" is generally used to explain peculiar behavioral responses by the patient in psychoanalysis and as an explanation of the cause of therapeutic change. Transference responses are associated with the concept of "regression," with the implication that the patient becomes more infantile as he projects upon the analyst unconscious ideas rooted in his infantile needs and strivings. We suggest that this description is perfectly valid if one focuses only upon the patient. If, however, the analyst is also included in the description, it is possible to see the transference in a different light. (Note that "transference" in this paper refers to the restricted use of this concept in the psychoanalytic situation. It does not refer to the general use of the term as synonymous with Sullivan's "parataxic distortion.")

When the analyst is included in the description, psychoanalysis appears to be a rather peculiar communication situation. This peculiarity is a result of the paradoxical nature of the relationship

Reprinted from THE JOURNAL OF NERVOUS AND MENTAL DISEASE, 137, No. 4:363-371 (October 1963). Copyright, The Williams & Wilkins Co., Baltimore; reproduced by permission.

between analyst and patient. As the patient attempts to deal with this paradoxical situation, he will exhibit a variety of behavioral tactics, many of them part of his past repertoire learned at an early age. However, the use of these tactics does not necessarily mean that he has regressed to that early age. Since psychoanalysis moves from the present backward, an anachronistic bias is introduced which influences both patient and analyst. As a result, there is a tendency to overlook the current interaction between analyst and patient and to consider only the patient's past.

Therapeutic change resulting from psychoanalysis may reside not only in the greater self-understanding which comes about as the result of analyzing the transference, but in the forced change in the patient's behavior which is required if he is to deal with the psychoanalytic situation. In emphasizing something other than transference interpretations as a cause of change, we join others who have sought other explanations. For example, Hans Sachs, Freud's first training analyst, is credited with saying that analysis terminates when the patient realizes it could go on forever. He thereby implies that the resolution which occurs in analysis is dependent upon something in addition to the patient's understanding the influence of his past on the present.

In Hinsie and Campbell's Psychiatric Dictionary (6), transference is defined as follows: "In psychoanalytic therapy, the phenomenon of projection of feelings, thoughts and wishes onto the analyst who has come to represent an object from the patient's past. The analyst is reacted to as though he were someone from the patient's past: such reactions, while they may have been appropriate to the conditions that prevailed in the patient's previous life are inappropriate and anachronistic when applied to an object (the analyst) in the present" (emphasis added).

The definition goes on: "During psychoanalytic treatment, the repressed unconscious material is revived, and since this material contains many infantile elements, the infantile strivings are reactivated and seek gratification in the transference. As the most important relationship of the child is that with his parents, the relationship between patient and analyst established in the transference becomes analogous to, or, at times, similar to the patient's relationship with his parents in childhood. The patient endows the analyst with the same magic powers and omniscience which in childhood he attributed to his parents. The traits of submissiveness and rebellion in transference likewise reflect the attitude of the child to his parents. The patient behaves irrationally in the psychoanalytic situation: it often takes a long time to make him see the irrationality of his behavior which is deeply rooted in his unconscious infantile life. "

In this standard definition, the only object of observation is the patient. The larger social field within which transference occurs is not included since transference is something which emanates from the patient and invests the analyst--a unilateral transaction. Yet in recent years the focus on countertransference has indicated that the personality of the psychoanalyst can be a distorter of "pure" transference and the patient may react to these new elements. With the inclusion of the analyst in the description, the point of view about transference must inevitably change. As Ackerman has pointed out, when countertransference was introduced as a concept, the psychoanalytic situation became a dyadic one even though the terminology remained monadic (1, cf. also 7).

While there is little doubt that the patient's past experience affects his behavioral tactics within the psychoanalytic situation, it is only by ignoring the psychoanalyst that the responses of the patient appear irrational and inappropriate. In fact, the question whether the patient's responses are appropriate or not <u>must</u> depend upon a description of what he is responding to and a value judgment by the analyst as to what is "appropriate" in this very complex treatment situation involving two people.

When the possibility is raised that a patient may be responding to the immediate psychoanalytic relationship rather than merely to his unconscious infantile life, then a definition of the analytic situation is important. A standard definition is provided by Stone (10), who lists eight conditions for psychoanalytic treatment:

1) Exclusive reliance during the hour on free association.

2) Regularity of time, frequency and duration of visits in a clearly defined finanical agreement.

3) Three to five appointments per week.

4) Recumbent position.

5) Confinement of activity of the therapist to interpretation, purely informative intervention, or occasional questions.

6) Emotional passivity and neutrality with abstention from gratification of the patient's transference wishes.

7) Abstention from advice, direct intervention, or participation in the patient's day to day life.

8) No immediate emphasis on curing symptoms.

Granting these conditions, and leaving aside whether they can be completely carried out, the question could be raised whether transference responses by the patient to this situation are irrational, inappropriate and regressive, or whether any other type of behavior is possible given these conditions.

What would be appropriate behavior in this unique situation? Ordinarily when two adults meet, they share information about each other either deliberately or unwittingly. In the psychoanalytic situation, such sharing is kept to a minimum. Similarly, adults attempt to phrase what they say in a reasonably logical and consistent manner so that the other individual can follow the meaning they are attempting to convey. In the analytic situation, the patient is asked to follow the fundamental rule and say what comes into his head, no matter how silly and no matter how lacking in context; that is, he must learn to omit those verbal cues which would acquaint himself and his hearer with the setting in time and in context of his remarks. In ordinary adult conversation, either member may comment on the manner and behavior of the other and his comments are accepted if they are not considered rude. In the analytic situation, only comments about the patient are permitted; comments on the analyst are turned aside or subjected to interpretation and so are not accepted at face value in the usual adult fashion. In addition, the analytic patient must respond to a regularity of time and duration of visits more reminiscent of his school days than adult social intercourse. Further, he must pay a fee for the company of the analyst and carry on his conversation while he is recumbent and the analyst is not, hardly a situation where adult behavior is possible, far less appropriate. Finally, the patient is expected to express himself freely and spontaneously to a man who shows the utmost reserve and inscrutability.

In this situation, the patient cannot possibly manifest the easy exchange of adult conversation and is forced to attempt an interchange more reminiscent of earlier learned tactics when he was small and others were large. In fact, to respond in a rational and mature way, the patient would have to refuse to follow the analyst's directions to lie down and free associate. Indeed, should the patient behave in an "adult" way, it would be said that the treatment was going badly; for example, the concept of resistance is employed when the patient does not follow the analyst's directives.

Viewing psychoanalysis as an interchange between two people provides an opportunity for explanation of the patient's behavior which is rather different from a point of view which is only patient-oriented. If one focuses only upon the patient, it is perfectly satisfactory to describe the analytic situation as one where primary mental processes are permitted to flourish and the skillful analyst offers progressively deeper interpretations until the infantile neurosis is resolved. With a patient orientation, unconscious factors are the subject of interest and the source of all explanations of behavior. Focusing only upon the patient, it is also reasonable to argue that to ignore unconscious processes is to view the psychoanalytic situation superficially.

Yet if one shifts one's frame of reference to include both patient and analyst in the description, unconscious factors assume a different position in the theoretical framework and other factors in the situation come to the fore. Let us take an example to demonstrate how a viewpoint can shift within the space of only a few years. When experiments on perceptual isolation were first reported, experimental subjects demonstrated hallucinations and disorganization of thinking. This appeared to be a situation where the forces of the id were given free play because of the restrictions on outside stimuli. More recent work, especially by Levy, demonstrates that the effects of isolation appear to depend upon the relationship with the experimenter. Levy reports that in a group of subjects who were unusually well prepared for their experience and had a good relationship with the experimenters, only two subjects out of one hundred had hallucination-like experiences and these were clearly hypnagogic (9). If one takes into account both subject and experimenter rather than just subject, the situation appears as different as psychoanalysis does when both patient and analyst are included in the description.

The current direction of psychiatry would seem to be toward including two people, at least in a description of therapy or a description of a psychiatric malady. (For a further consideration of this viewpoint, cf. 5.) For example, prior to Freud, it was assumed that an individual could change if he understood that his fears were irrational and groundless, and if he could not he must be suffering from an organic brain disturbance. If a man with a healthy heart handicapped his life because of fear of dying of a heart attack, it was thought that when he was reassured that nothing was wrong with his heart, this self-understanding would dissipate his fear. This rarely happened. Freud accepted the idea of change through self-understanding but added the concept of the unconscious. Thus, a patient who irrationally feared a heart attack had to understand that his fear represented, among other things, repressed hostile wishes and threatened self-punishment for having such wishes. At first, Freud assumed that if the repressed idea was merely explained to the patient, this self-understanding would cause him to change. This did not occur. Instead of discarding the idea that self-understanding causes change, it occurred to Freud that self-awareness alone was not enough and that the self-understanding must take place in a particular type of therapeutic relationship which involved the transference phenomena as we describe them today.

Instead of emphasizing the interpretation of the transference with consequent insight to the patient, it is possible to regard the analytic situation itself as largely responsible for a change in the patient, with self-understanding an accompanying but not necessarily crucial factor. This notion arises because when both analyst and patient are included in the description of the analytic situation, one discovers that they have a very unusual communication context. This viewpoint goes along with the current tendency to see the patient in terms of his interpersonal and social relationships and not merely in terms of his intrapsychic dynamics.

For example, if we include the wife in our description of the above-mentioned heart phobia patient, we get a different point of view about his symptoms. We may find that husband and wife have a particular sort of relationship, for example, one that is both controlling of and protective of each other through the use of certain behavioral tactics. Since the patient fears a heart attack, he protests that he cannot be left alone, thereby constantly supervising his wife. His wife finds that her life becomes organized around his state of health, since all family activities depend upon his reports about feeling better or worse. When the husband feels better, she struggles to be amiable so that he will not collapse again and lose his job, and when he is worse she struggles to be amiable so that he will continue working. At times she will threaten to leave him to stir him into activity. In this struggle, she settles for a man who will manage her in a helpless way but who still will not make the demands on her which a healthy man would make. This is to say that it is becoming generally known that when a patient has severe symptoms, the spouse has interlocking problems. Often the man who fears a heart attack has a depressed wife. If she has suicidal thoughts, her husband's expression of fears about his heart occur at those times she is withdrawn and he is anxious about what is on her mind and what she will do. When he takes his pulse or expresses his fear about his heart, she becomes angry at his irrational behavior and thereby comes out of her withdrawal and depression temporarily. Yet her depressions are responsive to his helpless managing and irrational fears, just as his fears are responsive to her depressions and threats of leaving as the two of them work out a vicious circle of psychopathology.

When such a patient enters psychoanalysis to overcome his fear of a heart attack, he is experienced at manipulating relationships by his phobia. Meeting the psychoanalyst, he finds that he cannot deal with this relationship in the ways he has dealt with others. He is forced to change his behavior and with that change comes a change in his fears and subjective sensations. Essentially what he meets when he enters analysis is a situation that is impossible if he continues with his distress because it is a thoroughly paradoxical one. We will list a few of the obvious paradoxes faced by the patient. By paradox, we mean those messages which the patient receives at one level which are in conflict with other messages he receives at another level. For example, if one person says to another, "Disobey me," the other person is faced with a paradox: he cannot disobey without obeying, nor can he obey without disobeying because a message at one level is in conflict with the message it classifies at another. Problems posed by such multilevel communication have been discussed previously (2, 4, 8).

When we list these paradoxes, we do not mean to imply that they are imposed in a Machiavellian way by the analyst. We suggest that they are implicit in a therapeutic setting which was designed without the deliberate intention of imposing paradox.

1) First, the patient faces a relationship which is defined in one way at the beginning and then undergoes an abrupt transition to quite a different sort. When the patient first talks with the analyst, the analyst spends a session or two diagnosing the problem. In these early sessions, the analyst wishes to encourage the patient to open up as much as possible and express what is on his mind. Therefore the analyst tends to be warm, encouraging and responsive. He defines the relationship as a benevolently helping one for a person in distress. When treatment begins, the analyst suddenly becomes a silent, unresponsive man, and the patient may

see him as cold and distant. Although the patient will inevitably feel deprived of the warm responsiveness he first experienced, he cannot easily get angry at the analyst for his unresponsiveness because he knows it is part of the method to help him; it would be like being angry at the surgeon's scalpel. The patient can only feel helplessly frustrated.

2) When the patient comes to the analyst, he expects an expert who will help him by taking charge and telling him what to do--as experts are supposed to. The analyst responds by putting the patient in charge: he indicates that he will not tell the patient what to do or how to do it. He is a kind of psychological midwife merely assisting natural forces, and the success of the treatment is the patient's responsibility. He emphasizes that he will not direct the patient.

3) While indicating that he will not tell the patient what to do and putting the patient in charge, the analyst takes charge by directing the patient to lie down, to free associate (which is a direction about how to talk) and what sort of material is acceptable (which the patient learns from the response of the analyst even if it is only uh-huh or silence). The analyst will also not let the patient direct him what to say, and may be silent even if the patient demands that he talk. Therefore, in a non-directive setting at one level, the analyst at another level directs the crucial behavior in the situation: who is to speak, what is to be said, and how it is to be said. (The rule that the patient must make no important changes in his life during the analysis is also an interesting communication. Although the analyst does not tell the patient what to do, he is taking charge of the patient's life by telling him what not to do and framing the message in terms of the patient's not knowing what is best for himself.)

4) The patient comes to the analyst for help in getting over his symptomatic behavior, and the analyst indicates that they will not deal with the symptomatic behavior, thereby indicating that he will change the patient but not by dealing with what he came to change. Yet typically when the patient free associates and deals with other matters, the analyst will use an interpretation to relate these other matters to the symptomatic behavior.

5) Not only is the patient unable to use his symptomatic behavior to manipulate the analyst because the analyst directs him to others matters, but the patient also cannot use improvement or getting worse in a manipulative way. The analyst does not re-

spond to threats, open or implied. In fact, the patient is faced with a paradoxical response no matter what he says in this direction. If he states he is getting worse, he is advised that this is a necessary part of treatment and affords the opportunity to better study his problem. If he improves and says he is feeling fine, the analyst indicates that he is resisting treatment by escaping into health. Thereby the patient becomes incapacitated if he attempts to control this relationship in the ways he has controlled other intimate relationships in his life.

6) The general framework of analysis is one of benevolent help. Within that framework the patient is put through a rather distressing ordeal. The patient is required to talk with as little censorship as possible about all his problems and all the unsavory aspects of his life. If he does not wish to discuss something that reflects too badly upon him, this is defined as resistance. It is not a pleasant experience to undergo psychoanalysis either emotionally or financially, and insofar as it is a punishing experience the patient faces a paradox: he is undergoing a punishing experience within a framework of benevolent help. If he refuses to accept the punishing experience, perhaps by resisting, he is further punished by being labeled as the kind of person who eschews help.

7) Another paradox resides in the question whether the analytic relationship is compulsory or voluntary. Typically the patient is excessively concerned in his personal life with the question whether his intimates associate with him because they want to or because they must, just as he is uncertain whether he is with them because he is ill or because he wishes to be. In psychoanalysis, the patient is told that his relationship is voluntary and his improvement depends upon his willingness to cooperate and attend sessions. Yet if the patient is late or misses a session, the analyst objects and so indicates that the relationship is compulsory. Similarly, the patient faces a man who talks to him only because he is hired to, while within that framework the analyst indicates that analysis offers an opportunity for a deep relationship and this concept is reinforced by transference interpretations which imply that the patient is being markedly influenced and controlled by the analysis. For example, if he is late he is resisting and if he complains about finances he is actually resenting what he pays the analyst.

8) Finally, the patient is in a situation where he cannot behave in an adult way, and when he does not the analyst points out to him that his childlike behavior is evidence of a point of view carried

over from childhood. Although the analyst has other purposes in interpreting the transference, from the point of view of the formal structure of the psychoanalytic situation the patient is responding appropriately only to find that his response is labeled as inappropriate and irrational.

Typically, patients have managed to control the responses of other people by symptomatic behavior, but they become incapacitated if they attempt to deal with a psychoanalyst in these ways. They are forced to develop new techniques to gain a response from an unresponsive man. In his attempt, the patient will go through his whole repertoire of past ways of gaining responses from people. This repertoire will include tactics that he has not used since childhood. When the patient uses these rather desperate tactics, the analyst will assume that the transference relationship has been established. After that, a change by the patient tends to be accepted. However, the patient's behavior is only accepted if he is agreeing with the analyst that his tactics are irrational and based upon childhood experiences. When the patient begins to say, "It isn't you, it's my father I'm really angry with," the last stages of therapy are reached, since the patient and the analyst are now using the same labels.

From the point of view we are presenting, the patient is forced to change his ways because the analytic relationship is one he cannot deal with by using the ways he has dealt with others in the past. The more desperate his attempt to deal with the impossible and paradoxical relationship he faces, the more an observer would say that a transference phenomenon is taking place. To restate: the essential paradox in the psychoanalytic situation and, indeed, in most forms of psychotherapy (including some which do not focus upon self-understanding) consists of the following conflicting levels of messages: First, the situation is defined as one in which the patient will be benevolently helped to change. Second, the patient is encouraged to continue his usual behavior (and symptoms) because of the permissiveness of the analyst and in order that he will demonstrate his problems so they can be studied. Third, the patient is required to undergo a punishing ordeal as long as he continues his usual behavior. The patient is caught in an impossible paradox: to change, he must continue unchanged, while being benevolently helped to go through an ordeal until he changes. A patient must behave differently if he is to resolve the situation, but his different behavior will only be accepted if it occurs on the analyst's terms--otherwise, it is mere resistance. It does not seem surprising that a patient caught in this situation will exhibit "irrational" behavior quite independent of his early infantile life and anachronistic forces that are also affecting his behavior.

The development and resolution of the transference (infantile) neurosis is the key therapeutic agent in most theories of psychoanalytic treatment. Authorities such as Edward Glover recommend five to six sessions a week in order to establish a sufficiently deep transference neurosis (3). Changes brought about by less intensive psychotherapy are regarded by such authorities as superficial and probably not lasting. It does not seem that the frequency of sessions alone can account for the intensity of the transference. Rather, we are suggesting that the analyst's behavior and how the patient views that behavior may be a factor in producing transference phenomena. If this is so, then it may be possible to expedite psychoanalytic therapy by sharpening the paradoxes posed by the treatment situation. The paradoxes are sharpened when the analyst poses the opposite extremes of the paradox quite sharply. For example, when the analyst clearly defines the relationship as voluntary and entirely up to the patient and then reacts quite sharply and firmly when the patient misses an appointment or is late.

From the point of view we are presenting, the analyst induces a kind of behavior in a patient which he then treats. However, this behavior need not necessarily mirror the infantile neurosis experienced by the patient in his early years. The patient's responses to the analytic situation are not necessarily a duplicate of moments in his early life history. He may respond idiosyncratically, but still his responses might be similar to those anyone would make who sought out this situation and cooperated within it. Under certain stressful situations the individual will exhibit unusual behavior which is related to his human biological possibilities as well as his experiential history. But his response is not necessarily repetitive of his life history. The adult patient who "regresses" in psychoanalysis does not behave as he did when he was a child; he behaves like an adult being childlike. The notion of "deep" when it is applied to phenomena occurring in psychoanalysis requires a good deal of further study. One area of study is the family situation where someone may exhibit inappropriate and irrational behavior quite similar to transference responses when he is caught in a particular kind of paradoxical relationship. These responses are not infrequently seen in family therapy.

The question of insight also appears in a somewhat different light when the frame of reference is the dyadic analytic relationship--although patients benefit from understanding their present behavior in terms of the past, a question can be raised whether this understanding is "causal" to a basic change in their behavior and their perceptions. Some patients manifest considerable insight and continue in their distress. Other patients improve in types of psychotherapy where insight of the psychoanalytic sort is not utilized. Yet the argument that insight causes change is essentially irrefutable if one wishes to make it so; one can always say that a patient who manifests insight but does not change has not yet sufficient insight, and if patients change with non-insight therapeutic methods it can be said they have not really changed. There is, of course, no answer to such arguments. But the question of what causes therapeutic change is of such profound importance that the relation between change and insight requires thorough scrutiny.

One important argument for the necessity of insight is the point of view that change can only persist if understanding has taken place. Yet if a broader description of a patient is made, other reasons for the persistence of change appear. For example, if a patient changes, he is going to behave differently with his intimate family members, and if he does so they are going to behave differently with him. As the patient establishes different sorts of relationships within his family, a change can continue because a different living context has been established. Although the patient might say that his life is different because he understands himself better and so is behaving differently, it can also be argued that his life with his intimates is different because he has been behaving differently and cannot go back to the old ways without disruption of a whole network of relationships.

Sometimes it appears that a fascination with Freud's brilliant contribution to the understanding of unconscious symbolism has contributed to a confusion over what causes therapeutic change. Some psychoanalysts appear to believe that if they can understand the patient's symbolic processes, and certainly if they can help the patient understand them, inevitably change will occur. But what we are discussing here is the context within which that understanding takes place with the suggestion that it is the context rather than the self-understanding which leads to improvement in a patient.

The idea that people undergo therapeutic change when they understand themselves better is as deeply rooted in psychiatry as the notion, once widely held, that the earth was the center of the universe. If only the individual is studied, one can only say that he has changed because he has learned to understand himself better. What other explanation is there? However, if both patient and the person attempting to change him are described, other possible causes of change appear. We suggest that an important causal factor is the paradoxical situation imposed upon the patient in psychoanalysis which forces him to change his ways. From this point of view, the notion of self-understanding has two purposes: it provides a subject for patient and analyst to talk about; a modus operandi for dealing with each other. It also provides the two people with an explanation of why change has occurred after it happens. In other words, the emphasis upon insight and self-understanding can be seen both as tactic and a rationalization. The fact that psychoanalysis could not be conducted without an emphasis upon understanding does not mean that self-understanding is causal to change: paradoxical factors in this peculiar relationship appear equally important as a cause of change.

When one shifts from a focus on the individual to an interpersonal orientation, many problems in psychotherapy appear in a different light. This does not mean that one point of view is more true than the other; each is equally valid from the point where the observer stands. Individual psychology has built a solid foundation; interpersonal psychology is just beginning to be structured. The ultimate choice will reside in which approach is most consistent theoretically and most practical in application.

REFERENCES

1. Ackerman, N. Transference and countertransference. Psychoanalysis, 46:17-28, 1959.
2. Bateson, G., Jackson, D.D., Haley, J. and Weakland J.H. Toward a theory of schizophrenia. Behav. Sci., 1:251-264, 1956. Reprinted in Don. D. Jackson (Ed.), Communication, Family, and Marriage (Vol. 1, Human Communication Series), Science and Behavior Books, Palo Alto, California, 1968.
3. Glover, E. The Technique of Psycho-Analysis, p. 20. Internat. Universities Press, New York, 1955.
4. Haley, J. Paradoxes in play, fantasy and psychotherapy. Psychiat. Res. Rep. Amer. Psychiat. Ass., 2:52-58, 1955.
5. Haley, J. Strategies of Psychotherapy, Grune & Stratton, New York. In press.
6. Hinsie, L.E. and Campbell, R.J. Psychiatric Dictionary, pp. 751-752, Oxford Univ. Press, New York, 1960 (3rd edition).

7. Jackson, D. D. Countertransference and psychotherapy. Progr. Psychother., 1:234-238, 1956.

8. Jackson, D. D. Guilt and the control of pleasure in schizoid personalities. Brit. J. Med. Psychol., 31:124-130, 1958. Reprinted in Don D. Jackson (Ed.), Communication, Family, and Marriage (Vol. 1, Human Communication Series), Science and Behavior Books, Palo Alto, California, 1968.

9. Levy, E. Z. The subject's approach: Important factor in experimental isolation? Bull. Menninger Clin., 26:30-42, 1962.

10. Stone, L. Psychoanalysis and brief psychotherapy. Psychoanal. Quart., 20:215-236, 1951.

INTERACTIONAL PSYCHOTHERAPY

Don D. Jackson

There is an increasing interest, in the past few years, in techniques which are utilizable in brief psychotherapy and during phases of long-term psychotherapy. This interest has existed since psychoanalysis was founded, as exemplified by the work of Ferenczi, Rank, and others. There has been relatively little recent work by psychoanalysts in this area and the majority of papers suggesting specific techniques to shorten the length of treatment are largely by non-analysts or by analysts who have renounced the traditional method and are looked upon as something akin to heretics. Attempts to change the prolonged course of analysis have really not amounted to much since Reich's epoch-making work on character analysis.

As one example, you may well recall the furor caused by Franz Alexander's introduction of the corrective emotional experience and of shortening the length of therapy in relation to the patient's dependency; but what does one hear of this work currently; and who has followed it? Who has attempted to validate his impressions? One problem, to paraphrase Freud, is whether the technique of analysis is so flawless that its pure gold should not be alloyed with a baser metal. Another problem is whether the controversy that is caused whenever one suggests innovations drives would-be innovators from the field. I would suspect that this disinclination to stomach controversy does play an important part in why so little is done in attempting to change techniques, if only for experimental study. But there are a few other reasons that I think are becoming increasingly important. One is that it is becoming obvious that psychoanalytic results have not always warranted the time, money, and energy put into them. Also, the number of young psychiatrists seeking psychoanalytic training is increasing so markedly that institutes do not have room; and yet,

Reprinted from CONTEMPORARY PSYCHOTHERAPIES (Morris I. Stein, ed.) pages 256-271, 1961. Copyright, The Free Press of Glencoe, Inc., New York; reproduced by permission.

these individuals want to practice a dynamic psychotherapy. In addition, the number of non-medical psychotherapists is increasing and these individuals may be freer to experiment with psychotherapy than are some of the more traditionally-bound medical therapists.

Another element, which is very hard to gauge, is that perhaps there have been modifications in analysis which are much more pronounced than one would suspect from, say, reading the most recent edition of Glover's book on psychoanalytic technique. That is, over the period of years, changes have crept into technique which have never been formalized and perhaps never been quite admitted, and yet they are there. I would say the most obvious such cumulative change is the importance currently paid to counter-transference and to the personality of the therapist.

One of the issues that is at heart in all attempts to change, to modify analytic technique and to apply these modifications to brief psychotherapy is the fact that interpretation is considered the real modifier of personality. That is, the changes brought about economically and topographically by a properly-timed interpretation of the transference makes advice, suggestion, and technical manipulations of questionable significance and they may even be given a negative value. But if one believes that interpretation has been given too high a value and that the analytic situation has been reductionistically under-evaluated, then the possibility of exploiting some other therapeutic innovations looms as more promising. Obviously, though analytically trained, I would not be giving this paper if I didn't adhere to this latter point of view. I think it is possible and useful in some cases to utilize technical interventions even in psychoanalytic therapy and to apply the understanding gained from these experiences to brief psychotherapy, where the therapists may never have the opportunity to analyze the effects of what they have done.

The problem is that the prolonged, intensive contact established with the patient in psychoanalysis is an excellent source of study of the effects of parameters or innovations. But on the other hand, if one is doing psychoanalysis, one isn't apt to be free to try innovations. In addition, the very training that has helped to create a skilled psychoanalyst may severely limit the kind of innovation that would occur to him. The stress placed on the almost surgical interpretation ignores all that interaction that would interest experts in communication.

My own interest in communication theory stems from work with schizophrenics and from a long association with Gregory Bateson. The rationale for the kind of interventions I shall describe strictly follows the importance I attach to double level messages, context, behavior as a message and the human's ability to simulate.

However, the use of psychotherapeutic interventions depends on a series of conditions without which their use would be meaningless or possibly harmful and I would like to name the conditions so that it is clear what I am recommending and that I am not, in a sense, suggesting that everyone go out and practice some interventions. First the therapist must have had enough experience within himself, preferably through personal therapy, so that he can recognize his own needs in therapy and distinguish between an interest in helping the patient and more power-oriented motives. He must be aware of his own value judgments in order to check whether certain suggestions or advice arise from the patient's needs or from his own wish to espouse a cause. Second, the patient must be seeking change and have a reasonable expectation to benefit from it. It is not necessary that the patient want to help in the overt sense because many patients who insist on "doing it themselves" are not especially suitable for certain techniques. The point here is that the patient's social field must be expandable so that the therapist does not whittle a square peg who has access to only round holes. Symptoms which have a family adaptive value are not treated <u>without</u> <u>due</u> <u>regard</u> <u>for</u> <u>reactions</u> <u>in</u> <u>other</u> <u>family</u> <u>members</u>.

Given these basic premises then, I would like to consider some of the theoretical notions as to why interventions should be used. Perhaps the first intervention of importance in psychoanalysis was Freud's discovery in the analysis of phobics that there came a point when the analyst had to tell the patient to take action, to face his phobia; and many of the attempts to modify psychotherapy or psychoanalysis depend on changing verbalizations into action. I think it is a simple fact that people can talk about something as a way of not dealing with it; and the therapist by merely listening to what they say may be unwittingly condoning procrastination. To give you a simple example, a young man, who had been under therapy for some time and was quite adept at expressing hostility toward his mother, which among sophisticated people is a rather common indoor sport, remarked that she had just sent him a muffler for his birthday and that he had a drawer full of mufflers which she had sent him on previous birthdays. He used this as an explanation of her lack of interest. It was suggested that he return the muffler with a note expressing his interest in having her exchange it for something that he could use and which would be more suitable for the California climate. He should also remind her that he had now several mufflers already on hand. He should not allow a simple five or ten dollar item to interfere with what little relationship he had with his mother. The patient was literally unable to do this. He rationalized the item as of small monetary value, that the mother would take this as criticism, that it wasn't worth it. After a number of hours of struggle he was impressed by his inability to do this small thing and recognized that he was more afraid of his mother than he had realized. More important, he realized that he was much less of a conforming and "good" patient than he had ever thought. In this instance, as in most instances which I will describe, the function of the advice is to point up the problem area just as an interpretation would do. But, advice also serves two other purposes, it aids the patient to translate intellectual understanding into action; and it forces the patient to focus on his relationship with the therapist regardless of whether he rejects the advice or accepts it.

Some of you may know of the interest of our research group in double bind communication, which is based on the fact that all communication is multi-level. Every message is qualified by another message, or by the context, and these qualifications may be congruent or incongruent. If I say I am angry and my tone sounds angry it is a congruent message and quite different from the incongruent message uttered when I say I am angry with a level tone and a smile on my face. It is, perhaps, easiest to think of incongruence in relation to messages in the hypnotic situation. Here the context is important. We assume that a subject is experiencing an involuntary phenomenon in hypnosis when, for example, his arm begins to levitate and yet he says in a surprised tone, "Why my arm is rising." He is doing something; and yet he is denying that he is doing it. In the hypnotic context, such incongruence is appropriate since the subject feels the hypnotist is really responsible for the arm raising.

On applying the idea of the double bind to psychotherapy and the general idea of multi-level communication to psychotherapy, we have noticed that there are a number of factors in therapy which automatically bind the patient to this situation and that this attachment can be utilized in maneuvers which we would call a therapeutic double bind. This term is used loosely since the therapist need not express two orders of messages, one of which denies the other, as in a typical double bind situation; but he may take ad-

vantage of the fact that the patient expresses such order of messages when he is confronted with a situation that taps his own ambivalence. How often in therapy we use the expression "the other
side of the coin." If the therapist wishes to get the patient to see
this other side, and this cannot be accomplished by verbal explora-
tions because of conscious or unconscious resistance, it may be
possible to bring out this "other side" by a reductio ad absurdum
approach to what the patient is revealing. The therapist uses,
even over-uses, what the patient offers rather than hunting by attitude and questions what the patient is hiding. The reasoning is:
if A is a function of B, but not all of B, then extending A to its ultimate may reveal the B that it does not include. This situation
may occur inadvertently with the inexperienced therapist whose
patient maintains a uniformly lovely positive transference whose
presence is discussed routinely by patient and therapist while the
patient creates all sorts of hell on the outside. A simple example
of the deliberate use of this technique would be one in which the
patient uses denial to cover up his critical feelings. He is presented with the idea that one cannot really like someone else unless he can be critical of that individual. If he is asked to think
of something critical, he is bound to experience some annoyance
at the therapist and in the process of being critical he may actually
feel the criticisms. In addition, the criticisms he makes against
others are almost certain to have been experienced against the
therapist as well.

A typical psychotherapeutic situation occurs when a patient
tries to please the therapist by talking about what he thinks the
therapist wants to hear; and the therapist accuses him of using
pleasantness as a resistance. The patient can only feel hurt and
insist that he is trying to do what the therapist wants. However,
if the therapist focuses on teaching the patient to be really more
pleasing, then he may be able to demonstrate to the patient the
areas in which he is not really pleasing and the patient can be
prevented from utilizing his standard technique of being pleasing
in the therapy situation. An actual clinical example would be a
young woman who had been married for some years and sought
psychiatric help because of urging by her physician, after years
of pills and shots for unexplained fatigue and listlessness. She
turned out to be a rather martyred soul who honestly felt that she
was doing her best to please her husband; but despite her efforts,
he was not satisfied. She was aware of not feeling loved but not
aware of anything resembling rage. When the area was approached
in terms of as mild a word as "dissatisfaction" she was literally
unable to agree that such an affect could be present. In the face

of such resistance the therapist recommended that, since her marriage was so important to her and since her husband's mood produced a marked response in her, then it was important that she learn to become really pleasing. A good deal of discussion went into her husband's likes and dislikes and how she might go about satisfying them with renewed vigor. The first dent in her martyrdom came when she was greeted by the news that she really wasn't pleasing after all. By implicitly accepting the therapist's suggestion that she learn to be really pleasing she admitted to a certain lack of her pleasantness. She also was caught up enough in her old patterns that she had at least to attempt to carry out what the therapist described. She was spurred on to some really superb efforts when she felt her husband liked what she was doing for him in her new efforts; but it also made him uncomfortable, and he was driven to protect himself by attempting to do something for her. In the process, both people found a few pleasant surprises. The manner in which they finally achieved closest collaboration was in a coalition against the therapist. They were able to delight each other with tales of what a stupid procedure he had instituted, how it didn't get at the real cause of their troubles, which lay much deeper. They then agreed to come in jointly for continuing psychotherapy. Thus, if the patient is taught to be more pleasing when she feels that she is already "too pleasing," and not fully appreciated for her efforts, then several events occur dynamically. In order to please the therapist she must do what he says but she does this with a tacit admission that she isn't pleasing enough; and, in addition, she is being pleasing only because the therapist orders it and not because she really is. If she is resentful at the implication that she isn't as pleasant as she thought, this shows up in the therapy situation. We now have a look at the other side of the coin.

If she reveals annoyance then she is really pleasing the therapist, who is searching for genuine affect. The therapist's intervention usually produces one of two reactions, either of which can be useful in the spouse or other significant individuals. A coalition can be established against the therapist if the patient is annoyed with him, and the spouse can seize on this opportunity to get out from his own load of guilt. Or, the spouse may switch complaints, and if the patient is able to carry out the pleasing campaign and thus demonstrates that the problem in their relationship is not solvable by the techniques of being pleasing, she may discover for the first time that her husband's complaints are not the basic issues between them.

This idea of developing messages which carry a multi-level significance and impinge on the patient's dynamics was first systematically carried out by our group with patients who had severe plantar warts. We have found that patients with severe plantar warts that have not responded to years of dermatological treatment could not have the warts removed by simple suggestion even though they went into a good trance. As you know, these are warts which are continually irritated by walking, since the bottom of the foot has to bear the body weight, and they are much more difficult to treat than the so-called juvenile variety.

In the course of talking with one such patient, a petite, attractive, feminine-looking woman, who nevertheless had strong masculine strivings, it occurred to us that the wart had brought her a good deal of attention and annoyance from her husband, whom she seemed unable to handle. It also accounted for her poor moods when it was hurting, and thus she tended to ignore other factors in her situation that might be producing unpleasantness. The wart was so continuously inflamed that she could not go dancing and this disappointed both her husband and herself, since she was vain, pretty, and a good dancer. As with the other female patients in this series, the wart mysteriously was connected with pregnancy and children and received the same ambivalence felt by the woman toward her children, especially males.

This particular patient was instructed to smoke a pipe each evening for nine evenings in the presence of her husband. The therapist provided her with the pipe and tobacco. Detailed instructions, which I'll not attempt to cover here, were given her, including reaming out the bowl and how to tap out the residue which had various possible bearings on her psychodynamics. When the patient awoke from the trance she was in no hurry to leave. She wondered how long it would take her to smoke a full pipe and stated that she would have to "pin her husband down" for that amount of time. She gave a slightly uncomfortable laugh at this and then said that she hoped that it wouldn't make her sick. She looked at the can and remarked "mild tobacco." Three days later, she called the therapist on the phone and her first statement was "I might as well return your equipment"; she went on to say that the thought of smoking the pipe nauseated her and that she was more nauseated since she had been in the office than she had ever been in her life. She remarked that "I'll never be comfortable holding that thing. The trouble probably is that I really don't believe in it, and I think one has to believe in something in order for it to work; you might as well tell me to plant a piece of me in the backyard and it will grow into a cow. It's obvious that I don't believe in that kind of thing. " She got increasingly angry as the conversation continued and she said that she had a small operation coming up in two months and that the pipe smoking was too much on top of this. "This on top of it is too much. Why do I have to have something difficult?" As she got increasingly angry, she stated that the practice of smoking the pipe would upset her whole household, especially her husband, and that since she was not allowed to tell him what it was for, it would cause more trouble. "Wouldn't it bother your wife if you wore a bra and panties around the house? Besides, it would take at least six weeks to get him pinned down for nine nights; it's just too long; must I be humiliated in order for this thing to work?" She was assured that the suggestions were tailored to her personality and not to humiliate her and that she could make up her own mind about carrying them out. Several months later, she called to say that she was asking another woman to drop my "equipment" off. She had had the pipe and tobacco on her bureau for six weeks or so and had not been able to go through with the experiment; there was now no need to go through with it because the wart had healed up. It is important to note that the equipment, and this is her term, was on the bureau where she saw it every day and there were undoubtedly other members of the household who could see it too.

The principle of developing dynamic insight through action suggestions is, of course, utilized in non-hypnotic cases as well. The theory on which such apparently ridiculous suggestions are based can be described again in a slightly different framework. This is the notion that people are constantly attempting to determine the nature of their relationships (Jackson, 1958; Haley to be published). This is done most directly by taking action and by uttering congruent messages, and most indirectly by uttering covert messages.

Every symptom may be considered as a covert message--that is, an attempt to bring something about in a relationship. I say "may be considered" since it is unimportant whether the symptom was unconsciously developed for this purpose or not. For example, if a headache develops on the basis of prolonged tension in the occipital muscles, it nevertheless becomes a message, since it is a report on how the individual feels and a command to be responded to. The intent is not important because the receiver of the message is influenced if he has a relationship with the headache bearer. He may be annoyed, sympathetic, deny that it has anything to do with the relationship, or whatever; but he does make an overt or covert response to the headache as a message.

If a symptom is seen as a covert message, then theoretically if the patient is persuaded to make the message overt, he will not need the symptom. Thus, if a woman with an easily tiring larynx is instructed to tell her family that her therapist won't allow her to speak to them, she may find that when she spontaneously has to make a protest against some injustice her voice rings out loud and clear. The therapist's instructions have made her message overt. The effect of changing the level of the message has been known for a long time, but not thought of in these terms. Thus, Ferenczi (1955b) suggested that if a patient is blocked in his attempts to free associate, the therapist get him to fantasy. He made this suggestion in order that unconscious material continue to be made available to the therapist. But there is a further aspect to this suggestion. If a patient can't free associate, he is merely an innocent victim of some unconscious force. If he also can't carry out any attempt to change the level of his method of communication, then it begins to dawn on him and the therapist that he is just plain stubborn. That is, we allow the patient one symptom or a group of symptoms, but if he extends these during therapy, it becomes apparent that this is a comment on his relationship to the therapist.

I am not sure how clearly I have been able to communicate the theory that these suggestions are based on, so let me make one further attempt. If a patient comes to a psychotherapist for headaches, he learns to label them as suppressed anger. Once he has accepted this labeling, the headaches no longer have the same meaning to him that they did. If he were to have a headache, he would now know that he was angry, and thus, his anger would not be covert and the symptom loses some of its meaning.

In the course of learning to label, the patient experiences resistance to change which comes about not only because he has learned about a new system of labeling but mainly because the old problem is also experienced in the relationship to the therapist. As he attempts to influence the nature of his relationship to the therapist, the same need for covert communication that he had on the outside will rise again. However, if the therapist does not deal overtly with the symptom as such, nor make its meaning overtly clear to the patient, but instead intervenes in a way that will help the patient change his level of messages, he may avoid the need for the symptom being used against him in the therapy situation. This idea is again most easily demonstrated in hypnosis. A patient with a tic involving the tongue that is creating annoyance in her husband because of the clicking sounds that she makes, is asked where she would like to have this symptom transferred to. It is subtly suggested that a wiggling toe is not a bad thing to have since one is free to wiggle it and no one else knows about it, and she accepts the suggestion. Once the symptom is transferred it wears off in a period of days or weeks because a wiggling toe is not annoying to one's husband and the toe is not connected with speech as the tongue is.

In describing how such a suggestion works, I would emphasize that the patient is given permission to have a symptom, whereas her previous symptom was reinforced because it was something she was not supposed to have and because it annoyed other people. Secondly, the therapist has tacitly labeled the symptom as a covert attempt to annoy others and he has changed the level of message by saying in effect, "you will be responsible for wiggling your toe." This taking of responsibility for a symptom (like toe wiggling) is quite different from a tic, which is merely mysterious to the patient and which, of course, she can't help. This was a pleasing person who had to accept the therapist's suggestion. Once she agreed to the notion that the symptom could be moved, she tacitly accepted responsibility for it, i.e., she changed the level of the message. At the same time, the implication that she was willfully causing her symptom was avoided by allowing her another.

In some brief therapy cases where a followup has been possible, it appears that the original symptom has not returned nor been replaced by another, as one might expect. This is not true of the majority of cases where only symptom transference by simple suggestion is used. If a change in the level of message is achieved and if overt behavior is brought about that will make overt the covert meaning of the symptom, then more lasting results can be expected. For example, the lady with the tongue tic could be instructed to bring her husband to a session, and, acting under orders from the therapist, she would have to be critical of him. Since both of them would be told that someone he really cares about is someone he is able to be critical of, and someone he knows well enough to have spotted his faults, then it is not as difficult to get the patient to be critical as it might seem. Once having been critical, even though it is under the therapist's aegis, the patient cannot retract it completely, nor will the spouse ever forget it. In this manner, a symptom is made a part of overt behavior and the behavior is made interactional by bringing in family members or by making the behavior appropriate vis a vis the therapist.

I would like to illustrate these ideas in a more complete manner in several case histories showing the type of thing that one may do, both in brief therapy and in utilizing them as a part of intensive analytic therapy.

A 64-year-old woman was brought to the office by her daughter-in-law, who was very solicitous about her depressed mental state. The patient had been having anxiety attacks for a year and a severe depression since her husband's death two months previous. She came from a distant town to stay with her son and daughter-in-law and their two children in a fairly small house. She was a conscience-ridden woman who was always aware of having done her best and she had a certain air of helplessness which was both an appeal to the therapist and an insurance that her son and daughter-in-law wouldn't kick her out. Although her constant self-recriminations annoyed other people, she felt justified in them because she felt that she may have contributed to her husband's death. She felt vaguely that there was something more that she could have done that might have prevented his heart attack. Under questioning she revealed that her husband had had twelve years of alcoholism and that this had been a terrible period for her, but that during the last ten years of their marriage, he had not touched alcohol at all. Also, his alcoholism was strictly confined from Friday night to Sunday morning, and she, without too much therapeutic leading, was able to see that he seemed more comfortable at work than at home. She had also taken care of her invalid mother for thirteen years, and under the pressure of her husband had finally sent her to another sister, who had never since masked her feelings of anger toward the patient. The mother's illness covered a good bit of the period of the husband's alcoholism and the patient spoke of feeling torn between her husband and her mother. Although the husband was consistently good to her mother, he resented having her in the home.

It occurred to her that her feeling that she had contributed to her husband's death from the coronary attack was related to her own anxiety attacks which had started a year previous to his death. When she was the one who was down and unable to take as good care of him, then he was obvious in his displeasure. There were hints that he was intolerant of her having difficulty, but there was little he could do about it since the family physician assured him that she had had heart spasms. Subsequently, several specialists diagnosed her condition as hyperventilation and stated that there was no medical evidence that she had had coronary disease. However, they would not go so far as to say that she could not possibly have had a heart attack. So this left her for a number of months, prior to her husband's demise, with a mixed feeling about whether she had been really sick or whether she had just been nervous and had taken advantage of him. She punctuated all of her history with statements like "I'm trying my best, doctor, I'm ashamed of myself; I am trying my best."

After the initial interview, the therapist decided that she was not an ideal candidate for insight therapy; she was deeply religious, conscience-stricken, and not especially sophisticated. She was not used to being introspective and she would probably be running into increased resentment if she remained indefinitely in her son's crowded home. Although the situation was currently being covered up by benevolence, it was possible to pick up hints from the daughter-in-law, and later from the son on the telephone, that they were not too happy about it. Her natural obedience and her conviction that she "could lick this thing" could be exploited by giving her explicit instructions. Also, since her son complained that she was appearing in rather undressed states in front of him, the therapist decided she would respond to a certain amount of flirtatious bantering.

She was told that she must get out of bed every morning, rather than have her breakfast brought by her daughter-in-law, that she must do part of the housework, and that she must engage in a graduated series of trips away from home. The first trip involved a junket to the local store about a block away and the final trip involved taking the train to another city several hours distant, eating lunch, and returning. She was assured that she need not spend any time in the city beyond meeting these requirements.

In actuality, her defiance of and attachment to the therapist allowed her to prolong this last trip for an hour and a half while she did some shopping. The son and the daughter-in-law were instructed not to be so benevolent, because their mother would pay for their benevolence by feeling increasingly guilty and depressed, and she couldn't stand much more of this. The one pleasure period emphatically allowed her was when her son came home in the evening. She was instructed that they must have a cocktail together. The son normally did this and the mother never touched alcohol. She was told that alcohol was a specific drug for depressions, equal in some respects to modern-day tranquilizers, and that she must have at least two ounces of bourbon before dinner. This was done in order to facilitate her acceptance of her husband and his drinking problem, as well as to allow her a structured context in which to enjoy her son's company. She complained initially that she couldn't stand the taste of bourbon, but that she was getting it down. Several weeks after this procedure was inaugurated, the son and daughter reported that she had honestly sparkled during her cocktail hour, and subsequently, she reported to the therapist with smiling annoyance, "You know, I think you had me drink deliberately in order to remind me of my husband." Little reassurance was used, but a somewhat teasing, provocative manner which both intrigued and irritated her was employed. She was heard by the secretary to mutter in the waiting room that she did everything that damn doctor told her, and he never gave her any praise.

Within two weeks after this regime had been inaugurated, she was noticeably better; she was able to deal with everyone but her son and daughter-in-law. With strangers and neighbors she could be gay and interesting, and not grunt, moan, or engage in self-recriminations. A period of several tiffs between her and the daughter-in-law, especially over matters of household cleaning (which I had anticipated when telling her to do some of the housework), increased her feeling that she was on borrowed time. She was then able to admit her terror of going back to her home town and living alone, and the therapist was able to help her arrange with a friend of hers to spend the first week with her in the empty house. After six weeks, she was asked how soon she thought she could make it home, whereupon she thought two weeks, and the therapist insisted that she take three. When she left, the therapist advised her to take six meprobamate tablets daily, although she had been on the drug for several months without noticeable effect. She had been engaged in a struggle with her previous psychiatrist who was fearful of the possibility of addiction. Again, her Presbyterian conscience came through, and two weeks after she had returned home she called to say that she had cut down the meprobamate tablets to four a day, but asked my forgiveness for still taking them.

In summary, a 64-year-old woman exhibiting characteristic signs of an agitated depression was handled by being seen five times over a period of two months. No claim of cure is made, but it did seem that she responded to a regime developed according to guesses about underlying psychodynamic factors. Evidence for conscious and unconscious insight existed in the fact that she made a connection between drinking bourbon and her husband's alcoholic period, long talks with her son in which they both decided that the husband had been a somewhat difficult character, and a statement that, despite her sending her mother to her sister after thirteen years of caring for this bedridden patient, the sister had perhaps had it coming to her, and the mother's death could not have been prevented whether she was in California or elsewhere. It is difficult in this kind of case, because of the lack of follow-up, to know what procedures the patient carries out on her own. All I know about this particular patient after about six months, is that she is still living in her home in another part of California from her son, and, according to her, is doing all right. She still is not happy about it, but she is not depressed.

An example of conscious insight occurred with a young man who had been in analysis for several years and whose progress was slowed by recurring quiet recriminations, mainly against his parents. Although they lived in a distant city he often felt misused by them in the present, as well as in the past, and duplicated this situation in many of his relations with other people. The analyst had had little success in analyzing this situation in a way that led to anything more than intellectual understanding. It gradually dawned on him that the patient was afraid of his parents and that there were not only deep religious overtones to this, but also the parents unconsciously, and to some extent, consciously, were perceived as all that he had in the world. Naturally, this kind of dependent hostile involvement kept him away from other people and kept his parents in their exalted position.

During one session, when the patient was complaining in his typical hopeless and non-productive manner, the therapist cut in to ask him, "What would you be willing to give up in relation to your parents?" He was rather taken aback by this, but stated after some thought that he would be willing to give up his right to his inheritance. He expressed definite annoyance at the idea of giving up anything in relation to the people he felt deprived him; it seemed inexplicable. He explained, however, that giving up his inheritance might not mean too much to him because his parents were relatively young. The money would go to his mother and then to him and other siblings, and by this time, he would probably have an adequate income of his own. He also felt that since his siblings had children they would be more in need of extra money than himself. The point of the therapist's question stemmed from the fact that the patient's father had kept an exact account of every penny spent on his higher education and the patient was engaged in paying this back on a monthly basis. The patient didn't believe this was fair of the father, but he continued to send the monthly allotment; and this, of course, kept him and his parent involved with each other. After the patient stated that he would be willing to give up his place in the will, the therapist pointed out that, since he had given up something, he was now in a position to ask for something. Therefore, he should write his parents a letter stating that he was renouncing his place in his father's will because he could no longer continue the payments on his education, since it interfered in his relationship to the parents, and it was not worth sacrificing this relationship for money. It took the patient nearly two weeks under pressure by the therapist to get the letter written. He and the therapist went over the document carefully, sharing a joint project. Following the writing of the letter, the patient experienced a good deal of anxiety and showed a noticeable increase in his self-confidence, and had a dream in which he became a father himself for the first time in therapy. Evidently, in giving up his place in the will, he gave up being a son and was able to conceive of having a son of his own. The therapist had little doubt that the father would respond favorably to the letter because of his and the mother's need for the son, and this turned out to be correct. The father stated that he hadn't realized the patient felt so strongly about the debt and that he was willing to cancel it. However, he didn't want the patient to give up his inheritance and suggested that he simply subtract the education debt from the amount coming to him in the inheritance. He assured the patient that he was as much his son as the other children.

Of course, the patient was delighted with this response and it immediately led to several more profitable and aggressive adventures in other areas, including his job and his girl friend. The anxiety toward the therapist for influencing him to such a degree was minimal. Although he immediately had some reaction after getting the letter written, out of fear that he had substituted one father who had pushed him around for another one, this was analyzed and, in addition, other successes on the outside made the patient feel that he was improving on his own.

As an example of how this anxiety manifested itself--following writing the letter and prior to having heard from his father, he industriously started relandscaping his house. He was concerned over how extensive a job he had started and he had a dream in which he was a patient in a mental hospital; he wandered away in a confused state and was brought back by the attendant. When the therapist mentioned that it was too late to take back the change instigated by the letter, he broke into spontaneous laughter. Any improvement in such a patient does result in some increased anxiety, which the therapist expects and accepts.

Most analysts certainly would be critical of the kind of intervention I have described, on the basis that the use of techniques like these irrevocably distorts the transference situation. They interfere with the use of abstinence as a motivating force, since the therapist is gratifying the patient by his activity, and they do an injustice to the patient's trust. I have certainly been told outspokenly that "with the kind of parents these patients have had, you know very well that what they need is absolute honesty and not manipulation." Let me try to answer these points individually. In regard to distortion of the transference, until there is better data as to the effect of the therapist's personality and of countertransference on the course of therapy, I would suspend judgment on how disastrous it is to deep insight when the transference situation is deliberately disturbed. If the therapist is covertly dissatisfied with the patient's progress, I am afraid the transference would be distorted despite his most avid attempts to remain a fly speck. Also the enduring nature of the transference phenomenon and the vigor of repetition compulsion has led most patients, as far as I can tell, to place interventions in the framework of their own past life. They do not see them as a continuing interruption in the therapeutic process.

Interventions may also be criticized on the grounds that they involve manipulation or trickiness. I think this is a value judgment which ignores the fact that all psychotherapy or psychoanalysis attempts to influence the patient. In psychoanalysis the use of the couch, of silence, and of non-gratification are technical devices employed to influence the patient. Recently Fairbairn (1958) stated that he has renounced the use of the couch because he feels that it is too humiliating to the patient. I think most psychotherapists operate implicitly by putting the patient in the "one-down" position. If he is able to extricate himself, he is cured, and if he can't extricate himself, he usually quits. The happy outcome is something like growing up and leaving home, it is achieving an equal status, and I think that if one follows a few rules, it will lessen the possibility that the patient may feel that he has been used or tricked.

Manipulations or interventions must not be employed if the therapist has any negative feelings toward the patient and if they are especially counter-indicated as a way out of some sort of therapeutic impasse. That is, when the therapist feels that he does not know what is going on, things bog down and then a bright idea occurs to him. This is exactly the time when an intervention should not be used. The therapist must frankly answer any questions that the patient asks in an attempt to understand the meaning of his recommendations. The therapist must be prepared to be wrong if his intervention fails or if the patient becomes angry, as mentioned in the description of the married couple who formed a coalition against the therapist. He should accept his position, non-defensively and be free to lose a patient.

I hope these remarks will not be interpreted as a "cookbook course," designed to get around the need for intensive training in order to do psychotherapy; the opposite is the case, for only an experienced therapist can tailor an appropriate intervention to each individual patient.

This is one of the paradoxes, and one of the stumbling blocks in psychotherapy: the experienced therapist is best able to conceive and execute innovations; yet his experience is apt to render him chairbound and a devotee of his own style.

CONTROL IN PSYCHOTHERAPY
WITH SCHIZOPHRENICS

Jay Haley

Most theories of schizophrenia were proposed at a time when it was thought the schizophrenic patient could not be treated with psychotherapy because, according to those theories, he was out of contact with reality. In recent years a variety of therapists have been developing therapeutic techniques which seem to produce some results with schizophrenics. It has been difficult to see a connection between the ways these therapists actually deal with a patient and former theories of the psychopathology. Such therapists may have a violent struggle with a patient, they may have a quiet, insightful conversation with him, or they may spoon feed him like an infant. It is possible to learn more about the nature of schizophrenia by examining these therapeutic methods. An attempt will be made here to demonstrate that the various techniques of therapy involve a similar pattern which can be related to a developing theory of schizophrenia. (1)

THE CONTEXT OF PSYCHOTHERAPY

Although ambulatory schizophrenics may occasionally be treated in private offices, the traditional context for treatment is an institution where the patient's entire life is circumscribed by the people in authority over him (3). What the patient eats, what clothes he is to wear, when and where he is to sleep, and what he is to do are in the hands of a supervisory staff. Within this context of total authority, a therapist attempts to change the patient by individual conversation with him. It is important to emphasize the context because it frames whatever is said between the two people. A quite different situation occurs with neurotic patients where the therapist has little or no actual control of the patient's life. Of course therapists in many total institutions do not have total power because of administrative needs or conflicts among the staff, but from the pa-

---

Reprinted from the A. M. A. ARCHIVES OF GENERAL PSYCHIATRY, 5:340-353 (October 1961). Copyright, American Medical Association, Chicago; reproduced by permission.

tient's point of view the therapist is part of the staff hierarchy and so controls what is to be done with him. How different it is for a therapist to be permissive when he has power over the activities of a patient and when he has no more power than the patient is willing to grant him. Similarly, if the therapist insists the patient do something when he can back up his request by physical force, the message is a rather different sort than when he cannot, even though that force might actually never be used.

Besides an authoritarian setting, the therapist of the schizophrenic works within a context where the control over the patient is said to be for his own good because he is within the institutional setting for help and treatment. This benevolent frame also affects whatever the therapist might do individually with the patient. If a therapist is harsh with a patient within a framework of benevolent help, his harshness is of a different sort than if it took place in a setting which was designed to mistreat people.

An equally important part of the context is the "involuntary" nature of the relationship. When a patient volunteers to be treated, as in other forms of psychotherapy, he accepts a certain sort of relationship by that act. The therapist of the schizophrenic must typically force himself upon the patient and impose a relationship on someone who has not sought his company.

AN AUTHORITARIAN APPROACH

The first example of a therapeutic interchange offered here is typical of one type of treatment of schizophrenics. It takes place in a benevolent context where the therapist maintains the patient in a private home with a staff in total charge of the patient's living conditions. This particular paranoid schizophrenic had previously escaped, was placed in a state hospital, and had just been brought back against his will prior to this interview. The session takes place in the living room of the home in the presence of several assistants and visitors. The patient's mother is present in the kitchen, within hearing distance, although it is unusual for a relative to be present during this therapist's treatment. This is an excerpt from a tape recording of the interview.

Therapist: Do you think you're going to get well this time, or is it going to be another business of going off to the insane asylum?
Patient: Well, I started off from there, and uh-when I figure out how I--where's my mother?
Assistant: She's in the kitchen.

Therapist: She's here. I-I will send her out--and she has to do what I say.

Patient: No, no, you got to do what <u>she</u> says, I...

Therapist: Don't you know who God is around here?

Patient: I am God. (Laughter in background.)

Therapist: You!

Patient: Yes.

Therapist: You crazy dope (laughs). Kneel in front of me!

Patient: No, you kneel in front of me.

Therapist: Boys, show him who's God. (The assistants struggle with the patient, forcing him to his knees in front of the therapist.)

Patient: Now listen...

Therapist: Kneel in front of me!

Patient: You're not supposed to use force against me.

Therapist: Don't be silly. I'm the boss.

Assistant: Now he's on his knees.

Therapist: Now---what are you doing?

Patient: Hey, mother!

Therapist: What are you doing to God?

Patient: Hey, mother!

Therapist: What are you doing in front of God?

Patient: Hey, mother!

Therapist: Let him up, boys.

Patient: (as he rises) There are conditions under...

Therapist: Who's boss here--?

Patient: You do what I say and we can make conditions for dealing...

Therapist: That's right, there's no conditions.

Patient: I am the creator and if you don't do what I say then uh-what can we...

Therapist: Who kneeled in front of whom?

Patient: Uh-I will destroy you.

Therapist: You can't destroy me because I'm God.

Patient: No, I am God.

Therapist: No, I am God.

Patient: Well, I happen to be a better thinker and more-more of a leader than you of human beings and I think what I am and I realize I'm God, and I see what you are and uh-

Therapist: Show him again boys, there's no use arguing with a crazy man.

Assistant: Kneel to God.

Patient: Look uh-mother. (Confusion of struggle as they force him to his knees.)

Therapist: Make it easy, make it easy.

Assistant: Why does God have to cry for mother?   (More noise and confusion.) Why does God have to cry for mother?

Therapist: That's true, I didn't think of that even.   That's true what he says.

Patient: Look, you're not supposed to use force against me.

Therapist: I'm boss here.

Patient: You're not supposed to use force--you're not boss here.

Therapist: Who's God?

Patient: I am God.

Therapist: Well, why don't you get up then?

Patient: Well, I'll push them away--tell them to get away.

Therapist: All right, boys, get away.

Patient: That was a mistake, I should have pushed them then. (The patient laughs and everyone laughs.) I should have obliterated them.

Assistant: (Laughing.) Obliterate, yeah.

Therapist: Obliterate, that's it. (Pause.) You're absolutely helpless.

(The interview continues)

The subtle aspects of this type of interchange will be largely ignored in this paper and only gross formal themes will be emphasized. The most obvious theme between the 2 men centers on who is in charge. Whether the question is phrased in terms of who is God or who is the boss, the apparent issue is which man is to govern the behavior of the other and so set the conditions for what sort of relationship they will have together. The therapist chooses to force this issue, apparently assuming it is a crucial one. The patient responds as if he too considers it of vital importance. When the therapist says, "Kneel in front of me!" the patient replies, "No, you kneel in front of me." When the patient says he is God, the therapist says he is God. This kind of one-upmanship struggle takes place between them with the patient attempting to win despite his obvious disadvantage. The patient has only his wits, while the therapist has on his side not only medical authority but the patient's mother, a number of strong assistants, and about 40 lb.

The simple way for the patient to win in such an interchange would be to say, "All right, if you want to be the boss, I will let you." By giving permission to the therapist to take charge, he himself would be in charge. Such a maneuver would incapacitate the therapist in this sort of struggle. However, such a maneuver is not part of a schizophrenic's repertoire. To either take charge himself, or to acknowledge that the therapist is in charge, would require the patient conceding a relationship with the therapist. Instead, the patient rigidly insists that he is God (and therefore he is not relating to the therapist) and that the therapist must do what God says.

DEFINING A TYPE OF RELATIONSHIP

A basic characteristic of the schizophrenic, either chronic or in an acute episode, is his unwillingness to follow directions and do what he is told. However, he does not refuse to follow directions. The schizophrenic does not say, "No, I won't," to a request any more often than he says, "Yes, I will." When he is told to do something, the schizophrenic typically does not do it but does not take responsibility for refusing. He may indicate that he did not hear what he was told, or that he is too preoccupied with his thoughts or "voices" to do it, or that he is helpless and unable to move, or that he misunderstands because of delusory thoughts about the situation, or that he is too suspicious or too excited to do it, or he may offer an argument in the form of some fantastically implausible reason for not doing it.

When a schizophrenic actually does what he is told, it is usually when sufficient force is threatened so that he must, and then he will do it in his own time and in his own way. The doing of it even then may be labeled as accidental, e. g. , when a schizophrenic is required to go somewhere with an aide and walks a desultory route, just "happening" to continue in the company of the aide. However, there are some schizophrenics who achieve a similar end by doing exactly what they are told. Waxy catalepsy is an example of this type of behavior; in milder form it was followed by rebellious soldiers in the army who followed orders so precisely that they caused confusion to their superiors. A pertinent example was a mute patient who was told to leave the ward and take a walk on the hospital grounds. It was necessary to push him out the door, and he walked straight ahead into a tree and stood there with his face against it, thus exasperating his helpful doctor.

It is not the existence of delusions or hallucinations which cause a patient to be hospitalized; a person can have those and still make his living in society. The schizophrenic is placed in a hospital in those periods when he cannot maintain the most ordinary sorts of relationship. One ordinary relationship he will not form is that type where one person tells another what to do and he does it.

Even though a person would not do what he was told, he might still survive as a social being if he could tell others what to do. However, if the schizophrenic is placed in charge, he rapidly arranges that he not be in charge. He does not take necessary action when he should, or he does not tell anyone to do what must be done, or he tells people to do things so fantastic that others are forced to take charge of him. The patient in this interview insisted that he be treated as God, which would seem to imply he would accept being in charge of his life and that of others. Yet when he was previously put in charge of himself he went to the police and told them he had been kidnapped and was God, thus forcing them to lock him up under supervision.

A third necessary type of relationship is that which exists when two people behave as equals with each other. If one tries to behave as an equal with a schizophrenic, he soon makes it impossible. Typically when faced with a competitive relationship, the schizophrenic will fail, thus forcing a relationship between unequals. If asked as a peer to cooperate in some joint endeavor, he will not hold up his end. (If schizophrenics could cooperate as equals, they would probably form gangs and attack hospital staffs as delinquents and criminals do.)

To say that a schizophrenic is unable to do what he is told, to tell others what to do, or to behave as an equal with others is to say that he cannot maintain either complementary or symmetrical relationships and so any type of relationship. A complementary relationship is one between two people of unequal status; they exchange behavior which indicates that one is giving and the other receiving, one teaching and the other learning, and so on. A symmetrical relationship is one where the two people exchange the same sort of behavior. One asks for something and the other asks for something, one gives and the other gives. Such a relationship tends to be competitive.

Any behavior exchanged between two people can be classified as defining either a complementary or symmetrical relationship. Whatever response a person makes must indicate one of these types of relationship. Should a person decide that he does not wish to define a type of relationship with anyone, he is faced with an almost impossible task. One way a person might try to achieve this task would be to become immobile and have no contact with anyone, therefore he would not be responding to anyone. Yet other people will inevitably intrude on his immobility to help him stay alive, and he must respond to that intrusion and so acknowledge some sort of relationship.

The only way that a person can effectively avoid forming a relationship with anyone is by behaving like a schizophrenic. Since any response made will define a relationship, he must qualify every response with a label that indicates it is not done by him in relation to the other person. For example, he may indicate that he is not responding to the other person (by labeling himself as God or someone else), that what he is doing is not a response (but merely random behavior which might occur no matter what anyone was saying to him--a schizophrenic denial accepted for many years by psychiatry), that he is not responding to the other person (but to someone else, such as a delusionary figure) or that he is not responding in this place and this time (and therefore he cannot be responding to the other person). (7)

It is these various ways of qualifying what he does which identifies the schizophrenic and also makes it so difficult to "reach" him. From this point of view, the goal of psychotherapy for the schizophrenic could be phrased in this way: It is necessary to persuade or force the patient to respond in such a way that he is consistently indicating what sort of relationship he has with the therapist instead of indicating that what he does is not in response to the therapist.

With a neurotic, the therapist may attempt to bring about a change in the type of relationship consistently formed by the patient. With the schizophrenic, the therapist must require him to form any type of relationship.

Gaining Control of a Relationship. The psychotherapy of schizophrenics requires unique techniques because of the peculiar unwillingness of the patient to indicate that what he does is in response to another person. To persuade the patient to indicate a type of relationship, it would seem obvious that the therapist must gain control, or direction, of the patient's responsive behavior.

Those methods of gaining control of another person's behavior which prove effective with normal people and neurotics are frustrated by the schizophrenic. For example, one can ask a person to do something, and if he does it then one has gained some control of his responsive behavior. Such an approach is not practical with a schizophrenic because he will not do what he is asked. It is also possible to gain control if the other person will refuse to do what is asked. By provoking rebellious responses, one can control what the other person does. However, the schizophrenic does not refuse to do what is asked, he just does not do it, and so one cannot easily influence him to rebel.

It is also possible to gain control if a person says he "cannot" do something. Typically neurotics, and resistant hypnotic subjects, do not do what is asked of them but indicate they are unable to. The hysteric "cannot" move a paralyzed limb, the phobic "cannot" enter a phobic area, the resistant hypnotic subject "cannot" levitate a hand or have a hallucination. A typical method of gaining control of such a person is to ask him to be unable to do what he is told. If he then indicates he is unable to, he is responding to direction (4). The resistant hypnotic subject, for example, is encouraged to resist the hypnotist's directions. If he does so, he is following the directions of the hypnotist who is thereby controlling his behavior. The schizophrenic, however, will not say he "cannot" do something. One discovers immediately how different is the schizophrenic response if one attempts to hypnotize such a patient. The usual techniques for dealing with resistant subjects simply do not work, since the patient is likely to preoccupy himself by responding to his "voices" instead of the hypnotist. If the patient cannot say "Yes" and cannot say "No" and cannot say "I cannot," he must respond by labeling whatever he does as not related to the other person.

The Forced Relationship. One way to gain control of a schizophrenic's behavior is to force him into a situation where he cannot deny he is responding to the therapist. Essentially the patient must be trapped so that he is following directions whatever he does and so is participating in a relationship. The physical assault by the therapist cited earlier requires the patient to respond to him. The patient may label himself as God and so indicate that he is not responding, but this contention is difficult to uphold when he is on his knees. This is a possible position for a helpless patient, but not for God. Not only is he forced to his knees, but his denials are brusquely dismissed by the therapist. When the patient says he is God, the therapist says, "Show him again, boys, there's no use arguing with a crazy man."

The patient is in a rather hopeless dilemma; if he denies that he is relating to the therapist by labeling himself God, he must acknowledge that God is subservient to the therapist; an untenable position. If he does not deny that he is relating to the therapist, he is conceding that he is responding in a complementary relationship with the therapist and so no longer is behaving in a schizophrenic way. Much of the violence that takes place in this style of psychotherapy centers on forcing the patient to concede he is responding directly to the therapist.

THE BENEVOLENT APPROACH

Although one can force a direct response from a patient by physical assault, subtle procedures may achieve the same end. A quiet conversation can also make a patient's denials ineffective. Fromm-Reichmann was once treating a patient who had a religious system which included an all powerful God. The patient labeled her responses as occurring in relation to this God rather than other people. Instructing the patient to go to her God, Fromm-Reichmann said, "Tell him that I am a doctor and you have lived with him in his kingdom now from 7 to 16--that's 9 years--and he has not helped you. So now he must permit me to try and see whether you and I can do that job." (1) This patient is also in a position where she must acknowledge a response to the therapist whatever she does. If she does not go to the God and tell him what she is supposed to, she is rebelling against Fromm-Reichmann, as well as rendering questionable the existence of God. If she goes to God and says what she was told, she is not only conceding a complementary relationship, but she is conceding that the therapist is more powerful than God. If she acknowledges her God, she must deny him. If she denies Fromm-Reichmann, she must acknowledge her.

Quiet directives may contain a formally similar pattern to violently forcing a patient to his knees and so may the opposing extreme of violence. A presumably polar extreme would be a therapist soothingly nurturing a catatonic patient. Many therapists typically treat extremely withdrawn schizophrenics by a benevolent nurturing. This technique is succinctly described by Ferreira who considers the term "mothering" most appropriate for the interaction (2). A few quotations from his article give the flavor of the technique. He describes the treatment of two mutes, chronic schizophrenics, and says of the first patient:

Disheveled, in a waxy immobility, she sat in a chair, aloof, staring fixedly into space while a tray of food was rapidly getting cold on her lap. I sat by her side and gently inquired as to why she wouldn't eat. She gave me a slow-motioned glance but remained immobile. I began talking about her food, that it would get cold while she, probably hungry and thirsty, was afraid to touch it. I continued; that I wouldn't let her be thirsty or die, that I would feed her myself. I raised a glass of milk to her half open lips, and continued talking in a soft and low tone of voice, tender and warm as if talking to a baby. "Come on...it's milk...so good, so white, so fresh...

gee! it's good milk...it's _my_ milk...I'll give it to
you."

Although this "mothering" approach seems rather different from
forcing a patient to his knees, the therapist is insisting upon a complementary relationship by indicating that he will take charge and
the patient should follow his directions. He continues:

She looked at me with a somewhat curious expression,
a quasi smile on her immobile lips, a spark of light in
her eyes. Slowly she reached for the glass. I commented: "I know you can drink it by yourself," and re-
linquished the glass to her. She took a few sips, while
I kept remarking about the "freshness" of the milk and
the pleasant sensation of drinking it. I spoon-fed her
some food. She took over slowly--more milk, then
more food. It took her about half an hour to eat half of
her food and drink a glass of milk. At that point, her
negativistic attitude became more pronounced again,
and, without the least insistence, I left her with a
smile and the promise of returning the next day to see
her.

When the therapist holds the glass to the patient's lips, she is
in a situation where it is difficult for her not to respond to him. If
she drinks, she is accepting the complementary relationship. If
she turns away her head or clenches her teeth, she is rebelling
against him and so defining a relationship. Instead, the patient responds by taking the glass herself, and the therapist immediately
accepts this symmetrical maneuver. In a similar way, when the
patient dealt with the previous therapist directly by asking him to
tell the assistants to get away, the therapist immediately complied.
In both cases if the patient indicates he is not responding to the
therapist, the therapist insists on a complementary response. If
the patient then responds in a symmetrical way, the therapist accepts this definition of the relationship.

The nurturing technique includes "taking over" the patient's behavior in other ways:

I would talk directly to her almost constantly. Facing
her, smilingly warm, I would intrude on her silence
and mutism with many statements and questions for
which I would then verbalize the follow up answers.
"You always sit in the same chair? I guess you like

this chair better... makes you feel it is your chair...
do you?   Oh, I know you won't tell me that... You
don't have to... but I wonder how lonely it must make
you feel to have only one chair to sit on... only one
chair that you want, that is..."

The patient cannot easily refuse to behave in relation to the
therapist when he is labeling all her behavior as responsive by
taking personally not only her slightest response but even her lack
of response. When he carries on both sides of the conversation
with her, he defines her as a person in a complementary relationship with him and she cannot deny this without responding to him.
She cannot even "happen" to be sitting in that chair after he has defined it as her chair. From that point on, whether she sits in that
chair or not, she is threatened with this action being in response to
him.

The patient's denial that she is responding to the therapist by
indications that she is responding to "voices" is handled in this way:

She nodded her head affirmatively when I stated (interpreting her silence): "Voices forbid you from talking?"
Then I embarked upon a line of dramatization. In a soft,
quasi-intimate voice I stated to her: "You and I will
fight those voices." Whereupon I addressed myself to
the empty corner of the room and, with shouts of rage,
I blasted the air and those invisible voices; "Go away,
don't bother Cathy!" The patient paid unusual and dramatic attention to my attitude, and later on began responding to such antics with loud outbursts of laughter.
This was the first time the ward personnel and I had
heard her laughing.

When a patient continues to respond to "voices," the therapist is
relating to the patient but the patient is labeling what is happening
as unrelated to the therapist. To frustrate such a maneuver, it is
necessary for the therapist to gain control of this symptom. The
therapist does so here by siding with the patient against the "voices."
If the patient then responds to voices, she is also responding to the
therapist who has labeled those voices as occurring under his aegis.

When the patient begins to accept a complementary relationship,
he typically carries it to an extreme and so requires the therapist
to continue to be disciplining or nurturing. In the second case reported by Ferreira, the patient not only began to accept things from

him but even arranged to be put to bed and tucked in by the patient therapist. He would also rather frantically masturbate in his presence which, instead of antagonizing the therapist, resulted in his verbalizing the pleasures of it for the patient. Beside accepting a complementary relationship, no matter how extreme, the therapist also accepts and encourages any move toward symmetry. For example, he first was willing to hand feed the patient milk, and then:

> I added a carton for myself, an action which increased the conventional tones in our relationship. Later I replaced the milk with orange juice or coke, and as the patient improved, I began to omit the bringing of a beverage.

PSYCHOTHERAPY AND ETIOLOGY

Although it is an almost absurd simplification to synthesize months or years of psychotherapy down to a few formal patterns, it seems reasonable if these patterns can be shown to be relevant to the nature and etiology of the problem. The various theories of schizophrenia extant were proposed in a period when schizophrenics were considered unreachable by therapy. The first and still persistent theory of the problem, the idea that schizophrenia is based upon an organic defect, does not help explain why particular techniques of therapy now seem to produce improvement in a patient. The intrapsychic idea that schizophrenia is an immersion in archaic and primitive thinking also does not relate easily to techniques of therapy. If ego should be where id is, one can wonder how the two entities are reversed by feeding a patient or forcing him to his knees. Similarly, to argue that a patient was irrevocably scarred in the first months of life by maternal deprivation does not help in understanding the responses a therapist obtains from an adult patient. The argument that schizophrenia is a maturational defect would seem relevant if we had more understanding of the process of maturation. If one thinks of maturation as steps up the ladder of psychosexual development with the schizophrenic on the oral rung at the bottom, the process of bringing him up is not clarified. However, there is a theory of schizophrenia developing which is relevant to a maturational point of view and to the techniques of therapy described here.

If we define "maturation" as a sequence of learning experiences in a family, then a maturational defect could be seen as a defective family situation. Although we know little about the subtle processes of interaction in a family which permit a child to develop normally, we do know that it is necessary for a child to proceed from a complementary relationship with his parents when he is young to a more symmetrical relationship as he matures and goes his own way. It would seem that the psychotherapy of schizophrenics described here institutes that formal process.

A human child, by the nature of the organism, must be taken care of or he will die. He must be offered food and accept it, he must be supervised and respond to that supervision, he must be directed and follow that direction if he is to live with others. At the same time that he is learning to define his relationship with his parents as complementary, he must also begin to learn to behave symmetrically in preparation for that day when he leaves his parents and establishes a family himself. He must "assert" himself, walk without support, attempt to compete with others, try to be superior to others, and ultimately behave as an equal with his peers. The usual family somehow manages to provide a learning context where the child can learn to form both complementary and symmetrical relationships. Current research on the families of schizophrenics indicates that the schizophrenic child does not have that opportunity. Although a description of the family of the schizophrenic with a review of the literature on research in progress is not practical here (5), a few points about these families which are generally agreed upon and relevant to psychotherapy can be described briefly.

The Family of the Schizophrenic. Perhaps most relevant to any therapy of schizophrenics is the fact that the patient's family is a part of the context of treatment. He came from a family when he entered an institution, and he typically must return home when treatment ends. Not only is he likely to have continuing contact with family members during therapy, but whether he improves or not may depend less upon therapeutic technique and more about his concern over the family waiting at the gate for him should he be released.

The influence of the family on this type of patient is particularly important because he usually has had little or no experience with people outside his family. In cooperation with his parents, the child who becomes schizophrenic does not have independent relationships outside the family. For many years he experiences only the responsive behavior peculiar to his family and suffers an almost total lack of experience with people who respond differently. When he is ultimately of the appropriate age and circumstance to leave home and go out into the world, he is incapacitated for normal social intercourse. Not only does he lack experience with people, but if he forms an intimate involvement outside the family he is breaking a deeply ingrained family rule against such relationships. It does not seem surprising that a psychotherapist must force his company upon a schizophrenic and so relieve the patient of the responsibility of forming a relationship which is forbidden and which he is ill-equipped to form.

Therapeutic change in the patient also has repercussions beyond his own life. It is the contention of many investigators that schizophrenia in the child serves a supportive, or homeostatic, function in this type of family (8). If the patient behaves more "normally," the parents become disturbed or a sibling may begin to develop symptoms. The continual conflict between the parents may also come out more openly and separation may be threatened. When the patient is ill, the family is drawn together by this burden they share in common. Family members can avoid facing their difficulties with each other by focusing upon their problem child. Although it is possible to conceive of schizophrenic symptoms as a defense against unacceptable ideas by the patient, it is also possible to see them as a way of perpetuating a particular kind of family system. Therefore therapeutic change may threaten a patient not only with a different way of life for himself, but the responsibility for a shattered family and the collapse of someone else.

For most people, family life is where they learn to form, and have freedom to practice, different kinds of relationships. The maturational defect in the family of the schizophrenic centers in the inability of the parents to let the schizophrenic child learn to experience complementary and symmetrical relationships, despite the millions of messages they exchange together over the years. Typically if the child behaves in a way which indicates he is initiating a complementary, or "taking care of," relationship, his parents will indicate he should be less demanding and so behave more symmetrically with them. If he behaves in a symmetrical way, they indicate that he does not seem to appreciate their desires to take care of him. This constant disqualification of his bids for relationship is a theme of their life together. If the child seeks closeness he is encouraged to be at a distance. If he attempts to put some distance between himself and his parents, they respond as if they have been criticized and indicate he should seek closeness. If he asks for something, he is too demanding. If he does not ask, he is too independent. The child is caught in a "double bind" (1) with all of his responses labeled as wrong ones. What other parents would consider normal behavior, such as the child making demands upon them, criticizing them, objecting to what they do, asserting his independence, and so on, these parents consider impossible behavior. Even positive, or affectionate behavior by the child, is responded to by these parents in a negative way as if they feel that too much more will be expected of them. This constant disqualification may occur immediately in response to a patient, particularly those who later give up trying to reach their parents, or the disqualification may be delayed. Paranoid patients would seem to have experienced an apparent acceptance of their behavior and a later disqualification when what was previously done is labeled as something else, and so they live in a world of booby traps.

The child also does not easily accept the behavior of his parents; typically he disqualifies whatever they offer just as they do. Because of the family inability to maintain a type of relationship with the child, there is thorough confusion in this type of family over authority and benevolence. Attempts to discipline the child usually end in confusion, indecision, and parental conflict. When parents attempt to be authoritarian, the attempt usually dissolves into helplessness and benevolent overconcern for the child. When they attempt to be benevolent, the benevolence dissolves into exasperated and futile attempts at discipline. Rarely can the parents insist the child do something because they prefer it that way; they must insist it is for his own good no matter how obviously their request is to satisfy their own needs.

Self-sacrifice by the parents is considered a virtue in these families; mothers will even say that they have done nothing for themselves in their lives and everything for the child. Such mothers have been called "overprotective" because of their persistence in doing for this special child what other mothers would let him do for himself. Not only will they help adult children eat, but they will converse with a quiet child by carrying both sides of the conversation.

What discipline there is in the family is usually sporadic and occasionally violent. Some fathers give the appearance of being stern authoritarians, but their directives are usually unsuccessful. Mother either interferes and incapacitates father, or he backs down when his orders begin to be followed. The continual conflict between the parents over whether one or the other is too mild or too severe with the child is easily spurred on by the child who may prevent discipline by behaving in a helpless or disturbed way. Even parents quite determined to exert authority jointly will end in a row if the child becomes upset. Not only does conflict between parents disturb the patient, but by behaving in a disturbed way the schizophrenic can instigate conflict between parents.

The problem of who is to control whose behavior is a central issue in this type of family. The parents appear to receive any attempt by the child to initiate a type of relationship as a maneuver to control them. However, if the child responds appropriately to a relationship initiated by them, the parents also respond as if this is a maneuver to control them. For example, if the child asks mother to do something for him, she indicates by her reluctance that he is too demanding. Yet if she initiates doing something for the child, and he accepts her behavior, she responds as if he is demanding too much of her. Similarly, if he indicates he wishes to do something himself, she will respond by showing him that she should do it for him. Conflict over even minor matters becomes a major problem when every response is taken as an attempt to be in control of the relationship. The schizophrenic solution is to label all his responsive behavior as not occurring in relation to his parents and therefore not indicating a type of relationship. Yet this psychotic behavior is also not a satisfactory solution; his parents are then unhappy because he does not respond to them. Should he attempt to respond to them directly, they become disturbed and encourage him toward denials that what he does is a response to them.

PSYCHOTHERAPY AND THE FAMILY

There are several major differences between the treatment methods described here and the family system of the patient. From a learning point of view, it would seem logical that in these differences resides the source of therapeutic change. The psychotherapy situation is by no means totally different from the parent-child relationship in the family. The authoritarian technique of the first therapist described here is reminiscent of the kind of assault some patients might suffer at home. The "mothering" of the second therapist is reminiscent of the ways the patient's mother does for him what he is capable of doing himself. Not only has the institution for treatment a peculiar mixture of overprotection and authoritarianism, but often what is done for the needs of the staff is benevolently defined as done for the needs of the patient. It would seem paradoxical that there are similarities between the processes of relieving a pathology and the process which nurtures it. However, besides the pressure which the schizophrenic puts on the world to build it in his expected image, one might assume that it is necessary to behave in a way familiar to a patient if there is to be understanding. The change would presumably come when the familiar is redefined and so becomes different.

The Double Bind and the Therapeutic Bind. In a situation where he cannot leave the field, the child is forced to respond to two different sorts of messages from his parents which are incompatible with each other and so is in a double bind. For example, he is asked to respond in a more self-assertive way to them, but he is not to criticize them. Or he is asked to respond to them in a way appropriate to a certain kind of relationship, but he is not to indicate what sort of relationship he has with them. When faced with these incongruent demands for a response, the child solves the problem by indicating that his responses are not in relation to them and so appears withdrawn from reality.

The psychotherapist too could be said to be imposing a double bind on the patient. However, the patient is not forced by this bind to respond in a schizophrenic way, he is forced to concede that he is responding to the therapist. In the example cited, the therapist prevents the patient indicating she is responding to "voices" and not to him. He "takes them over" by commanding them and siding with the patient against them. From that point on the patient cannot use "voices" to deny a response to the therapist; if she responds to the "voices," she is acknowledging a coalition with the therapist against them. If she does not respond to "voices" she is indicating a coalition with the therapist because his goal is to cure her of such symptoms.

A more clear example of the double bind imposed by the acceptance of voices was once described by the first therapist cited here. He reports that with some patients who once heard "voices" and have improved, he will insist that the patient hear them again. If the patient hears the "voices" on command, he is following the directions of the therapist and so responding in relationship with him instead of using the "voices" as denial of that relationship. If he does not hear the "voices" on command, he is also following the directions of the therapist who as a larger directive is encouraging the patient to stop hearing "voices." Whenever a therapist encourages symptomatic behavior, within a framework of helping the patient cease the symptomatic behavior, the patient is caught in this double bind (4). A similar example is the therapist who encourages the paranoid patient to be suspicious. The patient cannot keep him at a distance by suspicious behavior if he is being encouraged to behave in that way. Whether he is suspicious or not in this situation, he is following the therapist's direction and so is in a relationship with him.

Although the parents of the patient may feel more comfortable with him if he is denying a response to them, the therapist attempts to prevent that denial. Typically he either encourages the denial, and so takes it over, or he takes denials personally so they lose their effectiveness. For example, the therapist may say to the patient who is off in a psychotic flight, "Why do you deal with me in that crazy way. " The patient cannot then define the flight as not a response to the therapist.

When the therapist forces the patient to concede that he is responding to him, no matter what the patient does, the patient can no longer continue with schizophrenic symptoms. The further process of therapy is the clarification of what sort of relationship they are having and the encouragement of the patient in searching behavior to learn to define different types of relationship with the therapist.

The Acceptance of a Relationship. The therapist's willingness to accept the patient dealing with him directly may be severely tested. If the patient gives up his denials and indicates he wishes a taking care of relationship, the therapist will be nurturing. The patient may then persist in this demand to the limits of toleration of the therapist, if not beyond. Similarly, the patient will deal with discipline by provoking the therapist to continue it at length.

When the patient deals with him directly, it is often in such an intense way that the therapist will be tempted to encourage the patient back into schizophrenic behavior again. The reputed "insight" into the unconscious by schizophrenics can also be seen as a willingness to put the needle into a therapist's weaknesses to the point of provoking retaliation. Similarly, improvement in a patient may not only involve provocation of the therapist but also of conflict between the therapist and the patient's administrator. Quite a good relationship must exist between a therapist and ward doctor to weather the storms provoked by an improving patient.

Besides being willing to continue in a particular type of relationship, no matter how difficult the patient may make it, the therapist must also be willing to accept a shift in type of relationship if the patient initiates it. Although the therapist may impose "mothering" on a patient, he does not insist upon this type of relationship if the patient indicates he would prefer another type. In the example cited, when the patient reaches for the glass of milk, the therapist immediately lets her hold it and drink herself. The actual mother of the patient would be more likely to take the patient's indication that she wanted to do something herself as a criticism of mother and so prevent it.

Although the therapist is willing to let the patient initiate a type of relationship, this does not mean the patient is in control in the situation. The therapist indicates that he is _letting_ the patient define the relationship in whichever way he chooses. The total authority which the therapist has over the patient's life provides a continuing context which indicates that whatever the patient does is done with the therapist's permission. Therefore no matter what type of relationship the patient initiates, it is within a complementary frame at a higher level. (A rather different interchange is involved when the therapist sees an ambulatory schizophrenic in private practice.)

The _Frame_ of _Psychotherapy_. Perhaps the major difference between treatment method and family situation centers on the peculiar nature of psychotherapy as an interchange set apart from ordinary life. Neither patient nor therapist can actually be defining a "real" relationship with each other; they are not friends, not relatives, not acquaintances, not even doctor and patient in the ordinary sense. Typically the therapist behaves as if there is an intimate involvement with the patient, but actually there is not. Both patient and therapist will go about their own lives separately when they leave each other's company. The supposed intimacy which is defined between them terminates with the end of the interview, in contrast to a relationship between friends which extends into mutual social life or a relationship between relatives which includes sharing living conditions.

From the point of view of the patient, it is extraordinarily difficult to gain control of the relationship with a therapist when the nature of that relationship is so slippery. The patient cannot assume the therapist is merely harsh, because he is benevolently helping him. Nor can he assume that the therapist is only benevolently nurturing him, because their relationship is usually consummated in a rather grim authoritarian setting. Often the patient will attempt to relate to the therapist as a parent, and many therapists of schizophrenics will encourage this by literally saying, "I am your mother and I will take care of you," or they imply such a relationship by their behavior. Yet obviously the therapist is not a parent; there is no family life between them but only a series of interviews. Similarly, the patient and therapist may establish a relationship more like friends than other forms of psychotherapeutic relationship, and yet they do not move in the same circles socially. It is perhaps the multiple contradictions in the relationship which make it so difficult for the patient to find a handle to manipulate the therapist.

Not only is their relationship not an ordinary one, but one of the premises they establish together is "this is not real life," or "this is a kind of game." Within that framework the two people may become quite emotionally involved with each other, but this is also true of many games. Like a game, the interaction is confined to specific periods of time; unlike a game, the only rules are those the participants work out together as they go along. Not only must they define the rules as they interact with each other, but also they must resolve the conflict over who is going to make the rules. They have no outside authority to consult on what rules their relationship should be built upon, nor can they apply the rules of other types of relationship because this one is like no other. In the process of learning this, the patient tries to, and finds he cannot, use the rules typical in his family relationships.

The play-like quality of the interchange between schizophrenic and therapist is more apparent in this type of psychotherapy than any other. In all psychotherapy the therapist is both "involved" with a patient and at the same time sufficiently detached so that he can observe the type of interchange taking place. In this type of psychotherapy the same behavior exists but in a more active way; the patient is faced with a man who is "acting out" different kinds of serious involvement while labeling the situation in a play-like way. In the first example, the therapist forces the patient to his knees and insists that he is God, yet he does so in such an exaggerated way, before an audience of people, that it is like a game. Despite the grim seriousness of schizophrenia, the interview is even playful with considerable laughter from everyone involved. At one point the patient himself laughs, indicating he made a mistake and should have obliterated the assistants.

With the second therapist, there is again this play-like quality to the interaction. By exaggerating the "mothering," the therapist indicates that it is not "real," as it cannot be. This framework is further emphasized when the therapist sides with the patient against the "voices" and dramatically tells them off, provoking laughter from the patient.

From a communication point of view, the incongruity in levels of message manifested by the schizophrenic is met by a similar incongruity on the part of the therapist. For example, the message of the patient who calls himself God might be verbalized in this way: I am speaking, qualified by the statement it is God speaking qualified by the helplessness which indicates it is not God speaking. The therapist's answer is: I am being harsh with you, qualified by the setting of benevolent help, qualified by an indication that it is a kind of game they are playing. Just as the therapist has trouble dealing with any one level of the schizophrenic's multiple messages so does the patient have difficulty selecting and responding to a single level in the therapist's message.

The play-like nature of the therapeutic interchange is particularly striking if one observes the grim, realistic struggle between the patient and his actual parents. The therapist may insist the patient behave in a certain way, or he may take personally whatever the patient does, but he can shift his responses easily and treat the situation lightly. The parents of the patient rigidly follow a pattern of objecting to whatever he offers while encouraging him to offer more. The parents also become disturbed if the patient makes any comment on their behavior. The therapist encourages such comments and can accept them or decline them as he chooses so they do not interfere with the therapeutic framework. Of course the therapist has an advantage in a prolonged struggle with the patient that parents do not have. The parents may have to continually live with the patient and feel continually responsible for him. The therapist can maintain the play-like quality by absenting himself when he chooses and going about his own life, leaving the disciplinary problems to a paid staff.

Countertransference and Parents Behavior. When a therapist becomes "too involved" with a schizophrenic, the therapy is in difficulty. The play-like quality is gone and the patient can easily put the therapist at a disadvantage or provoke him to behave in ways he would rather not. At this point, supervision of the therapist becomes important to help him detach himself from too personal an involvement and reinstitute a psychotherapeutic frame to the interchange. The control of what sort of behavior is to be exchanged between therapist and patient then shifts back to the therapist.

Psychotherapy with a schizophrenic is generally agreed to be going badly if the therapist does any of the following sorts of things: (a) if the therapist lets the patient provoke him to retaliate in a way which encourages the patient to withdraw into schizophrenic symptoms, (b) if the over-dedicated therapist insists on continuing to take care of a patient when the patient is indicating a desire for more equality, (c) if the therapist pushes the patient toward equality, or independence, at a time when the patient is indicating he wishes more nurturing, (d) if the therapist institutes disciplinary measures and then retreats if the patient becomes disturbed, and (e) if the therapist denies the patient's perceptions about him when they are accurate because he cannot tolerate certain types of comment on his own behavior. One of the more convincing arguments that schizophrenia is of family origin is posed by the fact that this list of ways a therapist should not behave with a schizophrenic and the list of ways the parents behave with the patient are synonymous.

Countertransference can be seen as misperceptions of the patient by the therapist, but the interpersonal context of such a phenomenon is important. Those moments when an observer would say countertransference is occurring can be seen as those moments when the therapist has lost control of the relationship and is being forced by the patient into certain sorts of behavior. Subjectively the therapist may project various images upon the patient; in terms of formal behavior, he is behaving like the actual parent of the patient.

Psychotherapists who have developed specialized techniques for working with schizophrenic patients have usually never observed the patient interacting with his family. Yet the accepted procedures for therapy which have developed include systematically behaving differently from the actual parents. It would seem reasonable that a more careful examination of the family system of the schizophrenic would lead to more effective treatment techniques.

REFERENCES

1. Bateson, G., Jackson, D. D., Haley, J., and Weakland, J. H. Toward a theory of schizophrenia. Behavioral Sci., 1:251-264, 1956. Reprinted in Don D. Jackson (Ed.), Communication, Family, and Marriage (Vol. 1, Human Communication Series), Science and Behavior Books, Palo Alto, California, 1968.
2. Ferreira, A. J. Psychotherapy with severely regressed schizophrenics. Psychiat. Quart., 33:664-682, 1959.
3. Goffman, I. Interpersonal Persuasion in Group Processes. Transactions of the Third Conference, New York Josiah Macy, Jr., Foundation, 1957, pp. 117-193.
4. Haley, J. Control in brief psychotherapy. Arch. Gen. Psychiat. 4:139-153, 1961.
5. Haley, J. The family of the schizophrenic: a model system. J. Nerv. Ment. Dis., 129:357-374, 1959. Reprinted in Don D. Jackson (Ed.), Communication, Family, and Marriage (Vol. 1, Human Communication Series), Science and Behavior Books, Palo Alto, California, 1968.

168

6. Haley, J. Control in psychoanalytic psychotherapy. In Progress in Psychotherapy, Vol. 4, Jules H. Masserman (Ed.), Grune & Stratton, Inc., New York, 1959, pp. 48-65.

7. Haley, J. An interactional description of schizophrenia. Psychiatry, 22:321-332, 1959. Reprinted in Don D. Jackson (Ed.), Communication, Family, and Marriage (Vol. 1, Human Communication Series), Science and Behavior Books, Palo Alto, California, 1968.

8. Jackson, D. D. The question of family homeostasis. Psychoanal. Quart., 31 (Suppl.) 79-90, 1957. Reprinted in Don D. Jackson (Ed.), Communication, Family, and Marriage (Vol. 1, Human Communication Series), Science and Behavior Books, Palo Alto, California, 1968.

9. Rosen, J. N. Personal communication to the author.

10. Rosen, J. N. Direct Analysis: Selected Papers, Grune & Stratton, Inc., New York, 1953.

11. Jackson, D. D. Communication theory in psychoanalysis. To be published in Science and Psychoanalysis, Vol. 5, Grune & Stratton, Inc., New York (1962).

CONJOINT FAMILY THERAPY AS AN AID TO
INTENSIVE PSYCHOTHERAPY

By Don D. Jackson
and Irvin Yalom

In the past two decades the basic focus and format of psychiatric therapy has undergone significant change. The classical intrapsychic focus has been infinitely enriched by the cultural and interpersonal contributions of such innovators as Adler, Horney, and Sullivan. The classical one-to-one doctor-patient format also has been enriched by the rise of such new formats as milieu therapy, group therapy, and more recently, conjoint family therapy. At this stage of our knowledge, it is sagacious to consider classical techniques as being enriched by newer approaches rather than being challenged by them. Not only may different approaches be the therapy of choice for different individuals but several different approaches may be indicated in the treatment of one individual. These different approaches may be utilized concurrently or sequentially. This paper will present an example of the latter instance in which conjoint family therapy was utilized as one of a sequence of therapies. In this instance family therapy was particularly efficacious in abruptly motivating an apparently chronically hospitalized schizophrenic to leave the hospital, to find a means of supporting himself, and to involve himself meaningfully in further individual therapy.

The drama of sudden improvement can obscure the heuristic aspects of such cases and leave us with anecdotes rather than therapeutic insight. We present the case, however, not as a claim for the efficiency of conjoint family therapy but as an illustration of the basic theory behind family therapy.

Our basic theory stems, in part, from two observations made many years ago by innumerable therapists who came into contact with the families of hospitalized schizophrenic patients. One observation was that the families almost deliberately seemed to sabotage the treatment of the ill member. A harsh, even cruel charge, to be sure, and yet the behavior seemed so gross that no other conclusion could be reached. The other observation was that there occurred not infrequently an alternation or substitution of illness in the family. The patient's improvement was accompanied by the appearance of severe mental illness in some other family member--often the mother, less frequently a sibling or the father. What conclusion could be drawn from these two observations? It would seem that, despite the family's natural concern for the ill member, there are strong forces operating in the family to keep the patient sick.

Our major assumption, therefore, is that the family is a homeostatic system inextricably involving and influencing the patient.[1,2] Specifically, the family context of the schizophrenic is one in which the patient and only the patient has difficulties; and conversely, his position in the family is to be the problem. In addition to this we see the peculiar absence of personal problems in the cases of other family members. This assumption, of course, has many implications for therapy. The attempt to effect therapeutic change in a patient closely involved with his family without recognizing and dealing with opposing family forces is often foolhardy as well as futile. In fact, an important method of instigating some change in the patient is to tamper with the family system. Admittedly the schizophrenic family system is often ossified, and even when change occurs, it may be evanescent – the complex family forces quickly reinstating the status quo.[3]

The present case illustrates both the long-range use of family therapy and a specific technique for tampering with the family system in a crucial interview which appeared to be a turning point in therapy. We wish to call attention not only to the changes in the patient but to the changes in the family as well.

---

[1] Haley, J. The family of the schizophrenic: a model system. J. Nerv. Ment. Dis., 1959, 129, 357-374.

[2] Jackson, Don D. The question of family homeostasis. Psychiat. Quart. Suppl., 1957, 31, 79-90.

[3] Jackson, Don D. and J. Weakland. Conjoint family therapy. Some considerations on theory, technique, and results. Psychiatry, 1961, 24, 30-45. (See p. 223, this vol.)

THE PATIENT

The patient, David Brown, is twenty-five years old, unmarried, and when therapy was first begun by one of the authors (I. Y.), had been continuously hospitalized for one and a half years. Although in retrospect there were many ominous signs adumbrating his illness for a period of six years, he was first officially labeled a patient while in the service at age twenty. At that time, shortly after induction and assignment to Alaska, he was noted to appear confused, preoccupied, and withdrawn. He was unable to perform his work, had repeated episodes of extreme anxiety, and several inexplicable outbursts of anger and melancholy. The main thought-content involved the recent termination of a (largely autistic) relationship with a woman and marked indecision about future occupational plans. The confusion and withdrawal progressed to catatonia, and the patient was hospitalized and four months later medically discharged.

He returned home to live with his parents and his only sibling, a brother seven years his junior. His life pattern here consisted of numerous social and occupational failures. He dated often but characteristically misjudged the nature of the relationship and on several occasions made a premature and inappropriate proposal of marriage. Despite a high level of intelligence and a two-year college education, he was unable to negotiate even the least demanding jobs (janitorial work, messenger, etc.) and was invariably discharged because of his confused ineptness. He was seen by a psychiatrist in therapy during this time, but treatment was ineffective and hospitalization was advised.

The patient presented himself as an attractive, well-groomed young man, who, on casual examination, appeared to be in no distress. On thorough psychiatric examination, however, major impairment was obvious. His affect was peculiar--often indifferent, occasionally saddened, with periodic outbursts of inappropriate laughter or loud singing. He had had auditory hallucinations since the onset of his illness, chiefly derogatory, and resembling the voices of his family members. Present also were ideas of reference as well as bizarre somatic delusions that various parts of his body were decaying or vanishing and that maggots were infesting his blood stream. The chief impression one obtained from talking with him was one of vagueness, indecision, confusion, and a tendency to agree with everything the interviewer advanced. Because of his intelligence, attractiveness, good grooming, and presumably good potential, he elicited much interest and compassion from the ward personnel and on several occasions was involved in individual therapy. President of the ward community, editor of the hospital newspaper, he functioned well in the hospital setting, and the staff, like his family, tended to underestimate his inner turmoil. Student nurses and medical students identified with him, often vociferously taking issue with the diagnosis and ominous prognosis.

SUMMARY OF THE FIRST 18 FAMILY INTERVIEWS

Since individual and group approaches had failed to help, it was decided to involve Dave and his family in conjoint family therapy. His father and mother together with Dave were seen once a week in ninety-minute sessions. Because of school pressures, the younger brother, Charles, could attend only a couple of the sessions. (The meetings, incidentally, entailed some sacrifice on the part of the parents, since they lived over two hours away from the hospital.)

In the initial sessions, the therapist attempted to orient the family to the rationale of family therapy. He expressed the opinion that the other family members are invariably troubled, although the obvious distress of the identified patient tends to overshadow their pain. The family expressed a great desire to help and accepted this orientation albeit tenuously and quizzically. During the early sessions much historical data was discussed, developing the history of the family from its origins (the first meeting of the parents) as well as the early histories of each parent. These accounts, though seemingly complete, were strangely impersonal. Conspicuously missing were mentions of the typically human as well as the idiosyncratic problems of living. Aside from the appropriate concern for Dave's illness there was only happiness, cooperation, love, and inexorable social and financial success. Dave's response to this was, at one point, to pound on the table and shout, "My God, I come from a perfect family!" Mother answered, "Dear, have we said anything that wasn't true?" Dave replied, "No, but now I see what a goof ball I really must be."

Also absent was the occurrence of any "give and take" between the parents. They seemed to function as a single person or system. It was not until the sixth interview that the first semblance of individual differences occurred. Father, during the session, informed Dave that on his last job, he (father) had actually been paying Dave's salary and Dave's employer retained him only as a personal favor to father. Mother wept at this, saying that father shouldn't have told Dave. The first overt disagreement occurred much later when father accused Dave of not working because of laziness. Mother disagreed, gently serving as a peacemaker between father and son. It was especially difficult to obtain a multi-dimensional view of mother. A shadow figure, she smiled bravely and endlessly coined Norman

Vincent Peale-type cliches. When the therapist commented there-
upon, the family responded with disbelief or utter incomprehension,
leaving the therapist with the maddened feeling that he had been the
fall guy for father and sons, all of whom withheld their true feelings.
(The bewildering experience of the therapist who treats this type of
family is graphically described by Schaffer, et al.)[4]

Despite statement of the therapist's theoretical position, it
seemed impossible for the family to grasp that they were coming to
help themselves as well as the patient. The feeling prevailed that
they were there for Dave's sake, and the burden of keeping the discussions going fell on his shoulders. The parents after approxi-
mately eighteen sessions felt all "dried up"; there was nothing more
to say. The sessions became increasing unproductive, with all participants including the therapist growing discouraged.

CONSULTANT'S INTERVIEW
Because the family was losing interest and the therapist felt conjoint family therapy was still the patient's best hope, he asked a consultant (D. J.) to interview the family, primarily to get a feel for
them, but in addition to behave therapeutically if the opportunity offered itself. The consultant felt that like many of the families of
chronic schizophrenics, the Browns were well defended and most of
their energies were focused on maintaining the patient in the sick
role, as well as maintaining the status quo of the family inter-
relationships. He decided beforehand to see if the family could be
moved by placing them in a particular therapeutic bind; namely, they
would be asked: "What problems might arise for the family if Dave
improves?" Apart from that question, the interview was not
structured.

The usual framework for psychotherapy is a restorative one;
that is, we presume to remove the presenting complaint so that the
patient and those close to him can go about their lives without this
handicap. Clinical experience, however, often argues against this
view. The evidence concerning relapse and/or psychopathological
repercussions among other family members has led us to suspect
that we have tampered with part of an ongoing system and altered
its "normal" state in removing the labeled symptom of one member.
Thus, the usual assumption that things will somehow get "back to
normal" if the identified patient improves can obscure the possibil-

---

[4] Schaffer, L. et al. On the nature and sources of the psychiatrist's experience with the family of the schizophrenic. Psychiatry,
1962, 25, 32-45.

ity that the symptomatic behavior of the patient has a vital present function in maintaining the balance of family relationships.

In this case of a rigid family system, the physical presence of the other family members in a psychotherapeutic setting had not aided their understanding of their interlocking roles in Dave's schizophrenic symptoms. Indeed, these occasions only seemed to verify their myth that the family would be ideally happy but for Dave's misfortune, to which other problems could be traced with a truly remarkable consistency. The authors were in agreement that such a context was not likely to help the patient, and that family therapy was not going to succeed until each family member sought some help in it for himself. And no one at this point was even admitting to a problem.

The consultant felt that the situation warranted a sharp reversal from the prevailing view of Dave's psychopathology as aberrant behavior, and decided to use his authority as the consulting expert to focus the family's attention on their investment in Dave's illness. This was done by placing them in a particular therapeutic double bind. The question "What problems might arise for the family if Dave should improve?" is particularly forceful because it is a paradox in which the family as presently organized "can't win." The question encourages problems in a framework of help. Rather than arousing their guard by indirect probing, the consultant takes advantage of the family members' view of themselves as helpful individuals and implies they would be uncooperative if they did not produce some difficulties to discuss with him. Backed as it is by an expert, the question is heavily weighted to evoke at least token answers. Yet any indication of family difficulties which might be caused by Dave's remission can be amplified as barriers to his recovery and, hopefully, force the family to consider, at some level, that they must change before recovery is possible. If such a small dent can be made in the family's present rigidity, then further steps can be taken to get family members to assume some problems of their own.

This session was opened after polite formalities by the consultant's asking the above question. The family was incredulous at first, but the patient seemed intrigued by the question. The first breakthrough occurred when father admitted that if the patient improved and came home, he (the father) would be embarrassed socially. The mother was terribly hurt by this admission on his part, and the parents' usual coalition began to come apart at the seams.

Dave was helpful in suggesting several difficulties which might follow his improvement. He suggested that if he should fall in love and want to marry, it would be a problem for him to present his intended to his parents. Mrs. Brown said, on the contrary, she would be delighted, but qualified her statement by adding: " 'Course, I would always hope it would be the right one." The consultant agreed that this was a chancy thing, that every mother who loves her son is troubled by such questions as whether the girl is good enough for him or whether she might be too good for him. But while the mother agreed it was a "gamble," the rest of the family joined in to table this discussion on the grounds that it was a "natural" problem and, at any rate, "not that big of a problem."

The parents maintained that it was the opinion of many doctors that Dave should become "independent" of them if he were released, so therefore no problems for the family would arise. In the following example the consultant pressed them to admit that their plan for complete separation was neither practical nor desirable, and the patient attempted a rescue. Note that nonverbal intervention such as laughter is effective as interpretation while avoiding the sort of discussion in which the therapist must digress and risk becoming quite legalistic to make his point.

<u>Dave</u>:   Wh-What if it goes completely the opposite, what if I don't even wanna see them? (pause)
    <u>Consultant</u>: (laughs)
    <u>Dave</u>:   (laughs)
    <u>Mother</u>:   (joining laughter) What's happened...?
    <u>Consultant</u>: Mhm!
    <u>Dave</u>:   (still laughing)
    <u>Consultant</u>: How far away would you have to get---
    <u>Dave</u>:   (interrupting, laughs)
    <u>Charles</u>:   Tahiti or some other ---
    <u>Consultant</u>: (Interrupting) Yeah, I- I was wondering - I was thinking of Timbuktu... (Dave, still laughing) Ah, you don't think that wouldn't cause a problem.
    <u>Dave</u>:   Sure it would. But uh, I would... (sigh) I don't know what -- there's a - there's a problem in family relations that goes something like this: Unless you're actually in a psychiatrist's office you never want to hear - if you're on your own -- I don't -- I feel you never want your family to know just exactly how y- how bad things are or maybe...how...uh...realistically what things are really like. At least - I think you put up a front in both lines -- especially if y- the more you get independent and away from your family, the more you're likely to be like this. At least this is the way I see myself... So I see..uh..as I get well I see associations with my family more or less going down the drain.

Consultant: Mhm.
Mother: Well, other people's [relationships] don't.

Mrs. Brown's comment illustrates a typical double bind which pervades the schizophrenic family: While he is instructed, on great authority, to be independent of his family and thus avoid causing them trouble, he is told at another level that if he improves and breaks some family ties, he is behaving unnaturally and unlovingly.

In addition to this "stay away closer" position, the parents maintained that if difficulties ensued from Dave's improvement, they would be problems for Dave alone and not for the family:

Dave: What if- what if by some-some chance I should become more successful than my father, then how would my father feel about it?
Consultant: Well, predictably, he would say 'Great going!'
Dave: Mhm.
Consultant: But how would he feel about it?
Dave: Yeah.
Father: If you want an answer. . .from me; I'd be thrilled.
Dave, Charles and Consultant laugh.

Such a patently superficial answer illustrates that not only Dave is trapped by his role as receptacle of the family problems. The others are as obligated to feel and speak only the positive aspects as Dave is to accept the negative aspects of a given situation. Once this system is set into motion, the others cannot admit to "bad" feelings in the many situations where this is appropriate or even necessary. Here, by laughing, however good-naturedly, as the consultant did earlier, the sons indicate some preverbal understanding of the untenability of their father's position. Lest we be accused of advocating filial impiety, let us hasten to add that laughter often serves as a synthesis and release of paradox, as in formally labeled humor, and here, when family members have been forced to realize that something is vaguely amiss in their usual patterns of interaction. Further, laughing together is a vital form of interpersonal confirmation, which the consultant used frequently to ally the patient while forestalling distracting symptomatic behavior.

During the discussion of the drawbacks to Dave's improving, the younger brother had been silent but interested. When asked about Dave's weekends with the family (from which the patient usually returned quite agitated), Charles withdrew and relabeled Dave: "Before he comes home I'm a little nervous because I never know in

what mood or how he'll be. " The consultant pointed out that it
seemed as if Dave were being asked to bear the intolerable burden
of the whole family's solicitation. He was the total barometer of
how well or how poorly things went on the weekend. Surprisingly,
the patient burst in on this with:

Dave: Well, I feel that sometimes my parents and Charles
also are very sensitive to how I might feel, maybe overly sensitive
about how I feel, 'cause I don't -- I don't feel I raise the roof when
I go home, or. . .
Mother: Mhm. Dave, you haven't been like that either since
you had your car, it's just -- but before you did.
Dave: Well, I know I did. . .
Mother: (overlapping) Yeah, but even -- yeah, lately, twice
since you had your car.
Dave: Yeah, OK, anyhow, ah, (sigh) that's-ah, I wish I
didn't have to be that way, I guess, it'd be nice if I could enjoy my-
self or somethin'. . . (sighs, pause)
Consultant: You change your story in mid-stream when your
mother is nice to you, you know. Which. . . is understandable but
in your position you just can't afford to do it. (Dave: Mhm.) It
makes you kookier. Then you don't even know what you're thinking.
Mother: What did he change?
Consultant: That-ah, I can't read his mind so I'm just going by -
I don't know what he was going to say precisely, I have a general
idea, I think, just from experience --
Dave: Well, it's just, just the story that I'm the sick one
in the family and so this gives everybody else a. . . a chance to be
a good Joe and pick up Dave's spirits whether Dave's spirits are
necessarily down or not. That's what it amounts to sometimes, I
feel. In other words, I can't be anything but myself, and if people
don't like me the way they am -- ah, the way I am -- then I appreciate when they, if they'd tell me or something is what it amounts to.

The patient's slip of the tongue captures the puppetry in which
he is entangled; although he says "I can't be anything but myself, "
the question remains: is myself I or they?

At this point the consultant decided on a second major tactic to
tamper with the family system: to use as a foil Charles, the younger
brother, who was insipidly polite, smiling, and much too controlled
for a boy not quite eighteen. It was felt that his loosening up might
be beneficial to him and also would not make the patient's behavior
appear so out of line with the rest of the family. Further, the goal
of this single interview was not insight, but to set in motion family

forces which would alter the previously stable but unhealthy patterns of interaction. If Charles could be labeled as a problem, even if only to cooperate with the consultant, then Dave is not only somewhat relieved of his role but other family members must try new ways of coping with Charles, and those changes must have repercussions in other family relationships.

He was asked if he ever had any moods, which question elicited explosive laughter from the patient and his father. Charles carefully explained that sure, occasionally he had little problems, but in continuing in this vein he strained his father's patience to the breaking point. The father mentioned "slamming doors," schoolwork, and alluded to a rocky love affair mentioned earlier in the interview. This, it turned out, was a romance with a girl one year older than Charles, and though he had protested there was not much to it, the father had stated that he hoped Charles would not marry until he finished college. When the patient, in a brotherly manner, had asked Charles if he were thinking of marriage, father and mother had invoked the family rule that there were no problems and brushed the question aside.

In discussing Charles, Mr. Brown unexpectly confessed his feelings of inadequacy as adviser to his sons. But before this could be explored, Charles sought to restore the family facade:

Charles: And I think, I think it's better that way, too, because you get y-you -- in other words, of course a big problem I'll take to my parents but smaller problems 'n things I try to solve myself 'cause that way, even if I do make a mistake I learn that way.
Consultant: I didn't know there were any big problems. . .
Charles: Well, I say "if."
Consultant: (laughing, with Charles) If there are none then you haven't had the . . .
Charles: (overlapping) Well, I -- I. . .
Consultant: . . . experience of taking it to them.

Such examples illustrate the tenacity of the family rules even in the face of logical contradiction. Seeking to construct a situation in which it would be impossible to deny there were other family difficulties beside Dave, the consultant made a specific suggestion:

Consultant: . . . there's something, Charles, that you could do that would be, I think, of immeasurable help to your brother. And I think of help to you, but I can't prove that to you. And that is that you would agree that you would become more of a problem, during the time that Dave wasn't coming home. (pause). . .

Charles: You mean rebel against my parents, or. . .

Consultant: No. . . there are all sorts of ways of being a problem, what I mean is being a problem with a purpose, not just to -- not a troublemaker -- that's nothing -- but I mean you would be more of a problem in the sense that you would get a little more honest about some of the things that trouble you, or some of the uncertainties you may have, or whatever you don't share with your parents now because you don't want to bug them.

His father protested that Charles was already a problem.

Father: Well, ah, I'm thinking of Charles at home, though, it, ah, maybe you have a different idea of Charles than the way he is at home, ah, Charles, ah, yells and hollers around the house and there's no question about what it -- that something displeases him, you know it quick, and ah, he's very demonstrative, and ah, ah, ah, you sure do know what, what he likes and what he doesn't. He-he's not around trying to placate us.

Consultant: Do you -- are you aware of yelling, hollering around the house?

Charles: Well, sure, I mean, but this is my temper, I mean, just the way I am, you know, I -- I have a temper where -- it'll -- you know, fizzle out pretty fast and I'm all right again, you know, it -- it does -- it's not a lasting, you know, dislike. . .

Consultant: It -- there's no reason why it happens. It's just some kind of chemistry inside of you that. . .

Charles: No, no. There's something that certainly has to tee me off, but I mean, you know. . .

Consultant: Mhm. But -- you see --

Charles: Just a little thing --

Consultant: -- it's obvious, I would think, that what tees you off is something that the three of you don't have consensual validation about. You don't -- that, you know, there's no agreement; "Yes, this did happen, and this tees you off and it's going to continue to happen whether you like it or not, or we'll make some reparation . . ." It's treated as if you have a temper, not as if -- this is part of working out a relationship. If you're going to become more of a problem, in order to help your brother, then instead of just blowing up, you'll have to state, you know, what the problem is: "I feel unfairly treated," or "I'm not getting enough allowance," or whatever the thing, and have a discussion about it.

Mother: Well, it isn't those kind of things that --

Consultant: Whatever it is.

The only example the three could agree on was Charles' agitation at misplacing his glasses or keys. Charles agreed to become more of a problem, and the consultant ended the interview with the suggestion that unless they found some personal reason for family therapy, they should not burden Dave with their continued benevolence by attending sessions.

SUBSEQUENT FAMILY INTERVIEWS

The changes in the family following the consultation were dramatic; temporarily, at least, the therapist was able to break into the family system. Father began the very next session by stating that he had been thinking that he was tired of carrying all the family burdens and he would like to be a problem for a change. When he was asked how he might go about being a problem, he replied that he might come home late from the office one day without previously informing his wife. This opened up the crucial but previously unmentioned issue of mother's possessiveness, and immediately there was a deluge of pertinent and important material. The younger brother, Charles, commented that the family slogan or joke is "Mother has to know!" Everyone knew that mother became upset and worried if some family member went almost anywhere without "signing in" with her first. The issue was treated as gently as possible by the family, mother's contribution being to point out all the ways in which she had improved over the past few years. Following this meeting mother became quite depressed, and in the following sessions for the first time really began to talk about herself. She brought up the fact that her first marriage would have failed anyway even if her husband hadn't been killed in an automobile accident, since he had been flagrantly unfaithful to her. Mother suggested that this may have destroyed her trust in men and might explain her intrusiveness into the lives of her husband and sons.

She also related that her mother, who died when Mrs. Brown was six, was a severe asthmatic and had become addicted to narcotics. After her mother's death she lived in terror lest her father remarry, bringing an evil stepmother into the house. Some of these facts and others were heard for the first time by the family, and the two sons were quite astonished to hear of the previously unsuspected unhappiness in mother's life.

Father continued to bring up things that had been worrying him. He mentioned, for example, that during the family sessions he had often been a "nervous wreck" because he felt it necessary to walk a tightrope to avoid on the one hand upsetting Dave and on the other hand wounding mother if phrases were not carefully chosen. Father

again expressed his utter lack of confidence in himself as a parent
and his reluctance to counsel Charles about almost any matter because of his total failure with Dave. On several occasions when father
was trying to proceed, Dave attempted to focus the meeting on himself by direct request or by acting crazy in a fashion that demanded
therapist's and family's attention. The therapist commented on these
moves and in addition kept the family from focusing on them. Father
told Dave that the fact he (father) liked peace and quiet and therefore
kept things to himself was misleading. "If you think I'm superhuman,
that I don't have feelings or hurts or problems, that nothing inside
bothers me, then I've got news for you!"

And this was news for Dave as he began to see his parents with
their frailties and disappointments in a way he had not previously
perceived them. The parents became so involved themselves in the
sessions that there was a marked de-emphasis of Dave's problems.
He reacted to this at first with diversionary tactics as mentioned
above and then with sadness and fear at being extruded from the
family. He saw more clearly than before the dilemma which had
perpetuated his illness: that getting well and relinquishing his function as the problem meant losing mother and father and facing the
loneliness of life without them.

Charles was made an important part of the therapy by the pre-
scription given him to be more of a problem so that Dave would be
able to be less of one. Whereas previously he had attended only a
couple of sessions and remained on the periphery, now he attended
every one and was cast in a central role. His attempts to be more
of a problem were at first feeble, and he was dealt with severely by
the therapist and, surprisingly enough, by his parents, who objected
he was not trying hard enough to be a problem. If, for example, he
was able to tell his parents that he was worried about breaking up
with his girl friend he was criticized for not bringing it up earlier.
He was told that by waiting a couple of days and working it through,
he was depriving his parents of a chance of worrying with him and
helping him find a solution. Any protests by Charles were countered
with, "It looks like you just won't let Dave stop being the problem
in the family." Charles ultimately was helped to grow more spontaneous and honest with himself.

The third session after the consultation was an important one --
containing among other things, father's aforementioned "news" for
Dave about his own problems, and including a detailed description
of some of his early unhappy times. Immediately afterward Dave
answered a want ad and obtained a job on his own for the first time

in years. He worked at this for a month before being discharged because his employer obtained a skilled worker and possibly because of the patient's lack of manual dexterity (the job was making and installing awnings). When he lost this job the family response was appropriate and encouraging. When he expressed shame at failing them after all their effort in therapy, they all reminded him that they were also coming for themselves and pointed out to him the ways in which they had all benefited. It is of interest to note that once when Dave was working and could not attend a session, the family elected to meet anyway, an inconceivable proposition to them earlier in therapy. There was competition for the therapist's attention. After the brother's last session (before leaving for college) he privately expressed to the patient his annoyance at the parents and the therapist for not having devoted enough of the session to him. Later the patient passed this confidence on to the therapist with obvious relish.

SUBSEQUENT INDIVIDUAL THERAPY

At the time of this writing the patient has been out of the hospital for a year, living alone and supporting himself. He held one job for nine months, and then graduated to a more responsible, higher paying position. With Dave's gradual maturation and disengagement from his family, a new stage in therapy began and conjoint family sessions have gradually been replaced by individual sessions.

The family therapy context was directly pertinent to subsequent treatment and greatly enriched the scope of individual therapy. For example, Dave repeatedly created for himself a particular interpersonal dilemma. Early in a relationship he revealed everything about himself and later resented his friends for their premature intimacy and intrusiveness. The concept of roles was an utterly alien one to him. The idea that one has different roles (student, patient, employee, boy friend, etc.) and that one reveals different parts of himself in different roles seemed grossly dishonest and evil. However, when this dilemma was considered from the vantage point of the family and "Mother has to know," it became more comprehensible both to the therapist and to Dave. "Tell all to Mother" and "be strong and self-sufficient" were conflicting messages delivered to Dave all his life.

The examination of Dave's indirect methods of communicating with others was another crucial part of therapy. For example, one day he came to his therapy hour angry and discouraged. He had proposed marriage to a girl he had been dating and was rejected. It turned out, however, that the proposal had been far from a spirited one, and when he was asked what he would have done had she said "yes," he replied, "I guess I would've gotten the hell out of the state. " Therapy then focused on the task of finding more adaptive techniques of learning whether one is liked.

Another example occurred shortly after the patient was officially discharged from the Veterans Administration Hospital and began paying a fee for outpatient visits. The therapist was late for a session and, although he denied concern about this, during the hour he reported hearing a voice within him say, "You are robbing me." The therapist helped Dave to understand both that he was angry at the therapist and that he could, with safety, openly say so without resorting to indirect, crazy devices -- in this instance, a fledgling hallucination. On several occasions the patient found himself in an inextricable bind. His boss disapproved of psychiatry and refused to allow him time off for therapy hours. The therapist, of course, strongly urged him to remain in treatment, but only rarely could he offer him evening hours. This bind, which was constructed by two important survival figures, was experienced by him as one which he could neither attack, avoid, nor comment upon. It is interesting that this "independent-dependent" bind was similar to the previous one mentioned in relation to his mother. Dave's repertoire of responses to this type of life situation was limited -- almost stereotyped -- and he resorted to periods of confused, bizarre behavior or inappropriate laughter. In therapy Dave was helped to understand the nature of the bind and that more adaptive responses were possible. A discussion of this incident led to the development of tactics to handle Mother (especially humorous overstatement), and the patient seemed to benefit from these discussions, although he is still far from adroit in handling his parents.

The paramount significance of all these incidents, however, is that the patient repeatedly gets into difficulty because of his inability to label situations and to comment directly on his affective responses -- especially when his feelings involve anger or love. This defect is, of course, glaringly present in his family, and comparisons were frequently made between Dave's communication problems and the pathological communication in the entire family. It was at this point that Dave stated he finally clearly understood the role of his family in his illness and the rationale behind the family sessions.

Another important double bind that Dave's mother, like so many mothers of schizophrenics, created was in the area of achievement. Fundamentally, the contradictory messages that Dave received were: "You shall be a very great man -- the man among men" and "You cannot attend to even the basic necessities in life and without me would not survive." Dave's mother, who was somewhat of a mystic and belonged to a group of glossolaliacs, cherished a prophecy made by her sect when Dave was an infant that he "would one day be in India with an eagle on his shoulder." This prophecy was known by all and formed part of the family folklore. While Dave was in the hospital he ruminated endlessly about what he should be in life and subscribed to many correspondence courses. This rumination disconcerted the family who beseeched him to stop. Mother reinforced the double bind by frequently telling Dave, "Stop worrying about jobs because when you get well you can be anything you want to be." When Dave obtained his new job (which happened to necessitate a move to another apartment), he called home to give his parents the good news. Mother's response, however, was "What did you do with the clothes you had in storage at the old place?" Dave's response to this was predictable -- a feeling of confusion and a diffuse anger, culminating in his shrieking, "That's personal."

DISCUSSION

The utilization of conjoint family therapy as part of intensive individual psychotherapy is in need of further exploration. We have used conjoint family visits in connection with the psychotherapy of college students living away from home where the therapist would ordinarily not have the opportunity to meet the patient's parents. Many other situations arise that seem tailor-made for family sessions as a part of ongoing psychotherapy. Occasions such as contemplated matrimony, discharge from a hospital, moving of a relative into the home, divorced parents who share child visitation, and many others need study and documentation. If the psychotherapist is flexible in his approach, we feel that he will discover many indications for implementing psychotherapy with family sessions.

An increased flexibility of therapeutic approaches has been one of the concomitants of the developing maturity of the psychotherapeutic fields. Not only may different techniques be applied to different individuals, but different techniques may be employed concurrently or sequentially with the same individual as he passes through various stages of therapy. A course of therapy is described in which family therapy was used to liberate a chronic schizophrenic patient from a restraining family system which operated to impede his efforts at individualization. A therapeutic tactic, designed to rupture the premise system of the family, was employed. Some family disorganization ensued at first, but eventually the patient was able (at least temporarily) to relinquish his obligatory role as the problem in the family. The patient subsequently engaged himself gainfully in individual therapy which explored in depth many issues which had been raised in the conjoint family therapy sessions.

FAMILY INTERACTION, FAMILY HOMEOSTASIS
AND SOME IMPLICATIONS FOR CONJOINT
FAMILY PSYCHOTHERAPY

Don D. Jackson

In a paper entitled The Question of Family Homeostasis presented at the 1954 annual meeting of the American Psychiatric
Association, I focused on the upset that can occur within a family when one of its members undergoes intensive psychotherapy.
Since then, I have continued to be interested in family interaction
and family psychotherapy and would like to describe a way of
viewing the family and some of the implications this system has
for psychotherapy. These ideas stem mainly from two years'
experience in seeing families in conjoint psychotherapy, listening
to tapes of family interviews conducted by others, and occasionally studying sound movies of familial interactions. Recently our
group has had the opportunity of serving as observers during the
conjoint therapy of families of delinquents.[1] This experience has
provided some valuable contrast data to our own studies which
have been mainly concerned with the families of schizophrenics.

Our approach to understanding family interaction stems from
certain biases. We favor communication theory because it lends
itself to the descriptive study of tape recordings and sound movies.
It avoids the necessity of imputing effects to the subjects and allows outside observers more opportunity to see if the data war-
rant the conclusions.[2]   A second bias is our assumption that

---

[1]Courtesy of Dr. Charles Fulweiler.

[2]It is of interest that Dysinger, studying family interaction at
the National Institute of Mental Health, came to a similar conclusion. (Dysinger, Robert H. The action dialogue in an intense relationship. Presented at the American Psychiatric Association
Annual Meeting, Chicago, Illinois, May 1957.)

Reprinted from INDIVIDUAL AND FAMILIAL DYNAMICS (Jules
H. Masserman, M. D. , ed.) pages 122-141, 1959. Copyright, Grune
& Stratton, Inc. , New York; reproduced by permission.

there is no "not caring"; that is, the family member is only relatively independent, and whether he admits it or not, is continually responding to reflected appraisals from others in his family. Third, along with Maier, Halstead, the Russells and others we feel that the characteristic of frustrated behavior is its stereotypy or compulsivity, whereas motivated behavior is characterized by flexibility. In the study of family interaction, stereotypy may be indicated by the absence of behavior in certain areas as well as by inexorable, inflexible and characteristic transactions. Thus the absence of family arguments can be a pathologic sign, but to the superficial observer might be considered evidence of good adjustment.

METHODOLOGY

Given these biases there still remains the problem of how to collect data, what data to collect and how to process the data collected. Our approach has favored the group situation over collaborative data because although collaborative psychotherapy has established its worth, as a methodology for research it has certain serious drawbacks:

1. The most obvious is simply the flow of information. It is dependent upon the therapists' relaying data, and therapists tend to react to each other as well as to form coalitions with their particular patient.

2. In collaborative therapy, time sequences may be puzzling. Reactions in therapy may be of a linear nature; that is, from A to his therapist to B's therapist, to B. But these may also be out of phase reactions like the song that says: "I Can't Get Used To The You That Got Accustomed To Me." In short, it is difficult for the therapists to know if A is reacting because B was hostile, or because B was so nice A couldn't stand it!

3. It is nearly impossible to introduce planned interventions for experimental reasons in collaborative therapy. If you wish to see what parameter A does to the family interaction you cannot drop it into the family pool and study the ripples. There is the time problem already mentioned, and the fact that each therapist will drop a slightly different pebble in a slightly different manner.

4. There is an economic aspect to collaborative therapy which is not relevant here except as it pertains to the enormous difficulty in getting the therapists together to spend a significant amount of time going over their material.

Seeing a married couple together, the patient and his parents, or the whole family as a group does not completely overcome the above objections to collaborative therapy, but does offer some advantages as a scientific tool. Suppose, for example, one wished to study the kind of transactions that result in a homeostatic shift in the family. It is possible to get the family to play a game while being filmed. The game might consist of each member, in turn, introducing an idea much as he would play a card. The next member can add to the idea, trump it, or play a different suit, as it were. The therapist for his turn introduces the idea: "who is the boss in this family?" The response to this innocent question can be startling. One family appeared stunned, gazed uneasily at each other, and then the mother came through brilliantly with, "the cook!"

Although the therapist in conjoint therapy is on the scene and thus tends to correct the "time problem" of collaborative therapy, he has a huge problem in handling the manifold transferences and counter reactions. Recording or filming the sessions and supervision are important checks. Another possibility has been introduced by Fulweiler. [3] He views the family interaction from behind a one-way mirror and steps into the room only to make an intervention or interpretation. Unless you have observed this technique, it is difficult to picture how the therapist's resolute detachment forces the family members to turn to each other. Our group plans to employ this technique, as well as having the therapist speak to the group only via an intercom, and compare the experience with our present method of having the therapist present during the sessions.

PROCESSING THE DATA

Once one has collected tapes or films or simply impressions, the problem of what to do with the data arises. As a background for that I would like to emphasize that in studying the homeostatic mechanisms of the family it is useful to make a distinction between variables and parameters. If a thermostat is set at 68 degrees there are constant oscillations which turn the furnace on and off in order to maintain a relatively steady state. The better the thermostat, the wider the range of variables that can be handled without a new set being necessary. When the thermostat is moved to 70 degrees we have a new parameter and a new level of homeostasis. If the neighbors buy a new car there are apt to be

_____

[3] Personal communication.

oscillations in the family around the point of what it takes to make them happy. However, in some families such a variable may require a new parameter being introduced; for example, the concept of how lovely it is not to be mercenary. It might seem that the introduction of a new parameter could be treated like a simple learning experience, that is, if we are frustrated by our own not having a new car we make up a rule that says we wouldn't want one anyway. Actually new parameters are apt to be of the order of learning to learn. This is because in a family we do not have just a linear system where A affects B who affects C and so on; nor do we have merely circuits in which A affects B who is affected by C which alignment augments or diminishes A's effects. Family interaction is a system in which A can also anticipate an effect on B, and this modifies his subsequent behavior; and B in turn modifies his response in anticipation of what he thinks A anticipates. When C and perhaps some little Ds and Es are thrown into the picture one is faced with a problem that Univac is unprepared to handle.

Many of you perhaps remember the game, "paper, scissors and rock," or one of its many modifications. Paper covers rock, rock breaks scissors and scissors cut paper. You are playing the game and about to make the sign for paper when you think, "My opponent thinks I'm going to make paper so he'll make a scissors. I'll fool him and make a rock." Meanwhile your opponent is thinking, "He thinks that I think he's going to make paper so that he'll make a rock and break my scissors so therefore I'll make paper." In such games of two, with dedicated players, there are no random moves. The dedicated player discerns what system his opponent will use in anticipation of such and such a move on his own part and, in addition, at a higher level he anticipates what changes his opponent will make in response to having his system unveiled. In such a game of two, one possibility for successful gamesmanship occurs when a player randomly varies his play; that is, ignores that the other is an opponent who changes his system of systems. This does not seem a possible gambit in the family unless one of the members has outside experiences which increase his independence to the point that he ignores the moves of the other members. As I will mention later, this is one possible explanation of why psychotherapy for one member can upset the whole family. Or conversely, why progress in psychotherapy may be impossible for one member if the rest of the family is left out.

To return to the thermostat analogy, it is obvious that oscillations can be measured in some kind of heat units, and that a new parameter can be detected by the clustering of oscillations around a new point. In the family, because of the inexact state of behavioral science currently, we are faced with a variety of measures or units. Such units as anxiety, dependency processes, and role-playing have been utilized but it has seemed to us that they have disadvantages some of which our own system avoids. The system we use might be labelled "control theory." In essence, it is the belief that all persons implicitly or explicitly are constantly attempting to define the nature of their relationships. "Control" in this sense does not mean anything as simple as one individual explicitly telling another what to do. Rather, it refers to the fact that every communication can be seen as a report and a command, and the command may be of a higher order of messages than the explicit message. Thus A may use a "one down" ploy to influence B to take care of him. B would thus appear to be in control, but as far as A is concerned, he is determining the nature of the situation.

Evidence for the attempt to define the nature of the situation can be inferred from the individual's communication when context, verbal and nonverbal communications are all regarded as capable of modifying each other. Rather complex possibilities occur when as in a recent New Yorker cartoon, the boss says with a smile, "But, Jones, I don't want you to agree with me because I say so, but because you see it my way." This is as confusing a ploy as the mother who orders the child not to be so obedient. The communicative behavior that we view as an attempt to define the nature of the relationship consists of labelling a relationship or aspects of a relationship in one of two ways: complementary or symmetric. A complementary relationship consists of one individual giving and the other receiving. In a complementary relationship the two people are of unequal status in the sense that one appears to be in the superior position, meaning that he initiates action and the other appears to follow that action. Thus the two individuals fit together or complement each other. The most obvious and basic complementary relationship would be the mother and infant.

A symmetric relationship is one between two people who behave as if they have equal status. Each person exhibits the right to initiate action, criticize the other, offer advice and so on. This type of relationship tends to become competitive; if one person mentions that he has succeeded in some endeavor the other person mentions that he has succeeded in an equally important endeavor. The individuals in such a relationship emphasize their equality or their symmetry with each other. The most obvious symmetric relationship is a pre-adolescent peer relationship.

This simple division of relationship into two types applies to all two person systems. No relationship between two people will consistently be of one type in all circumstances. Mature relationships, we label "parallel" since there are frequent complementary and symmetric crossovers. In the ideal husband and wife relationship each defines areas in which he determines the nature of the relationship, in which he typically behaves in a symmetric or complementary manner. The determination of areas of control obviously are determined by cultural factors as well as by special skills such as the fact that the woman is the only one who can have a baby.

In a pathologic relationship, we see rather than areas of control a constant sabotaging or refusing of the other's attempts to define the relationship. The communication methods used to refuse, negate or sabotage the other's attempt to define the nature of the relationship may range from a simple, direct "no" to complex multi-level messages in which a covert denial is further obscured by itself being denied. This is the essence of the "double bind" situation which our group has described. (1)

A pathologic situation may also be evident because there is a direction in the two person system. Consider the following examples. The husband, in a culturally acceptable complementary maneuver says to his wife, "I'll take you to a movie." The wife (not accepting his benevolence) states, "There's nothing good playing." The husband replies (not accepting her denial of his benevolence), "Are you sure? Where's the newspaper?" Whereupon the wife responds: "Besides I have a headache." The husband running into a rather impervious ploy states, "Okay, I guess I'll watch some TV." The wife responds: "Fine. There is a program I wanted to see."

We would expect in this situation where the wife increasingly appears to define the nature of the relationship, that the husband will resort increasingly to withdrawal techniques thus increasing the wife's apparent control of the relationship. The relationship will thus exhibit a tendency, a direction rather than a healthy oscillation.

Every child begins life in the secondary position of a complementary relationship since someone must take care of him. However, as the child grows older, in the normal family situation he is encouraged more and more to determine the nature of his own activity, and ultimately he is able to behave with his parents as one equal to another. From the moment the child is old enough to

"assert himself" he begins to learn to make symmetric maneuvers.
When he insists on walking by himself or tying his own shoes he is
learning to act with others in a symmetric way. In the normal situation his parents let him behave in this way. They are willing to
encourage him to tie his own shoes, and they are willing to tie his
shoes for him if he requests a complementary maneuver on their
part. Within a general framework of taking care of their child,
the parents encourage him to experiment and to learn to behave as
an equal in preparation for that time when he leaves his complementary context and achieves symmetric relations with other people. The child also learns to make these maneuvers in fantasy
prior to the time he is capable of making them in reality. Such
practice often takes place during play. For example, the child
may ride on his father's back and treat the father like a beast of
burden who must be directed in his activities. Thus the child
assumes in play the superior end of a complementary relationship. Of course, daddy knows that he really isn't a horse and he
can show this at any point by bucking the child off, which he may
do to end the game.

Obviously, the adult's ability to interact in different types of
relationships can be inhibited by the ways his family encourages
or discourages his maneuvers during childhood. For example, a
mother who resents taking care of her child may make it unpleasant for him to accept the secondary position in a complementary relationship. The child will learn that he should not maneuver
her to take care of him because this provokes punishment. As an
adult he could not accept the secondary position in a complementary
relationship. When ill he might insist on continuing his own activities and refuse to let anyone take care of him. Although he
might be capable of competing with others, he would be unwilling
to be dependent on others. Similarly, a child might be discouraged
from learning to behave in a symmetric way. If he behaved as an
equal, for example, by trying to tie his own shoes, his mother
might punish him by withdrawal, and the child learns that he must
let her tie them for him. These problems are complicated by the
fact that a child not only learns to respond to his parents, but
learns to use them as a model for how to respond. If a mother resents taking care of her child, the child will not only avoid requests
that she take care of him, but he has before him a model of how he
should take care of others. Because of that model, he might only
be capable of resentfully taking care of others, as well as being inhibited in letting others take care of him.

Each individual in a relationship is constantly commenting on
his definition of the relationship implicitly or explicitly. Every

message exchanged (including silence) defines the relationship implicitly since it expresses the idea, "This is the sort of relationship where this sort of message may be given." There are also relationship messages (or maneuvers, or ploys) in which the purpose of the message is to test the other's acceptance of one's definition of the relationship. The obvious relationship messages are requests, commands or suggestions but in a more important way relationship messages can also consist of letting the other individual define the relationship. For example, one individual might act passively in order to force the other to take over. Such a ploy may not appear to be defining the relationship and thus may be acceptable to the other person, but the introduction of a new parameter may reveal the ploy and cause an upheaval. Thus a wife might behave in a helpless fashion and her husband accept the role of the strong one. However, if he takes to bed with a cold and she says, "I'd love to take care of you, dear, but I feel so terrible myself," the horrible thought may intrude on the husband's consciousness that "she's been doing this to me right along."

CATEGORIES OF FAMILIES

Since relationship messages are constantly being exchanged, it is likely (within certain limits) that a family can be characterized by the maneuvers used. The extent to which relationship messages are implicit (e. g. , symptoms of various kinds), explicit, commands, helpless or "one-down" ploys, will vary from family to family. It is possible to classify families or relationships into four types on the basis of the transactions used to define the nature of the relationship. [4] These four categories are: stable satisfactory, unstable satisfactory, stable unsatisfactory and unstable unsatisfactory.

These categories may be used to describe a phase of a relationship, a relationship that has perduring features or a family that shows a predominant trend. A couple may have an unstable satisfactory relationship until their first child, and by their third, have settled down to a stable unsatisfactory existence. The range, or richness of maneuvers, makes a certain amount of prediction

---

[4] Apology is made here for the fact that "complementary" and "symmetric" are mainly useful in describing two person systems. In describing a family, we can use two person terms since it is possible to talk about alliances, coalitions, disalliances, etc. ; however, a three or four person terminology would be far more appropriate. Unfortunately, we have not yet developed it.

possible as to the relationship tendencies; however, fate, acts of God and one thing and another make accurate prediction unlikely. One of our families went through an unstable period with much overt battling between father and mother until the father developed tuberculosis and was more or less out of the home for four years. After he returned the family situation jelled into a stable unsatisfactory state.

I would like briefly to describe each type of family and to emphasize that this description is temporal, and no attempt has been made to relate these types to socio-economic classes.

A stable satisfactory relationship can be defined as one where both parties can explicitly reach agreement that one or the other is in control of the relationship or in control of areas within the relationship. A person defined as being in control of the relationship is the one who initiates action, decides what action will be initiated or establishes what areas within the relationship shall be controlled by the other person. Note the emphasis on "explicitly." In this type of relationship, it is possible for each person to discuss the relationship and comment on the effect of the other person's behavior on him. Thus the stability is maintained by the possibility of reinstituting a stable state when the relationship becomes unstable through a disagreement. "Stable" does not mean an entirely smooth functioning of the relationship and implies brief periods of instability. Further, it is not implied that discussing the relationship means psychiatrizing. The fact that one may comment on the relationship may mean that no comment is necessary.

An unstable satisfactory relationship differs from the stable satisfactory relationship only in the length of the periods of instability. It occurs when two people are working out their definition of the relationship during a time when internal or external forces are creating frequent unstable periods which are stabilized with difficulty. These periods occur frequently enough to make the relationship unstable, yet the stable periods are satisfactory to both parties.

For example, mother and daughter may begin to reach an unstable but satisfactory relationship when pubertal forces plus the behavior of her friends encourage the girl to seek more independence and more adventures as a female rather than a child. The mother may at the same time feel reluctant to see her daughter growing up, feel competitive as the daughter becomes a woman, or fear the criticism of her friends if her daughter doesn't behave. The issue immediately becomes one of who is in control of the relationship as the daughter seeks to define it along the line of a relationship between two equal women and the mother tries to define it as a mother and child relationship. The girl may stay out too late on a date as a maneuver to show that she is defining the relationship in her way, and the mother may restrict the girl to the house for a week to prove that she is defining it in her way. The relationship can continue to be satisfactory only if mother and daughter explicitly deal with the relationship and eventually reach compromises. Explicit, I must point out again, does not necessarily refer to verbal processes. In the example above, neither the mother nor the daughter need speak to each other about their definitions. They might interact with the father in such a way that he eventuates a set of apparently new rules that result in a compromise.

The unstable satisfactory type of relationship is characteristic of any new or changed relationship since it must be progressively defined by the parties until a shared definition of the relationship is worked out. For example, a newly married couple must go through unstable but satisfactory periods in their relationship until the question of who is in charge of particular areas of the relationship is agreed upon. The introduction of parameters like toilet training and sexual intercourse into a relationship are bound to produce at least temporary instability. If the mother feels the child does it on the potty because she said to, and the child feels, "it's my feces so I don't mind doing what she says," then stability can return because areas have been agreed upon. It is quite another matter if the child feels vaguely that mother makes his bowels move.

An unstable unsatisfactory relationship is one where no explicit or implicit agreement is reached upon the question of who is in control of the relationship or areas within it. It is characterized by the need to redefine the relationship the moment it becomes defined so that stable periods are brief, and unstable periods are long. The discussion that takes place between the parties is apt to be not at a relationship level, but at a level of details. Each party tends to take the behavior of the other party as a challenge at a relationship level without this ever being discussed. Maneuvers to control the relationship are made with simultaneous denials that these are maneuvers. Often psychosomatic or hysterical symptoms are used as ways of defining the relationship since they are messages which can be denied as messages. A wife may get a headache whenever she is with her husband, yet both can discuss how unfortunate it is that she has headaches. Having the headache may permit her to control an area of the husband's behavior without any need to take explicit responsibility for defining the relationship. Thus, she can ask that he leave her alone because she has a headache rather than defining the relationship explicitly as one where she has the right to be alone if she wishes to be.

The unstable unsatisfactory relationship is often characterized by "helpless" maneuvers to control the relationship. Neither party can say "I'm the boss," nor can they say "You're the boss." Thus transactions are apt to consist of complementary maneuvers which are redefined as soon as they are accepted by the other individual. Or to put it another way, there is competition over dependency as well as alleged independency.

The mother and daughter in this type of relationship might quarrel about whether a blue dress is prettier than a pink one or whether someone else is allowed to stay out until one o'clock instead of twelve. The quarrels would not explicitly deal with whether the mother has a right to define the limits of the daughter's behavior or whether the daughter has the right to define her own limits. The mother cannot let the daughter choose her time to come home because this would mean the daughter was boss in the relationship. Similarly, she cannot set a time for the daughter to come home and insist that her instructions be followed because this would mean that she was defining their relationship. The result is the setting of a time by the mother which the daughter either ignores, or complies with by indicating she was tired and wanted to come home anyway. Should the daughter truly comply, the mother would indicate concern over her submissiveness. In this type of relationship rebellion by the daughter might be handled by hurt and helpless maneuvers on the mother's part so that the daughter constantly feels she must volunteer to do things which would please her mother. That is, she must initiate action in response to indirect commands by her mother, but since such actions appear to put her in charge of the relationship they must be sabotaged by the mother. Neither mother nor daughter can overtly and explicitly take responsibility for the action nor assume the initiative in setting the limits of the relationship. The relationship thus never becomes stabilized because mother or daughter become panicked or hurt if discussion is threatened at the relationship level.

We have been impressed by the virtual absence of completed transactions in the unstable unsatisfactory family. As soon as

agreement is apparently reached by two members the issue is
reopened either by the participants or a third party:

In an interview with such a family, the mother arrived drunk
in order to be able to tell the therapist that her daughter had to
change her ways or leave home. The daughter, who had begun
to define her relationship to her mother as symmetric, stated she
would be glad to leave home. The therapist tried to force father
to state his opinion but he allowed mother to speak for him. The
therapist then stated he had found a rather ideal place for the
daughter to stay and perhaps she should move out of the house for
awhile. The mother ended the session stating the therapist should
find a place for her also because she was leaving her husband!

A stable unsatisfactory relationship is one where the parties
have agreed never to make an issue of who is in charge of the relationship nor of areas within it. Neither party dares signal dissatisfaction with the relationship nor dares recognize such signals from the other party. The relationship is stable in the sense
that those problems which might make it unstable are avoided,
yet it is unsatisfactory since there is so little giving or receiving.
Typically, this is a withdrawn, distant kind of relationship although the "stability" may make it appear to the outsider as more
satisfactory than it is. Both Lidz (5) and ourselves (3) have mentioned it may be several months before the therapist sees the
underlying pathology. This is particularly true because of the
initial "united front" of the parents, or their "pseudo-mutuality"
as Lyman Wynne and his co-workers have called it. (7)

The stable unsatisfactory relationship is characterized by tremendous inflexibility and compulsivity. Cultural and social rules
such as religious principles are important because they involve
outside authority and thus apparently free the family from conflict
over who is determining the nature of the relationship. Role playing may be stressed for much the same reason; thus "mother" has
certain agreed upon rights and privileges that go with the title.
There may be gigantic distortions of ordinary social definitions
in order to impersonalize the actions of the individual. The lack
of contact with people outside the family aids this process.

A problem arises for these families on the rare occasions when
they encounter a psychotherapist. In order to show agreement and
cohesion, the parents especially may apologize for, or explain,
each other. In doing so they are making a symmetric maneuver
and it may be rebuffed by the spouse. A mother, wanting to ac-

count for the father's being away from home a great deal, but not wanting to imply that it related to his feeling toward her, stated that he was a very hard worker. The father retorted that he didn't work "that hard"; thus giving the therapist an opening to inquire about what he did do with his time.

John Weakland and I recently reported on a patient from a stable unsatisfactory family. (6) His psychotic break occurred at the point when he had to separate long letters from short letters on his post office job. The "in-betweens" proved too much; he was unable to define explicitly which should go in which pile. When a co-worker told him he looked ill, he realized he felt sick and went home.

In our experience, the stable unsatisfactory family is difficult to get into therapy and nearly impossible to keep in therapy. If they produce a schizophrenic, current hospital practices in the handling of relatives protect them from coming under scrutiny, and the patient remains the patient.

THE PSYCHOTHERAPEUTIC APPROACH

The three categories of families from which patients come — namely, unstable satisfactory, unstable unsatisfactory, and stable unsatisfactory— present different problems in terms of optimum psychotherapeutic intervention. While no hard and fast rules obtain, since the dividing lines between these categories are arbitrary, it does seem that an appraisal of the kind of family interaction aids the therapist in planning his treatment. Thus a young schizophrenic from a stable unsatisfactory family probably could not recover while living at home if he were seen only in individual therapy, or if the family were seen only once a week. I would like to give an example or two of psychotherapeutic experiences with each category of families, while emphasizing that our knowledge of tailored techniques is very limited.

The unstable satisfactory family. Obviously the most joyful results come from this group. If the spouses are seen together there is usually enough mutual regard between them to withstand some fairly straightforward intervention on the therapist's part. The presenting complaint can usually be traced to an event or happening--a new parameter. Occasionally, it is as obvious as the couple who felt they were in love until they made it legal. Sometimes it is a concatenation of events that crystallizes into a gestalt that the psychiatrist can help clarify.

A young man was sent to the psychiatrist by his wife because of three recent episodes of infidelity. It became apparent during the interview that 1) he had become successful recently after some years of working toward it in dubious battle; 2) his wife had recently had their third child, a boy, and the patient was the third child in his family. The wife had a younger brother who was the favorite in her family and who was referred to as "a juvenile delinquent"; 3) the wife was unbelievably naive or else she was pushing the patient toward his extracurricular activity; 4) the patient did all that one can do and still manage to remain unaware of it in order to signal to his wife that he was being unfaithful.

The patient was told to bring his wife to the next visit since his cure lay largely in her hands. This was done since it was obvious that she felt unimportant and also felt uninvolved in his sins in the typical manner of the injured party. Although she came initially with the attitude of "anything to help George get over this nasty business," by the end of the second session she was able to accept the comment that her finger was also in this particular pie. They were seen altogether for only nine sessions with two follow-up visits and made remarkable progress. The brevity of the therapy was partly financial, and partly because of the amount of work they did together between sessions.

I would say that the danger in the unstable satisfactory category lies in overestimating the extent of family fracture and not utilizing positive forces present. If one member is focused upon as the sick individual, and if he is closeted away from the others with his private therapist and instructed not to blab about his therapy, the richness of the situation is largely ignored. A case in point was the subject of a recent paper. (4) It concerned a little girl with Pavor nocturnus who did not respond to therapy until the psychiatrist got the whole family together and discovered that the real patient was an older sister who was calculatingly mean enough to be whispering horror stories into the little girl's ears after the lights went out.

The unstable unsatisfactory family probably comprises the large bulk of what the psychiatrist or social worker would immediately spot as a sick family. We feel that many of the serious psychosomatic disorders and possibly psychoses of rather acute onset come from this group. How terribly unsatisfactory things are for the family members need not be immediately apparent.

This is because medical practice usually dictates that the sick one be removed from the household and the label helps keep other members from speaking their piece. Then when the sick member returns home and falls ill again it is all the more apparent that he is the rotten apple in this particular barrel. After several bounces back into the hospital, he adds a layer of institutionalization to his difficulties, and that is usually that.

What I am trying to say is that current mores regarding mental illness may seriously complicate locating and diagnosing both the unstable and the stable unsatisfactory families even though the former's difficulties are much easier to ferret out than is the case with the stable unsatisfactory group.

We have found in our limited experience with the unstable unsatisfactory families in conjoint therapy that the patient's recovery poses a serious threat to the parents and occasionally to a sibling. We have seen, without any doubt, many patients who have sacrificed themselves and returned to the hospital rather than upset the family.

Such an incident occurred in the therapy of a young woman who had improved during the family sessions and was to be released from the hospital. She came home for a trial visit prior to her release and the mother and father had a serious fight. The patient and the mother left and went to a nearby town. The patient called the father to let him know where they were, and he joined them and made up with the mother whereupon the patient "misbehaved" and both parents joined in chastising her. At the next session the mother announced that the patient could not live at home and that she was becoming upset by having her around. It was interesting that during her description of the way the patient bothered her she used almost the exact words of the patient's delusions in her initial breakdown. That is, she spoke of the patient sitting in her room alone thinking evil thoughts about the mother, spying on her, being full of hate, and so on. The patient's initial delusions contained exactly similar references about the neighbors. The patient returned to the hospital, promptly threw a tray of food on the floor and was put in a locked ward and was given electro-shock therapy. The patient knew the hospital and her particular physician well enough to know that acting up was regarded as worthy of punishment.

The unstable unsatisfactory family is a classic example of not being able to live with someone and not being able to live without them. Considering the terrible struggles that go on within the walls, it is surprising that so many of these families stick together. Some investigators had hoped to demonstrate that schizophrenia comes from fractured families without taking sufficiently into account that clinging together can be a particularly vicious malady. As Clausen and others have shown, the socio-economic group also plays a part in whether an unstable family continued to stick together or falls apart. (2)

We feel we have been having some success in the treatment of these families. Our main focus has been on aiding the parents to realize how self-depriving they are and thus to avoid the guilt and blame that are strewn about. It follows from our theory that we hope to enable them to make symmetric maneuvers and this in turn will allow the patient to do the same.

A husband was hinting that his wife relaxed in the afternoon by taking a few drinks and was also covertly complaining that by the time he got home she was no company at all. The therapist asked her if she was not offended by the husband's delicacy in handling the topic whereupon the whole issue came out into the open. His light touch on a touchy topic was a maneuver defining the nature of their relationship and she would not accept it.

Although in the few families we have treated, the mother had been the more dominent figure, it appears to be something of a relief for her if the therapist can help her husband to be more assertive. At some level, the mother recognizes her intense self-depriving ways and longs to be taken care of. This fact becomes the therapeutic toe hold.

Our dealings with the stable unsatisfactory family have to date not been encouraging. There are several such families at whom we are currently chipping away but movement is very slow. The family is so aligned toward keeping the patient sick, and the patient himself so willing to accept the role that therapists can easily despair. On the other hand, if some movement is made, it can be quite upsetting to the group since the cardinal rule of such families is that no one must comment on the nature of the other's behavior. There is no tolerating of symmetrical behavior. The following incident illustrates rather tragically this fact:

During a family interview the patient's brother encouraged by his relationship to the therapist tentatively ventured that his mother might be a little hypocritical in her dealings with the patient. The father, with a liberal sprinkling of alibis for her, agreed with the son and his wife quietly accepted the verdict but with an air of "that's what I get for trying my best." Unfortunately, the therapist had the impression that the mother was accepting the comment and since it was near the end of the session nothing further was done with it.

Early the following morning the mother was taken to the hospital for an emergency cholecystectomy although she had had no previous history of gall bladder distress nor stones. Upon her return home the father was hospitalized for a coronary attack and in the midst of this psychosomatic melee the brother, who had initially introduced the damaging remark, had three automobile accidents all of a similar nature. He simply crashed into the rear end of the car ahead. At this point the family decided that they could no longer afford our expert help and placed the patient in a state hospital.

THE RELEVANCE OF COMMUNICATION THEORY AND FAMILY HOMEOSTASIS FOR CONJOINT FAMILY THERAPY

It is one of my private notions that the method of description presented above has practical uses for the psychotherapist interested in the family. His appraisal of interfamily communication will help him establish how the patient got to be the patient, and how serious the consequences might be for other family members if the patient alone is treated.

As the therapist notes the families' communication behavior he should pay special attention to how messages are qualified or labelled. Are messages labelled congruently; that is, the context, nonverbal communication etc. is appropriate to the message and does not deny, conceal or alter it but affirms the message. The most serious form of incongruent message has been described by our group as the double bind. [5] In this situation, two incongruent messages are accompanied by a prohibition against noting their incongruence. If no one in the family can deal with double bind statements, we would suspect serious pathology and would suspect that one member's receiving psychotherapy might seriously upset the family since incongruences will become more apparent to him with the therapist's help.

---

[5] Clausen, J., & Kohn, M. Parental authority behavior and schizophrenia. Orthopsychiatry, 26:300, 1956.

A rather typical situation occurred in the family of a hospital-ized schizophrenic the session following one in which his mother urged him to participate in hospital activities. The patient an-nounced he was on the baseball team and that they were going to an air field some miles away to play a game. His mother beam-ingly replied, "Oh good, they'll have doctors there too!"

If one considers the context, which includes the mother's in-structions the previous week, this is a deadly statement. Were the patient able, as he was not, to say, "Mother dear, how come you refer to doctors and my being sick just at the point I'm doing what you asked me to?" the mother would reaffirm her interest and love and the patient would realize he was a cur for doubting. However, the therapist can ask the mother (if he's not too angry) if she notices anything at all peculiar about her remark and can judge the depth of her unawareness.

In families who tend toward incongruent statements, the thera-pist can judge the effect of a symmetric maneuver; that is, a de-fining of the relationship statement that is not handled incongru-ently. The patient mentioned above once, appropriately enough, sent his mother a beautiful card on Mother's Day. However, the card stated majestically across its colorful surface, "For Someone Who Has Been Just Like a Mother to Me." When he was confront-ed by her at the next therapy session, he was able to make a sim-ple, quiet, symmetric statement, "Look Ma, maybe I meant to sting you a little bit"; and, under the increasing pressure of his parents' attack, stated the maneuver was linked to feeling she hadn't been as good a mother as she might have been. The cat being out of the bag called for heroic measures on mother's part and she was up to them. By threatening abandonment, and with an assist from father, she soon had the patient declaring he didn't know what was on the card, he didn't remember sending it, he could obtain no other card, and there was a Communist in-spired plot to plant such cards to get boys like himself into trou-ble.

The forty-five minutes of the interview were a tribute to the effect of a symmetric statement in such a family. Not only did the parents' defensive techniques cause the patient to back down, but at each step of the way his psychotic processes were reinforced. For example, crying he stated, "I don't even remember what the thing was," and his mother replied triumphantly, "Well, that's all I wanted to know!"

At the patient improved, he began to label the incongruencies
in his parents' messages. Conforming to our experience with
other schizophrenic families, he began with the father.[6] The difference in his responses not only upset the parents, but produced
strife between them. It is not entirely safe to notice that the Em-
peror is not wearing a fine new suit of clothes.

CONCLUSION
I have tried to demonstrate a method of thinking about family interaction and family therapy. The emphasis has been on theory
rather than on technique because we have had so little experience
that comments on therapy are rather premature. In spite of this,
our group has a definite feeling that conjoint family therapy has
some advantages over collaborative therapy. It may be that the
peculiar pathologic sticking together that these families demonstrate can be used to keep them in therapy. Perhaps our therapy
should be called homeopathic family therapy since we proceed on
the notion that the particular communication devices the family
uses can be in turn used against them for therapeutic purposes as
in the homeopathic idea that "like cures like."

REFERENCES

1. Bateson, G., Jackson, D. D., Haley, J., and Weakland, J. Toward a communication theory of schizophrenia. Behav. Sci.,
1:1, 1956. Reprinted in Don D. Jackson (Ed.), Communication,
Family, and Marriage (Vol. 1, Human Communication Series),
Science and Behavior Books, Palo Alto, California, 1968.
2. Clausen, J., and Kohn, M. Parental authority behavior and
schizophrenia. Orthopsychiatry, 26:300, 1956.
3. Jackson, D. D. A note on the importance of trauma in the genesis
of schizophrenia. Psychiatry, 20:181-184, 1957. Reprinted in Don
D. Jackson (Ed.), Communication, Family, and Marriage (Vol. 1,
Human Communication Series), Science and Behavior Books,
Palo Alto, California, 1968.
4. Liebermann, L. P. Joint interview technique: an experiment in group
psychotherapy. Brit. J. Med. Psychol., 30 (Part 3): 202, 1957.
5. Lidz, T. Schizophrenia and the family. Psychiatry, 21:21-27, 1958.
6. Weakland, J., & Jackson, D. D. Therapist's and patient's report
of circumstances surrounding a psychotic break. Arch. Neurol.
Psychiat., 79:554-574, 1958.
7. Wynne, L., et al. Pseudo mutuality in the family of the schizophrenic. Psychiatry, 21:205-220, 1958.

[6]Dr. Murray Bowen confirms this observation (personal communication).

FAMILY THERAPY IN THE FAMILY
OF THE SCHIZOPHRENIC

Don D. Jackson

I became interested in family therapy about seven and a half
years ago, when I went from Chestnut Lodge to Palo Alto. At
Chestnut Lodge, we had treated schizophrenics with psychotherapy, so I of course did so in Palo Alto. But, at the Lodge, we had
never had anything to do with their families. This, I understand,
has changed somewhat now. But in my day, it was really a dis-
grace for the therapist to encounter the parents. This was something he avoided and always left to the administrator. In Palo Alto,
which is a small university town, I couldn't avoid the relatives;
and this led to a lot of surprising and sometimes not very pleasant
results. I became interested in the question of family homeostasis,
which seemed most marked in the families where a schizophrenic
patient was able to live at home. If he then went through psychotherapy and benefited from it, any move on his part would usually
produce all sorts of disruptions at home. Surprisingly, there is
very little written on this topic. It is something that people who do
p sychotherapy can confirm, and to which they can add horror sto -
ries of their own of what occurred when they undertook psychotherapy with schizophrenics and ignored the patients' relatives.

Since schizophrenics have been treated largely in hospitals away
from relatives, the idea has only recently received sufficient attention that schizophrenia could be, in part, an adaptive disorder
which links itself to family pathology--a situation in which change
in the patient's symptoms produces feedback into the family situation.

At any rate, then, for practical reasons, I started seeing the
patients' parents, and then eventually, largely for research pur-

Reprinted from CONTEMPORARY PSYCHOTHERAPIES (Morris
I. Stein, ed.) pages 272-287, 1961. Copyright, The Free Press of
Glencoe, Inc. , New York; reproduced by permission.

poses, started seeing the parents and patient together. About this time, I joined forces with Gregory Bateson and his staff and we decided to work on data obtained from conjoint interviews with the family. These interviews usually take place for an hour or an hour and a half once a week; the longest follow-up we have had concerned a family which was in treatment for about two years. We have had perhaps fifteen families in therapy and have now been able to add several delinquent families for purposes of contrast, but we have almost no normative data. At least, if there is such a thing as a normal family, we haven't encountered it because we haven't focussed on that aspect, but we would like to enlarge our data and see how these families compare with families with other sorts of difficulties.

The lack of normogenic data limits our ability to generalize. However, comparisons between the families of so-called "process" schizophrenics with "reactive" schizophrenics reveal such marked differences, that we assume _mutatis mutandis_ there will be observable differences along the continuum to healthy families.

Initially, the patient was seen in individual psychotherapy as well as in sessions with the family, because traditionally the schizophrenic is the patient. We now tend to see the family together right from the beginning in order to avoid the bias of patient-oriented sessions. We may start with the patient in the hospital and have him brought to the session. But however it is done, we usually see the family right from the beginning as a group, and tell them that we will only meet when we can meet as a group. If the father is a travelling man or something of that kind, we will meet without him; but if we do, we cannot talk about him. In other words, a session is deliberately structured to make the focus a family one, and to avoid focussing solely on the schizophrenic patient. Despite the rules, the parents constantly try to break them because they are used to thinking in terms of having a sick member of the family, rather than of being a sick family. Thus, the first several sessions almost characteristically begin with statements to the effect that "We would be just fine if it wasn't for poor John being in such terrible shape." But this doesn't continue for long.

The other thing we do initially is to make a movie of the family and, again, it is in a structured situation. The game might consist of everyone offering a thought, much as you would play a card, and then the next person can trump that thought or can play another suit; that is, have a completely unrelated thought, and so on. We do this because it is easier for us to get non-sick families whose data are used for comparative purposes to come for a short movie-making period than it would be to ask them to come for a number of conjoint sessions. These movies are another source of data about how these families operate. Insofar as therapy itself goes, without any reference to its research aspects, at this juncture, after about three and a half years of experience, it looks promising. We have been surprised by the amount of change that has taken place in some patients. We have been surprised at how ill some patients can be and still remain out of the hospital, if the family and its own difficulties are being attended to in some fashion. But it is too early to say whether conjoint family sessions will ever be a contribution to psychotherapy.

Our goals at the moment are limited. Our main goal is to get the family to live apart. Now, this doesn't mean that we want to ship, say, one to Chicago and another to New York. We simply want them to be able to live in some sort of autonomy so that they then can live together. This is very difficult to achieve. We will listen for months to the story of how the patient is upsetting the whole family, but as soon as the patient improves and, let us say, wants to get a room by himself, it usually is another matter of months or longer before we can get the parents to permit that. This is one of the really striking things about these families. They just don't seem to be able to do without each other when the patient is living at home. We have seen other families where the patient has been hospitalized for a significant period of time. The parents, in effect, form a coalition against him so that he cannot return home. Hospitalization is one acceptable way for these families to be apart. It is obvious that the patient is labeled as sick--and usually as organically rather than psychologically ill. Hence the hospital. We try mainly to get the family to see how much they intertwine with each other. We are not attempting to bring about profound personality change, but in the course of trying to get them separated, a fair amount of change can occur. Following is an example of change that occurred in one of the families.

In the first case, this family consists of a mother, father, a 32-year-old daughter, who looks really about 18 or 20, and her 18-month-old child. The daughter has been having catatonic attacks since she was 19, and has had a total of five years of hospitalization off and on. Many of the times when she has been out of the hospital, she hasn't been able to function but has been cared for at home. She got married a couple of years ago during one of her periods of being out of the hospital, and had a child, and then promptly went back into the hospital. So, she has never cared for this child and has actually seen very little of her. When she got out of the hospital, she made arrangements with her husband to divorce him, and went to stay with her parents. The child, meanwhile, was in a foster home in the town where she had lived with her husband. I started with them, the family, about the middle of October, 1958, and after five or six sessions the patient, who is usually fairly mute and rigid, began to respond, in that she looked more alive at the sessions, more interested, and would comment occasionally. The mother told me that she had cared for the patient for so many years that she had sacrificed a good bit of her chance to be an artist; that not only was the patient a problem, but that her very successful father was subject to spells in which he folded up and couldn't go to work. During these spells, she would take him off to a cabin in the woods, or somewhere, and stay with him a couple of weeks until he got back on his feet. She also said that the brother, just before he went to Korea, had a similar episode and that she nursed him out of that. I asked the mother if she ever had had the privilege of breaking down, or if she always had to be the one who was strong. She looked as if she had been kicked in the stomach. She gasped and got red. She couldn't talk for a little while. When she finally could say something, she simply muttered, "Well, it is over with now, it was just a silly business anyhow," and literally would not permit me to return to that topic. At the end of this session, the patient, sensing the session was drawing to a close, said, "Would it be all right with you if I went to get my baby?", and I said, "Of course, if you want to." She looked surprisingly in control of herself. The mother protested vigorously because the plan had been that she would go get the baby after things were squared away with the patient. The grandmother would, in effect, take care of the baby. It wasn't assumed that the patient would be in good enough shape to take this responsibility. Late that afternoon, the patient came to my office with her mother in tow to get a letter to the foster home saying that she was in shape to bring the baby back from the foster home on the plane. The mother said, in a pitiful way, "I haven't been able to cash a check; I don't have enough money for your ticket," appealing to me somehow, not for money, but for something. The patient calmly told her that she had already checked with the travel bureau, that they would take a check, and that there was no problem. They left, with the mother again sort of following along behind the patient in a little pitty-patty kind of way. And the patient went for her child.

Let me present the initial session with the family I described. It is similar to all initial sessions we have had with the very sick, or what I call stable, unsatisfactory families. It is characteristic in that the parents focus completely on the patient's illness and indicate no problems of their own. The patients usually cooperate with such an endeavor and the net result is an impression of a family being victimized by the patient's illness. In fact, after many months, it invariably turns out that the parents not only have problems of their own, but that the patient's illness has become an explanation for their way of life.

M (mother): (to father)--You talk.

F (father):--It's your show.

T (therapist):--No, it's all of yours.

M: It was very pleasant. We had a very nice weekend. Barbara wanted to see the Van Gogh exposition so I drove her into town Sunday morning and we had a very pleasant weekend, didn't we, Papa?

F: Yes, yes.

T: (to father) Did you go along?

F: No, I stayed home and worked Sunday morning, as usual.

T: Do you like to work around the place or on your scientific work?

F: Yes.

T: (to mother) What seemed to be pleasant about it?

M: Barbara was her old self.

F: It was Barbara's proposal to go in and see the show.

M: Her proposal--

F: We were happy about that.

T: Well, does she have the responsibility of determining how things in the family go--happy or unhappy? Is she sort of your weather vane?

M: (laughing) Well, anyway, we're just fine when she is happy, then everything is all right.

T: I was thinking of what a tough spot that is for her to be in. You know, the feeling: "When I'm down the rest of the family is down; and if I get up again, they'll come up again with me." It's like walking around with a huge weight. Do you see that it might be difficult?

F: Well, it can't very well be any different. The girl has had a shock and naturally--

M: I was just so glad that she wanted to go in and I was so tickled to death we saw the pictures and came back. It isn't always that way. We had quite a full life and so on. You see, she hasn't been at home for six years.

T: Well, what else? You went in to the museum on Sunday morning.

M: Came back, had a late dinner and Barbara looked at the TV and then we all looked at it.

T: You watched.

<u>M</u>: (interrupting)--And while we slept, Barbara wrote a letter
to her best girl friend while we took a nap because we had been out
Saturday night and Barbara very nicely wanted us to go and we were
out from 8:30 to 10:30.

<u>T</u>: Well, what did you do, where did you go?

<u>F</u>: Oh, just visited this friend's house and the friend's apart-
ment.

<u>M</u>: That was the first time we really left her and went out. She
wanted us to and it went very nicely.

<u>T</u>: Well, that's fine. (To patient) What did you do while they
were gone? Watch TV or read or what?

<u>P</u> (Patient): I think I read (very quiet voice).

<u>T</u>: (approvingly) At least it wasn't so bad that you weren't able
to concentrate while they were gone? (To parents) How long has
it been since the two of you were out together, would you say?

<u>M</u>: All three of us?

<u>T</u>: No, I mean just the two of you.

<u>M</u>: Well, since she's been home, I guess, isn't it?

<u>F</u>: Yes, one other time.

<u>M</u>: Oh, yes, we did. Saturday afternoon, a cocktail party. We
had my cleaning woman in. She is a very nice woman that just
loves young people and children. She offered to come anytime she
could and the first time she came she stayed for two hours. But
this is the first time in a long time that Barbara stayed alone.

<u>T</u>: Well, that might encourage you to do it more often, do you
think? Is that all right with you, Barbara?

<u>F</u>: Yes, she's been very good about letting us go out.

<u>M</u>: Oh, yes.

<u>F</u>: She's very cooperative.

<u>T</u>: (to father) I imagine in some ways you might feel a little
roped into this. I am aware that your wife can be pretty persuasive.

<u>M</u>: (laughs).

<u>T</u>: As I told her it was more or less up to me over a period of
time to see if we could sell you on the notion that there was something here for you. Otherwise, if you come along, it's just another
body in the room and doesn't amount to much. In order to help me
get some picture, is there anything currently about your own situation you would like to change? In terms of your responses to
other people?

<u>F</u>: The problem is simply to help Barbara get adjusted to the
way of life and I think we're making reasonable progress. I think
it's going to work itself out all right so I'm not going around under
the burden of a terrific problem. Of course, we are facing it and
getting along all right.

<u>T</u>: Apart from Barbara's difficulties, everything would be fine?

F: Yes, I think so. Just the usual problems and it doesn't pay to worry about those.

M: Yes, that's our major problem. It's just a period of readjustment.

T: (turning to mother) What would you say about that?

M: I agree with him one hundred per cent, because they are both the same kind of people, (looking at her daughter) enjoying the same kind of things and if she could just get well and ask for records occasionally to be played and to play the piano together occasionally, well, I agree one hundred per cent.

T: Now I'm not sure that you are agreeing with him. Let me see, you lost me. Your husband was saying there was nothing about himself or his way of life--that everything would be fine if Barbara's problem would be solved.

M: Her being sick. There would be no problem at all if she were well.

F: Sure, we are in agreement on that.

T: Do you feel that if Barbara were well and living somewhere else?

M: No, not necessarily, if she wants to, okay, but right there with us is perfectly okay. We like the same kind of things, the same kind of people. There isn't any problem.

F: Let's not make problems where none exist.

T: Believe me, I don't want to do that either. On the other hand, I don't want to overlook any that do exist. Otherwise I wouldn't be of much use to you. You see, it's a little puzzling to me how Barbara would get sick in the first place if there wasn't something wrong, except for her being sick. I don't quite understand it.

M: Oh, well, perhaps you won't understand the gravity of what she's been through and that she has been sick before this and so on. I feel sure, at least, I hope, that when things get settled down. Now yesterday she had a bad day because she tried to write to her girl friend. She thought the one she had written Sunday, while we were sleep--she had said too much, has asked too many favors. So she struggled all morning trying to do this letter and I went out and left her alone. She got rapidly worse until I sort of persuaded her to stop and rest and then it got too late, about five o'clock, for the mail and so I said it didn't have to be written anyway. I didn't say that in the beginning because she really wanted to write. I let her go along but when I let her write, a whole sort of crisis developed about it. I...

T: I don't want to go off on a tangent, but I wonder if this happens very often; that is, I would say there seems to be something in the family situation that contributes to this difficulty.

<u>M</u>: Okay, that's why a doctor has to help me. Maybe I did wrong to let her write the letter, when probably the day would have been different. After all, I want a doctor to help me. I try my best but I just play by ear, sometimes it works and sometimes it doesn't, that's why I want you to help me not to play by ear. But, tell me what I should have done and point out what I should do. Should I have let her gone ahead and write the letter--what would you have done? Everything I've done ever since she was born, I've tried to do my best. I'm willing to do everything for her--if she likes to sleep, I let her--what would you have done? We had a bad day yesterday, not nearly as bad as two other days we had but it was sort of bad. We got the letter yesterday about the settlement. She told you she was willing to sign it. Now it would be a very nice thing if she could sign that today and we could get it in the mail. Because it has nothing to do with the divorce. It is to get it signed so we can get the child. Dr. X said it was important for the child to get settled. Her paternal mother-in-law was taking care of her and it's not very good if the father doesn't come and see her as when I was there in July. She says he has to go and have polio shots for the child and buy her a pair of shoes and the child gets hysterical so we should get the child as soon as possible, provided she will sign. I haven't told Barbara the letter just came last night at 6 o'clock and that was no time to tell her on a bad... Now provided she signs this and we send it right back, then the foster mother has nicely offered to come here and bring the child. She doesn't want the child to have to go through another siege with her father.

You will notice several things about this excerpt. One is the mother's tremendous devotion to her daughter. Notice that as soon as I mentioned that the patient might get well and live some place else, the mother, in a somewhat anxious tone, stated that it was all right if she lived with them. The father's reply to this is very obscure. He states, "Let's not make problems where none exist." What does this mean? Since it is said to me, I assume he means, "Don't try to cause trouble by intervening between my wife and daughter. I have learned not to do this myself." Note also that the parents are able to agree on the topic of their daughter's illness being their major problem. This is the only thing they are able to agree on. Even on this topic, they don't agree completely since there are implications about who is more at fault and about how sick she is and the nature of her illness. The father espouses a more strictly organic cause, whereas the mother feels that the fact that they were away from her so much when she was a child may have played a part.

Notice also that at the end of the excerpt, the mother produces a letter which she wants Barbara to sign. This is typical behavior and one reason why the patient has learned not to trust her parents. My position in this was that I did not know the family well enough to suggest whether Barbara sign or not and that I did not want to take sides. Naturally, the mother denied that there were any sides. I suggested to Barbara that she take the letter home, read it, think about it, then decide whether she wanted to sign it.

Let us consider an excerpt from another family session for comparison. This is a family being seen by John Weakland, in which the patient is a 24-year-old male schizophrenic. The family is interviewed in their home, in a structured situation. In this situation, as with all of our families, we ask them to plan something together and the therapist leaves them alone while they discuss a plan. Next, the therapist asks the question, in the context of a game, "Who is boss in the family?" The game is that each person is allowed to ask a question, much as he would play a card, and then the next individual can comment on the question, as one would play a card of the same suit, or he may trump it or play a different suit. The therapist's question, "Who is the boss in the family?" usually causes all sorts of hell. In the excerpt I am going to play, the therapist says to the mother, father, sister, and patient that they might discuss in detail something they would like to do together. He then leaves the room.

D (daughter): I have a wonderful idea.
M (mother): Bridge.
D: Oh, no, fishing in Guaymas.
M: Oh, would you like to do that?
F (father): What?
D: Go fishing in Guaymas. I think that would be fun. Paul (the patient) likes to fish.
F: He likes to fish.
M: Don't you think it might be a slightly expensive thing to do? Maybe we could fish in the Bay.
D: (turning to Paul) Oh, Paul, you'd get a kick out of this. The M's went fishing down there and caught 45 pounds of sailfish, each of them nine feet long. It was exciting. They jump out of the water like marlin or something.
(Overlapping) Oh, it is thrilling.
It is, it really is. And they only run in certain seasons. He said that they go down there and...
M: Can you eat them?

D: No, I don't think so. You just hang them up and have your picture taken and give them to peasants, probably, or something like that. But it's sort of exciting.

M: How long did it take to land them?

D: What?

M: How long did it take to land them?

D: Oh, forty or fifty minutes, I guess it was.

M: (to patient, Paul) Did you ever fish for sailfish?

P: No, I guess not.

D: I figured that you and I would get a kick out of something like that. Of course, that's my idea (laughs).

P: I'd love it too (laughs).

M: (short laugh).

F: Well, Paul, as Mother said, it's kind of expensive, we were down there once. It's better fishing.

M: It was...

D: You have to go down there at the right time. You didn't go when the fish weren't running, I mean. If you go when the fish are running or something, then you are bound to get something because everybody... all the boats are out and what not and they have marlin and sailfish, a few marlin. I don't know if they have something else or not, I don't know, but it would be exciting. I am just suggesting that it might be kind of fun or something like that (laughs). You know my ideas.

F: (laughing) Catalina would be closer and cheaper.

M: Yeah.

D: Or a river or something. I just happened to suggest that because the M's were talking about it so much.

M: What kind of... This is the only time of year I would think... It's not too hot.

D: Oh, yeah. Well, I guess it is as a matter of fact. But if you can go to a place where you're--you know you can catch a fish then you always have a good time.

M: What would you like to do, Paul?

P: What?

M: If you had a choice, what would you like to do?

P: Oh, I don't care.

M: We could plan something together. I was sure Mary was going to say, "Bridge."

D: No, I think Paul likes to fish. I know he does, as a matter of fact.

Here you have an interaction that is again typical in that the patient occupies the central position. This is not obvious because he doesn't say much but it is obvious when you break down the communications. It is exactly like the first interview I played for you, in that the only thing on which the family agrees is the patient's illness. This is shown by the fact that the daughter suggests fishing because that is what her brother likes, it is alleged, and although both mother and father disqualify her remarks as well as each other's, they do return the topic to the patient. One small indication of this is shown by both the mother and father. The mother states to the patient, "If you had a choice, what would you like to do?" The point of the game, you see, is to plan something that one might do and the position of the patient is shown by the fact that he has no choice. He then appropriately replies, "Oh, I don't care."

The same sort of thing occurs when Father asks him, "Did you ever fish for sailfish?" Since the patient has always lived at home, except when he was in the hospital, it's difficult to account for the father's not knowing whether or not his son had done anything so spectacular as fishing for sailfish. Notice, too, how much the daughter is disqualified with her remarks by the parents and also disqualifies herself. If she states something positively, even if it's only in the framework of a game, she must take it back or else the parents pull the rug out from under her. For example, she is talking about how exciting a time the M's had and the mother asks her if sailfish are good to eat. When she attempts to answer that question, Mother says, "How long did it take to land them?"

I would like to say something more about the sibling question, since I mentioned that the daughter in this family disqualifies herself. But first, let me describe the physical setup we use so that you can appreciate the surroundings and a family's expectations. They are seated around a table with a microphone suspended vertically above it. There is a one-way viewing glass and they are shown the control booth and recording setup. They will be observed from time to time but only at irregular intervals. They are aware that this is research, and they cooperate because they usually have tried everything else and nothing has worked. The patient may be in the hospital or may be living at home. Usually the patient has an administrator, that is, someone to take care of medication, job questions, etc., in order to leave the therapist free to deal with the entire family at once. The various members of our research group, Gregory Bateson, Jay Haley, John Weakland, Bill Fry, Virginia Satir, Jules Riskin, and several of the psychiatric residents, all have somewhat different ground rules. In my own case, for example, I will see the other members of the family if one member has a good reason for not showing up. However, the absent member cannot be talked about.

Now, to return to the siblings. As you know, there have been
several papers written about the siblings of the schizophrenic and
the general conclusion has been that they are fine, which proves
that schizophrenia is a recessive disorder, since it only hits one
in four or so of the siblings. Our own experience has not been that.
We find that the patient has had a special relationship to the parents but that the siblings have not escaped completely. It has been
difficult to keep them involved in therapy but to the extent that they
have come, we find that they are not as unlike the patient as they
would like to think. Take the first family I discussed. The patient's brother was described as a paragon of virtue by the parents.
He was working for a company in India and we were fortunate enough
to get him for three visits. Although initially I had the same impression of him as the parents did, namely, that he could not possibly be more different than the patient, this facade quickly broke
down in the family setting. He told me specifically that he worked
in India in order to stay away from the family. He had married a
girl who had his mother's artistic temperament and who ran him
from hell to breakfast. Here is a short excerpt from one of his
initial visits. Previously, he had denied having any recollection
of his sister whatsoever. However, under direct questioning, he
responded to the statement, "We used to fight a lot."

B (brother): We used to fight a lot. Until, let's see what age,
maybe as late as twelve.
T (therapist): When you were twelve you mean?
B: Yes, maybe not quite that late. Around there, up to there.
T: What kind of thing would you fight about?
B: Probably I was just teasing her. As I recall, I wasn't ma-
ture enough to fight about anything specifically. Well, for some-
thing to do. Bored.
T: (to father) Do you remember the fighting? What is your
impression of what it was about. Did you feel it was a teasing sort
of a thing?
B: (cutting in) On my part I don't think there was any animosi-
ty. It was a pretty superficial thing, as far as I remember.
F: (remains silent).
T: (turning to mother) Do you remember the fighting?
M: Well, all I remember is that on the back seat they used to
kick each other's shin sometimes. We didn't have a car until the
war because we were always living in New York and didn't need
one. And then suddenly, '40, I guess it was '39, we got the car so
that made you how old when we had it?
B: About nine. '39, so that makes nine.

<u>M</u>: That was something. I don't ever remember fighting on the boat. You were a bit older then. Couple of years older.

<u>B</u>: You got rid of it in '41. It was around then.

<u>M</u>: He (father) didn't have any interest in boats. He wouldn't have anything to do with it or work on it or do anything with it. I don't think either of them were very interested in the boat. We couldn't go to Europe and I happened just that time to get some extra money. We bought a boat and as I was raised on the water, and used the boats and...

<u>T</u>: Was it some kind of a sailboat?

<u>F</u>: A thirty-two-foot cruiser.

<u>M</u>: And as I talked him into it then he went all overboard for boats much more than I did. I was so tired of it. It was so much work to keep up and neither of us had time to do it and I told him and he still likes boats and I can't bear the sight of them but neither of the children took much to the boat...

<u>T</u>: Quite a bit of boat.

<u>B</u>: Yup, thirty-two foot.

<u>T</u>: Where did you cruise?

<u>B</u>: On Lake Michigan right across the canal, and on the Mississippi River, and St. Paul one summer when we were staying on a farm there.

<u>M</u>: We took them from the Mississippi down.

<u>T</u>: (to Barbara) Well, was this the summer that you were in that camp you've spoken of?

<u>M</u>: (cutting in) Yes, Minnesota. And Barbara came home feeling pretty low...

<u>B</u>: (cutting in) It was during the war and...

<u>M</u>: Minnesota it was. They were staying in Minnesota. So this summer we went up and brought them back in the sailboat.

<u>T</u>: Well, you had the cruiser too?

<u>B</u>: Yeah.

<u>T</u>: You had the sailboat at the time, though?

<u>M</u>: No.

<u>B</u>: Also the cruiser.

<u>M</u>: Of course. We didn't go out all the time but we had fun.

<u>T</u>: You had the cruiser before...

<u>F</u>: Sold the cruiser.

<u>M</u>: That's right, the sailboat.

<u>B</u>: Didn't get the cruiser either until we came back from Europe in '39 or '40.

<u>M</u>: '40. But we couldn't take it through the locks so it had to be the cruiser.

<u>B</u>: Well, now (tentatively) every summer we were in a sort of camp-farm or farm-camp something like that.

M: It's always been that he's wanted to (firmly looking at her son).

B: Well, yeah, as she got older (looking at sister).

T: Whatever that means (puzzled at switch in topic).

M: Well, then she didn't go. Well, then she didn't go because he continued to go and she didn't. Well, kid's stuff. I hate to talk about this.

B: Well, as I remember, all through this I don't think Barbara played a very big part in my life, well not a conscious part, because I really had difficulty in recalling her, how she acted and how she felt and so on to the age of twelve or so.

T: You might have been a little less close than some brothers and sisters are?

B: Perhaps.

M: Age difference was about three years and three months.

B: Well, as I recall, I don't think she was particularly happy in this period. When we were always together up until eleven or twelve. These summer camp sessions and other times.

T: And she would not be apt to let you know that she was pretty unhappy. So I wonder what cues you picked up to tell how she felt?

B: Well, we were usually at different camps... it's hard to remember.

You notice how confused the discussion is. Yet, at several points, the mother speaks up rather loud and clear. This occurs especially in two places, one, when the brother states that every summer, he and his sister were in some sort of a camp and the mother replies that he wanted to. When he switches to his sister from himself, his mother again firmly states that this is a forbidden topic. The brother complies by saying that he doesn't recall much about his sister. I might mention that during the brother's third visit with us, he got into quite a tangle with his mother over the exact circumstances of his marriage. He indicated at this time that he wished he could stay longer because there were problems he would like to get clarified. The parents, however, kept emphasizing that he was short on time.

One of the most rewarding occurrences in family therapy is the concordance between a symptom in the patient and a piece of family interaction that explains the symptom. In this sense, I am stating that schizophrenia or schizophrenic symptoms are adaptive behavior. For example, Barbara's parents complained more about her indecisiveness than about anything else. Evidently, it is a problem when she gets up in the morning as to what she will wear and everything else in the day becomes a similar crisis. When one listens to the sessions, it is striking that when Barbara makes a decision, the parents refute it in some fashion and then she backs out. Yet, they in no way see themselves as having anything to do with her indecision. One striking example was an incident in which a friend of her ex-husband was going to visit them. The mother implied that this was a friend of Barbara's although it had been the mother, in fact, who had invited this girl to stay with them. Barbara exhibited some paranoid symptoms, speaking about spies, and the mother wrung her hands and said, "She's getting worse." In that session, I asked Barbara, "Are you talking about Genevieve acting as a spy for your husband? That she is going to tell him what is going on in the house and whether she approves of the way you treat your child, etc. ?" To this, Barbara was able to reply quietly, "Yes." The parents keep insisting that this was a friend of hers, that it was a silly idea, but I suggested that since the divorce was not final, and since the husband might ask for the custody of the child, perhaps it was not silly to look on Genevieve with suspicion. I suggested that they have her stay in a nearby motel, rather than in an already crowded house. They also had no idea of how long she would stay because they failed to clarify this.

The parents felt that to have her stay in a motel would be inhospitable, and I asked Barbara what she thought. She said, "It would be simpler." She then looked at her parents and stated, "I suppose some people would see it as inhospitable." So the father immediately stated, "You see, she agrees with me. She thinks it would be inhospitable." I then stated: "Well, I thought she said: 'It would be simpler,' but let's play it back." One of the advantages of having a tape setup is that we can play back into the room through an external speaker and check what was said. We don't do this very often because it makes all of us too tape recorder conscious. However, I thought it was worthwhile on this occasion. I had to run that piece back three times before the mother and father could hear Barbara say, "It would be simpler." The father couldn't hear it at first because he kept saying, "She agrees with me." The mother couldn't hear it because she kept saying, "I sound like a man, I sound like a man." This was the first occasion on which she had heard her own voice.

Another example of this kind of thing is a patient of John Weakland who spoke very little, saying mostly, "I don't know," or "Mental illness is all a matter of physics and chemistry." The parents constantly undercut anything that he said so that he had reason for feeling, "I didn't know." And the mother on one occasion literally stated that mental illness is a matter of physics and chemistry. One amusing incident occurred some months after family therapy had been started, when the patient was much improved. We felt this was because the parents were talking about their own relationships and the patient was learning some family matters for the first time. The heat was off him, so to speak. Then mother accidentally discovered that the administrator had put the patient on chlorpromazine about the time that his apparent improvement began. Immediately she claimed that it was the drug and not the family sessions that caused the change. The dosage was small and we thought it could not account for his change, but there was no way of proving it. However, one day, a nurse in going through his bedside table found a huge mound of tablets that he had been collecting over months. He had not taken any. I don't know whether the patient was clever enough to play it this way, but it had quite a surprising effect on his parents.

Perhaps one of the most impressive things about family therapy is the rigidity of the family structure and the difficulty that is encountered when the patient makes a change for the better. An improvement in the patient's symptoms may be very detrimental to the parents, for the patient himself may have to renege on his getting better. With the young man I was just talking about, there was a striking episode in which it became clear that he was responding violently to the tendency of his ward doctor to forget about promises that he had made. The therapist then brought this up in the context of knowledge he had about the parents having reneged on promises. Immediately the patient got very upset and angry, swore at the therapist, and told him that he was crazy, that he was dangerous, and didn't know what he was doing. This tape was played at the next session to show the patient and his parents how afraid of them the patient was. When the patient responded that "mental illness is all a matter of physics," the mother commented, "I agree with him that it's all a matter of physics." Attempts to clarify what she meant became exceedingly vague. She made general statements like, "Well, you know, what you read in newspapers." She thus stopped any attempt on her son's part to stand up to them, and this was followed by an increasing emphasis on both parents' parts on the importance of not being rude. This topic was stressed so much that the therapist finally had to say on one occasion, "Look, you have a choice. You can either choose between rudeness and letting your son stay sick." The mother replied, "I don't think there is any choice. If he is rude, there is no sense in being well." This sort of thing is very difficult to break through. I mentioned earlier that we use a structured situation during our filming sessions which includes the question, "Who's in charge of the family?" or "Who's boss of the family?" The difference in response to this question between the stable, unsatisfactory families and more average families is very striking. For example, here is the response to this question in Barbara's family:

T (therapist): Anyway the idea I want to throw out to you now is the question, "Who is in charge of the family?"

F (father): (Slight laugh) Well, you could only answer this question, uh, if you ask who is in charge of what aspects of the family. It's a very simple question. Why, my wife is rather obviously in charge of what goes on in the household from day to day but, uh, I'm in charge of the check book.

M (mother): (slight laugh).

F: In the many questions connected with the more practical aspects...

M: I guess that's very... (slight laugh). Naturally, I do the marketing and see that we eat well because I like to eat well. (Ends with slight laugh.)

F: (slight laugh).

M: And then I take his shirts to the cleaners and his laundry to the cleaners and see that he has clean shirts and pants.

F: Yes.

M: ... cleaners. And his laundry to the cleaners and sees that he has clean shirts and pants are pressed and whatnot and there are a good many parties and things I arrange, not however, without consulting my husband first.

F: Hmmm.

M: Because he likes to be consulted on such things. Any serious amount I spend, of course, I wouldn't think of going out and doing it even without consulting him.

T: (to patient) Do you have any comments on who is in charge of the family?

P: (in rather low voice) My mother keeps things going.

You will notice how tentative and cautious the parents are in defining each other's roles. They usually manage to keep things so literal that they are difficult for interpretation. You will notice also that Barbara's remark is obscurely clever. "My mother keeps things going." That is a difficult remark to argue with and yet it could be a loaded remark. We find that these patients are capable of clever bombshells which have little to do with brain deterioration.

I would like to conclude by saying that our work is far from complete. Although we have studied a number of schizophrenic families and a good bit of data on them, we need many more control studies. We need normal families, delinquents, etc., and then we will be in a better position to describe the uniqueness of the schizophrenic family. I am sure that someone will ask, "Couldn't the parents' response be because of the patient's illness?" This cannot be answered with finality until we have longitudinal studies. My present opinion is that mother, father, and child are caught in a reverberating circuit. None escapes wholly, not even the siblings, and there are a number of reasons why the child who becomes schizophrenic is the chosen one.

CONJOINT FAMILY THERAPY:
SOME CONSIDERATIONS ON
THEORY, TECHNIQUE, AND RESULTS

Don D. Jackson
and John H. Weakland

The paper presented here is a product of the Family
Therapy in Schizophrenia Project of the Palo Alto
Medical Research Foundation and thus reflects the
ideas and experiences of the entire project staff and
associated therapists. In it we should like primarily
to report some observations based on this particular
experiment in conjoint family therapy with schizo-
phrenics--that is, in treating the identified patient and
other members of his family together as a functioning
natural group. We shall have little to say about the
work of others, except by way of acknowledging and
illustrating a growing trend toward this form of treatment. There is still only a limited amount of such
work being done, and less published, so perhaps the
best way to introduce something that is bound to be
somewhat new and strange is to have the reader accompany us on our voyage of exploration and discovery,
in part. As we go, we shall also attempt to formulate
more systematically what we ourselves have been learning along the way.

Our research group stumbled onto conjoint family therapy by
accident, or at least tangentially. In 1954 we wished to view the
schizophrenic patient communicating and behaving in his natural
habitat, which was not the hospital, and we inevitably turned to
the family as the proper milieu in which to view his interactions.
Our thinking in this direction was spurred by experiences with

Reprinted from PSYCHIATRY, 24 (Suppl. No. 2):30-45 (May 1961).

relatives in our private practice; by chance home visits made in connection with schizophrenics we had in individual therapy; and by stories we heard from various staff members at the Veterans Administration Hospital about their encounters with families.

In order to study the patient directly in relation to his parents and siblings, it was necessary to bring them together and, more important, to observe them together over a period of time. An answer to this practical problem seemed to lie in interviewing the schizophrenic patients and their family members as family groups, a procedure which would provide data for us (especially since all our interviews are recorded) and some therapeutic help for them. In setting up this work, we had no clear plans for family treatment, nor did we know at the time that family therapy was going on elsewhere. However, our experience soon demonstrated that, once one begins to talk directly with these families with a schizophrenic member, there is rapid development of pressures to treat them. Situations arise in which it is important to consider them from a therapeutic point of view, both to keep some control of the family's tendencies to involve the interviewer in their problem and to help them with their increasingly evident difficulties. So our own work in family therapy began.

Against this background, however, it is interesting to note that, as has happened repeatedly in the history of science, similar developments were occurring about simultaneously elsewhere; and in retrospect a rationale for this broad development, and a pertinent need to which it is a response, can be outlined rather clearly.

As we have been increasingly involved in studying and working with families over the past five years, we have been struck to come upon various other people who have independently gotten into similar work. Some of these--for instance, Lyman Wynne and his co-workers, Murray Bowen and his group (both originally at NIMH), and Ivan Boszormenyi-Nagy and his associates in Philadelphia--have like ourselves been most interested in schizophrenia. Others have been interested in a range of psychiatric problems, like Nathan Ackerman in New York, Kalman Gyarfas and Virginia Satir in Chicago, John Bell of the U.S. Public Health Service, and Eugene MacDanald in Galveston; while still others have been primarily interested in another particular problem, as in Charles Fulweiler's work with the families of delinquents in Alameda County, California. But all share a basic orientation toward understanding and treating the family as a unitary system.

Some of the background of this development is clear enough. Ever since Freud's early work, the fact that the patient's family is important has been recognized at least conceptually. But, practically, this fact has been dealt with mainly by segregating the patient and therapist and excluding all relatives from contact with the patient's treatment. An important and increasing exception to this practice, however, has been in the treatment of child patients; here at least the mother has become more and more an object of therapy also. Yet this leaves some problems hanging—for example, what to do about the father?—and raises new ones about the need for time and for adequate communication between therapists if parents and child are not seen by the same therapist. Similar problems arise in the treatment of marital partners. Meanwhile, there are serious practical problems attending individual treatment that are made especially evident in the case of hospitalized schizophrenics. On the one hand, hospital personnel frequently experience difficulties in necessary dealings with relatives, sometimes in being unable to get together with the relatives effectively when necessary and sometimes in being unable to get the relatives off their backs. On the other hand, when patients are successfully helped in relative isolation in the hospital, their return to the family too often is marked by upsets—of the parents, or of the patient, who then relapses, or of both.

The essential point to be gleaned from all these matters of common knowledge is that treatment of a psychiatric patient necessarily involves dealing with members of his family, and with family relationships, either directly or indirectly. Clearly, even setting up a rule of excluding the family from the therapy involves handling these matters, and drastically, though perhaps simply. The question at issue, then, is not whether the members of a patient's family are to be dealt with, but how they are to be dealt with. This paper is concerned with describing our work with conjoint family treatment as a means of dealing with this problem in the case of schizophrenic patients particularly.

THEORETICAL BACKGROUND

To understand our attempts at treating these families and formulating our treatment approach, it is necessary to understand the theory under which we labor, since our present practices and present conceptions have both developed out of the interplay of some very broad original orientations and our groping attempts at treatment of actual families.

At the outset of our program of work with families of schizophrenics our two main concepts were (1) the double bind[1] and (2) family homeostasis.[2] The concept of family homeostasis arose from observations that psychotherapeutic efforts with one member of a family might be hindered by the behavior of other members, or that another member might become disturbed as the member in treatment improved. These observations, in connection with existing ideas about homeostatic systems generally, suggested that a family forms such a dynamic steady-state system; the characters of the members and the nature of their interaction--including any identified patient and his sick behavior--are such as to maintain a status quo typical of the family, and to react toward the restoration of this status quo in the event of any change, such as is proposed by the treatment of any member.

The double bind concept is grounded in our most basic conception about communication as the chief means of human interaction and influence: that in actual human communication a single and simple message never occurs, but that communication always and necessarily involves a multiplicity of messages, of different levels, at once. These may be conveyed via various channels such as words, tone, and facial expressions, or by the variety of meanings and references of any verbal message in relation to its possible contexts. The relationships among these related messages may be very complex. No two messages, at different levels of communication, can be just the same; however, they may be similar or different, congruent or incongruent. Difference and incongruity appear fundamental to the richness of human communication, as when certain combinations of words and tone define styles of expression, such as irony or humor; however, they also appear fundamental to the origin and character of much psychopathology, as in the symptom "inappropriate affect," considered as an evident incongruence between words and tone or expression. Further, the use of double-level messages seems increasingly central to therapy in ways we shall mention later.

The double bind concept refers to a pattern of pairs or sets of messages, at different levels, which are closely related but sharp-

[1] Gregory Bateson, Don D. Jackson, Jay Haley, and John Weakland. Toward a theory of schizophrenia, Behav. Sci., 1: 251-264, 1956.

[2] Don D. Jackson. The question of family homeostasis. Psychiatric Quart., Suppl., 31:79-90, 1959.

ly incongruent, occurring together with other messages which by concealment, denial, or other means seriously hinder the recipient from clearly noticing the incongruence and handling it effectively, as by commenting on it. Instead, he is influenced toward incompatible behavioral responses while enjoined not even to notice either influence or incompatibility. We believe that, within an important relationship, where messages cannot merely be ignored or avoided, the combination of extensive experience of such communication being uttered and the recipient's learning to participate by accepting incongruence without question can be productive of schizophrenic behavior.

It is not hard to note that these two main concepts are both concerned with the description and specification of interaction among actual persons, by various means of communication, at a level of directly observable behavior. This focus implies further an emphasis on what is real and on what is current and continuing to occur. Taken together, these emphases define a broad 'communicational' and transactional orientation to the study, understanding, and treatment of human behavior--including that special class most interesting to psychiatrists, symptomatic behavior. This orientation, while related to earlier work, especially Sullivan's, and currently increasing in acceptance, still is considerably different from the strong traditional orientation of psychiatry emphasizing the individual patient and constructs about the unreal or unobservable: fantasies or misperceptions of reality; past, mainly childhood, experiences; and intrapsychic organization and content.

In brief, we are much more concerned with influence, interaction, and interrelation between people, immediately observable in the present, than with individual, internal, imaginary, and infantile matters. It is worth making this difference in basic orientation explicit, since to do so helps clarify the nature of our main specific concepts, indicates some important connections between them, and provides a background essential for understanding our whole therapeutic approach--what we do and what we do not do, especially some of our differences from other therapeutic concepts and practices.

The family homeostasis and double bind concepts, with some expansion and modification, [3] continue to be of major significance

---

[3] For instance, John H. Weakland. The "double bind" hypothesis of schizophrenia and three-party interaction. In The Etiology of Schizophrenia, Don D. Jackson (Ed.), Basic Books, New York, pp. 373-388, 1960.

in our family work. Since these ideas have not always been clearly understood by others, particularly the importance of difference in levels of messages, some more concrete discussion of them seems to be in order here. Some of our critics have felt that the double bind situation is essentially an either-or situation, a damned-if-you-do and damned-if-you-don't predicament, or merely a complicated way of describing ambivalence. 4) The double bind situation is all of these things. But it is more. As an illustration, take the predicament of an innocent person who undergoes a lie detector test. It is common practice in such tests to invoke a standard situation for the establishment of a base line. One such situation is to have the subject draw a card from a deck, look at it, and replace it. He is then told not to reveal which card he drew even should the examiner guess it. When the card drawn is guessed and the subject answers, "No, " the squiggles on the tape reveal how much he reacts to a lie. However, a theory merely invoking guilt over the telling of a lie fails to account for some of the complexities in the situation. Most subjects in this situation cannot be confident of innocence because a person cannot know a priori what his body will do and thus the subject's literal innocence is no protection against the context being one in which the power rests in the hands of the examiner. Since the examiner has asked him to lie, is this really a "lie" or is it not the truth--that is, a correct perception of what it takes to make the machine work? The double level situation renders the subject especially vulnerable because if he denies what he totally perceives, he has put into play a self-deception that does not come equipped with clear boundaries. Suppose at the completion of the test, the examiner stated to the subject, "You have been lying. " Could the subject be sure that the examiner was referring only to his deliberate 'cooperative' lie? Could he be sure that he is not a person who is in a chronic state of not processing all the data available to him and thus subject to self-deception?

THE THERAPEUTIC PROCESS--ARRANGEMENTS AND
TECHNIQUES
    "The family" we are talking about in practice usually consists of father, mother, and patient. They are seen together once a week for sixty to ninety minutes in a room equipped with a micro-

---

4) Despite our previous discussion of the "illusion of alternatives" in John H. Weakland and Don D. Jackson, Patient and therapist observations on the circumstances of a schizophrenic episode. AMA Arch. Neurol. and Psychiat. , 79:554-574, 1958.

phone for tape recording and a one-way window for occasional observation and supervision. The meetings may be conducted more frequently than once a week when indicated, but time limitations have not made this possible on a regular basis, and it does not seem essential. Any combination of the basic group's members may be seen as outside necessity--such as trips or illnesses--dictates, or if the therapist feels it is technically wise. We used to be fairly rigid about meeting only if all members could be present. Now, although the general emphasis remains on the whole group, there is variation on this among our several therapists.

The status of the patient's siblings remained obscure for some time and is still only partially settled. We have found them reluctant to be drawn into a potentially unpleasant situation. In retrospect, it appears that we attributed more health to them than they had in fact, and unconsciously went along with their characteristic defense: "This is a situation I am not involved in." For example:

The younger brother of a chronic schizophrenic was visiting this country on vacation from his European job. The therapist had anticipated his arrival by getting him to agree to three family sessions during his visit, since it appeared likely that he would not be available again during the course of therapy. At the first session, the brother appeared to be everything his parents claimed he was and everything the patient was not. During this session, he maintained a pleasant aloofness and claimed amnesia for any events that the therapist felt had been important in the patient's life. At the end of this session, his mother stated that she knew he would be happy to return, but the therapist, discouraged, made it clear that he realized this was a great imposition on the brother's limited time and, without realizing it, left an excellent opportunity for the brother to back out. However, he did return for the next session, and the several days he had spent with his parents brought to the fore more data than could have been hoped for. He expressed genuine regret at the end of the third session that he could not continue to participate in the family meetings and stated that his life abroad probably protected him from a crack-up.

Currently, we have no hesitation about trying to include one or more siblings in the family sessions if they are living with the parents. If they have established other residences, we generally limit the contact to occasional meetings, usually for our own data needs.

Given this basic group of at least three persons, what is the therapist's orientation toward them and his goal? In other words, how does he envisage the therapeutic process, and how does he structure the situation for the group?

When we started to try family therapy in treating schizophrenia, we assumed from our previous work that the identified patient was on the receiving end of double binds from a parent or parents; and we knew that we needed the parents' cooperation, about which we were uncertain, at least to the extent that they keep coming for a period of time. Accordingly, our initial efforts were crude attempts to protect the patient from his parents and to impress the parents with how much help we might derive from the data that they might furnish about the patient. It rather quickly dawned on us, however, that: First, the patient was not a delicate violet and was quite capable of upsetting his parents and blocking the therapist's ambitions; and, second, the parents were unhappy people who potentially could benefit from psychotherapy.

By now, the ten or so therapists involved in the schizophrenia project appear to be reasonably uniform in their impressions as to why they and the family are in the room. All of the therapists while still inexperienced were patient-oriented, but they quickly achieved the realization that the three persons confronting them are bound together in a mutually destructive way and that the primary symptom presented by all three is a crippling entanglement that from the surface is apparent only in the patient. The parents initially try to preserve this surface view, and hence every initial session is replete with remarks about poor X and his unfortunate illness. Once, however, they respond to the lure of the therapist's curiosity about them, the brittle surface cracks and the utter desolation that can only be experienced by two people living together in apartness begins to ooze from below. It is at this point that the therapist's humane interest can still save the day. It is at this point no longer enough that the parents come for the patient's sake. An abbreviated but typical sequence in early family sessions is as follows:

The patient is a 30-year-old man with some five years of hospital experience who is currently living at home. The parents are disturbed with his inactivity, sloppiness, and delusions. Their attempts to push him into activity or to get him out of the house boomerang and result in unpleasantness not only between them and the patient but sometimes between the parents themselves. In the initial interview, the patient is hugely sloppy, quiet, and makes a point of not appearing involved. The parents are careful to point out their own attainments in contrast to the patient's many faults, which of course are labeled sickness, and there is a sticky back-and-forth exchange between them and the therapist over the details of therapy time--the frequency of sessions and so on.

During the second session, the parents have been thinking about the patient's illness and recall anecdotes from the past having to do with outside events or acts of God that they suggest may have caused it. Typically the schools and school teachers are mentioned as culprits. In this session, the patient demonstrates some of his symptoms with obvious encouragement from the parents.

During the third session, the therapist expresses curiosity about the parents, their background, how they met, ar.u their early marriage. He introduces these topics deliberately, at the suggestion of his supervisor. Although the parents start out initially to report factually, there appears to be more tension in the air. Finally, well along in the session, the mother says to the father, "Why don't you tell the doctor about New York?" Her reference is to a not completely estimable escapade on the father's part, and he responds with an unhappy but gallant attempt to face the music. But the focus does not stay on the parents and off the patient for long. In the course of recounting this episode, it is stated that the patient was living with the father temporarily. This is quite correct, but largely irrelevant. The son was only about ten at the time and his staying in one city with the father temporarily, while the mother remained in another, was the parents' arrangement and indeed one related to their problem being discussed. But once the son is mentioned, the parents are soon off again on his difficulties and the father is off the hook.

During the fourth session, the therapist attempts to clarify the experience alluded to in the previous session and to discuss further some aspects of the parents' marriage. During this session, the patient appears interested and laughs heartily on several occasions when the father is willing to make himself the butt of a particular story. There is more of a feeling that, however unhappy they are, these people do share something together.

In the next session, the father appears alone. The mother is said to be down with some vague illness, and the patient is waiting in the car. The father has come in only to tell the therapist that they won't be arriving that evening. However, he stays to

chat and, to the therapist's surprise, writes on a matchbook
cover (presumably so it won't be overheard by the tape recorder)
that he and his wife are having terrible fights. He then retrieves
and destroys the matchbook cover. The father is almost totally
unable to break down and to allow the therapist to sympathize
with him over his marital discord; nevertheless, a breach has
been made, and subsequent sessions reveal that the mother was
not ill but that there had been a family quarrel before the session
and she had refused to come. This leads to further consideration
of their difficulties as well as those of the patient.

This example illustrates some of the typical characteristics
of our families and typical responses they show to the situation
posed by initially entering into therapy together. We may explicitly summarize some of these before going on to list and illustrate certain standard initial moves we have developed to
deal with the problems these features pose, and then to consider
the further course of therapy similarly.

In most of the families we have seen, perhaps especially in
middle-class ones, the mother appears as the prime mover about
therapy, with the emphasis on her concern for her child; many
mothers also appear as 'lay experts' on schizophrenia and its
treatment on the basis of long experience with their child's illness,
often plus reading up on the subject. In some cases the father is
more in the foreground, but on closer inspection he seems usually
to be so largely as a spokesman or front man for the mother.
Often it is found that the father is physically absent from the family a lot, as by being very much occupied with his business. In
fact, in many of the families it seems that the members hardly
ever get together except in the therapy room, although they have
little independent life as individuals either.

The father and mother both center their initial discussion on
the subject of their child, especially on his illness; this might
seem natural in the circumstances, except that this focus is extreme while at the same time it often centers on minor aspects of
the illness, such as details of the patient's dress and manners.
The parents are able to get together and agree fairly well when
the patient's illness is thus the topic of discussion, although they
may both speak of this in a disjointed or incongruent way--that is,
at one moment they may insist that the patient is too sick to be
held responsible for anything, and the next complain in extreme
ways about his irresponsible misbehavior, making this abrupt

transition without giving the cues or structuring that ordinarily accompany such a shift. Yet this area of agreement stands out, especially as it soon becomes evident that these two people can agree very little on any other matter. The patient, meanwhile, is appearing helpless and hopeless, yet by withdrawal or acting-up is influencing everyone and upsetting the therapy situation in part. It is thus very easy to see from these early sessions why observers without further experience would naturally tend to draw big distinctions between the "sick" patient and the "well" parents and siblings. Yet, on closer and more extended contact with these families, we have been struck by the observation not only that the parents also have considerable personal difficulties, but that their difficulties are apt to be fundamentally like those the patient exhibits via his symptomatology. [5]

A number of problems connected with these characteristics tend to arise very quickly in the therapy. The parents keep their discussion centered on the patient and by this avoid talking of themselves and their relationship. The patient often helps them in this by some kind of overt "goofing up" or going too far which aids in keeping him labeled as the patient; this may occur especially at points when the parents do happen to approach some topic that is hot for them, and so strongly that even the therapist is likely to turn on the patient, away from the parents, without quite noticing what he is doing.

If the therapist does attempt to put the focus on the family, or to define the parents as equally patients with their child, certain other difficulties are expectable. Either the mother or the father may move to involve the therapist in individual and private com-munication, by phone calls or before or after the family session. Fathers tend to avoid involvement in the family therapy by dis-tancing devices; sometimes actual absences from meetings, some-times withdrawal by silence, or intellectualization under the label of "objectivity." Mothers seem to feel more guilty about their pos-sible relationship to the child's illness, and they tend to be cor-respondingly active in one way or another. In some cases, there is danger that the mother will be so concerned as to terminate therapy very rapidly once the "family therapy" idea really is clear. In others, sessions may continue but be dominated by the mother, who may take over the therapist's position by endorsing everything he says, by being more expert and scientific than he, usually with biological and chemical theories of schizophrenia which deny her guilt, or even in a few cases by taking blame on herself so strongly and indiscriminately that examining actual family interactions again is badly hampered. Indeed, such examination is difficult at best, since it is a real project to get clarity about anything with these families; the statements of the various members do not agree, and each tends to be vague and shifting, or to bury everything in details, or both. Of particular importance is the fact that the family members present their behavior in terms of responses to outside situations, so that it is difficult even for the therapist to keep in mind and in view how much they are responding to each other, and to begin to clarify this with them.

FRAMING OF THE THERAPY

If such typical initial problems are not dealt with adequately, they are likely to become acute or chronic, ending the therapy quickly or leading into a repetitious stalemate similar to the family's usual circle of interactions, only with the therapist drawn in as one more player in this game with no winners. On the other hand, effective dealing with these initial problems is correspondingly valuable. As we see it, 'patient management' in family therapy, which includes management of all the family members involved in the therapeutic situation, is a central part of therapy, and by no means only superficial in its effects. Thus, the standard procedures we have evolved to utilize in the initial family sessions represent much more than merely a means of avoiding limited particular difficulties. They involve a framing of the therapy as a whole, a setting-up of continuing broad standards and expectations. Also, the means by which the therapist does this framing are illustrative of much about our over-all technical orientation and practice.

In the initial session, the therapist customarily expresses a philosophy of "We are here to work together on better understanding one another so that you all can get more out of your family life." Such a statement implies that the parents are as much involved in the family unhappiness, specified or unspecified, as the patient, and also that they equally have something to gain from therapy. This replaces our former tendency to open the initial interview by asking what they would like to get out of the sessions, an approach that resulted in the standard answer, "Nothing is wrong except poor Bill," or whoever the identified patient happened to be. Such mention of "working on understanding" also implicitly focuses on communication as deeply involved in their difficult relationships and as a means of therapy. There are similar implications in our usual handling of the problem of private communication. Formerly, it was customary for the therapist to receive a phone call from one or both parents during the early weeks of therapy asking if the patient shouldn't be put on tranquilizers or shouldn't be getting more exercise, and so on. Then the therapist would feel awkward about bringing this up at the next family meeting and awkward if he did not bring it up because it implied a conspiracy with one or the other of the parents. Now, in the initial session, the therapist casually announces that all parties are privileged to all information about contacts with the therapist; and, like most rules that are brought up matter-of-factly, this is accepted.

Alternatively, the therapist may sometimes handle similar matters less by implication and more by making fairly explicit statements, while attaching to these a prefabricated framing interpretation. For example, he may state that all families develop habitual patterns of communication, including some avoidances by which the family members protect each other, and therefore part of the therapist's job is to clarify these patterns and avoidances when they stand in the way of resolving important blocks between the family members; it is the therapist's responsibility to them all--while treating them impartially, although naturally each of them will feel at times he is not doing so--not to let the solution of such problems be missed even by such protective tendencies. Thus the family is given credit for their good intentions, while the therapist's position of stirring things up at times is defined as a positive duty for their benefit. Also the therapist will point out that they must have some important relationship with each other, regardless of their difficulties, since they have stayed together for a long time; in addition, they really know each other better than anyone else, including the therapist, can, and thus they are the best possible therapists for each other. This framing places responsibility for helpful participation on all the family members equally, which both calls on the more withdrawn ones to take more part and undercuts the usual tendency of some one family member to take over the situation from the therapist.

The members of our group also tend to be active in similar ways in connection with many of the more specific issues that arise initially. For example, we commonly avoid some dreary time-wasting by politely interrupting the parents' attempts to focus exclusively on the patient's illness. In addition, we tend to discipline the patient if he attempts to utilize the "I am the sick one so I am not responsible" ploy, as the following example shows.

The therapist was questioning the parents in the initial session about their living. The mother was uneasy, apparently about her alcoholism which had not yet been disclosed. At this point, the schizophrenic son broke in to announce how much he had benefited from shock therapy in the hospital. Immediately both parents discussed this with him, and the father asked if he wished more. The mother stated that maybe he needed tranquilizers and then thought to ask him if he was currently taking them, to which the patient replied, "No." At this juncture, the therapist broke in to ask the patient in a rather commanding tone, "Bob, you're not on shock therapy now? Right?" The patient replied that he was not. The therapist added, "And you said you were not on drugs." Again the patient acknowledged that this was true. The therapist continued, "So it's fortunate then that you are you this morning here with us. In other words, you and mom and dad and I are all responsible for what we say and that makes it easier to understand each other."

The patient's rescue operations which dig his own hole deeper are usually an issue in the first few minutes of the initial session. The therapist's criticism or irritation at these attempts implies not only that this kind of thing is not acceptable, but also that the patient can do better. This attitude is in contrast to that of the parents, who usually will drop whatever they are engaged in and follow up the patient's intervention like a hound dog in pursuit. (However, an alternative approach that is sometimes feasible is to accept this line of joint interest in the patient's symptoms but to press the inquiry in such a way as to include more of the family circumstances surrounding symptomatic behavior and their relevance to it.) Another matter that comes up in the first session is the question of what to do if someone in the family is absent from one of the sessions. It may seem to be borrowing trouble to anticipate such a happening, but experience has taught us that the multitudinous excuses proffered for someone's not appearing would delight a sage truant officer. It seems more efficacious to announce to the family that there will be times when they do not wish to come and that such absence is a rather powerful lever to use against the therapist and against family members; or to announce that they are likely to feel reluctant to come just when important progress is occurring. Such announcements also emphasize our philosophy that family members do have a great effect on each other and that there is no such thing as not commenting even if the "No comment" is attempted through silence or through a nonappearance.

In summary, a few principal means that the therapist may use --separately, jointly, or alternatively, according to taste and circumstances--in handling the typical problems arising at the start of family therapy might be listed as follows. First, there is a certain place for being very clear, direct, and explicit. This is comparatively limited, applying mostly to practical details such as the schedule of meetings; unless the therapist is quite clear and definite, even such a simple matter can set off a long, inconclusive discussion. Second comes the making of certain matter-of-fact statements whereby the important messages are conveyed implicitly. Third comes the making of statements about some aspect of the therapy which are accompanied by some comment that serves to anticipate and disarm resistance--for example, "I intend to be impartial, though each of you will surely doubt that I am at times." This may be carried all the way to an "inversion of meaning" statement such as "There will be times, just as real progress is being made, when you will feel like not coming to the meetings."

From the discussion so far it must now be evident that active intervention in and management of family interaction has an important place in our initial work; and, indeed, this holds true of the further course of family therapy also. This active orientation, however, grew out of our experience and was not a predisposition except that experience in treating individual schizophrenics presses one toward an active and varied style of therapy. Nevertheless, in beginning our work with families, we were concerned lest activity on the part of the therapist would obscure family operations and dim the light of our research. Actually, it has been so difficult to keep the sicker families involved, to produce shifts and not mere repetitions of the standard patterns characteristic of any one family, that we are no longer so concerned about the therapist remaining a flyspeck by his own design and efforts and more concerned with avoiding being put into such a useless position by the family.

If it is kept in mind that families have horizontal as well as vertical layers, then the pattern of response to the therapist's intervention can simply be viewed as a further unfolding of the range of this particular family's transactions. By vertical, we mean going back in time; by horizontal, we mean layers of complexity of communications or, as they might be called, layers of defense in concentric circles. One of the things that the tyro therapist must experience is that he will have to deal with the same problem over and over again in different forms and guises, as the following example suggests.

Initially, the father of a paranoid patient complained to the therapist of his son's obesity and requested a diet for him. He and his wife expressed futility about "doing anything with him." They occasionally took action of an interesting sort, considering their son's suspicious nature; for example, the father sneaked out early one morning to tell the milkman that he was to ignore any requests for ice cream. The therapist held fast to his recommendation that the patient would change himself when he was ready, and several sessions later the patient announced that he had lost some weight. As the therapist tried to congratulate him, the mother cut in to discuss her own weight problem, and the father topped her by recounting a rather bizarre episode in which he was found unconscious and taken to a hospital in peril of his life.

This sequence was characteristic for this family. The patient's statements tended to be ignored or rationalized away, the mother usually sounded a serious note about something, and the father topped it by telling something on himself which, while dramatic, inevitably made him out to be slightly foolish. A kind of closure was usually attained at the end of these sequences by the father, mother, and son all chuckling slightly at the father's expense. This sort of closed sequence, however, constitutes the sort of pathological family homeostasis that it is the therapist's business and duty to alter.

FURTHER TECHNICAL MEANS

As family therapy proceeds, we are ordinarily not much concerned with the topics and content of the family discussions, except perhaps when there is evident talking of one matter to avoid something else. Indeed, it may be valuable at times to shift the discussion from a hot topic to a less important one involving the same sort of family alignment and interaction, in the hope that the nature of the interaction can better be seen and some revision inaugurated while dealing with a more minor matter.

Such alteration of self-reinforcing and mutually destructive networks of interaction is the most general goal of our work with families, and our emphasis correspondingly is on means of influencing these patterns rather than on examining their content, or even on describing the pattern as such.

Our experience with this kind of repetitive pattern is that pointing it out to the family does little good. However, its meaning, intent, or focus can be shifted by the therapist's intervention; and after a-series of such interventions, the pattern loses some of its highly stereotyped repetitiousness. Various means may be essayed in relation to this formidable task, several of which have already been mentioned. Implication is a powerful tool in the therapist's hands; but making explicit what the family members communicate only implicitly can be equally important. Framing or interpretation of messages—in a communicational, not psychoanalytic, sense of interpretation—is most important, and occurs in many varieties: the therapist may frame his own message, and, equally important, he may reframe and reinterpret the messages of family members. By this means, the positive side of difficult or provocative behavior in the family can be shown, sense made out of craziness, and congruence out of incongruence. Such inverting is a powerful lever for change. Certain sorts of dualistic positive-and-negative messages also are important, such as criticism administered with personal attention for easier swallowing or a strong comment given in a mild tone; in this sort of "quiet bombshell" there is an evident similarity between our communicational orientation and more orthodox psychiatric thought and practice.

We may also give advice. However, our aim in advising is not to tell family members the proper thing to do; rather it is to enable them to accept interest, advice, and help, for they ordinarily are so defensive as to disqualify and reject whatever is offered, even if they have been demanding it. If we can present a little advice in an acceptable way, in accepting it from us as experts, they take a first step toward accepting from each other.

The giving of some rather specific instructions as a technique in therapy illuminates this area still further. We do not expect to achieve change directly by giving instructions on how to behave, and we ordinarily avoid doing so, especially on matters of obvious practical importance—although this is where our advice and instructions are most likely to be solicited. Instead, we are apt to choose an apparently minor matter—which still will be involved in some significant pattern of interaction—and give an instruction to do A, expecting that the person, from our knowledge of his reactions, will in fact do B, which will cause change C in a family relationship. An example may clarify this complicated but significant situation:

The mother of a 15-year-old schizophrenic boy was a very managing woman, taking over everything from her nearly mute son, her rather quiet husband, and also from the struggling therapist. Yet she was very unhappy and anxious. Finally she was able to say one day that she was upset because she felt that her husband was distant; she couldn't get in close touch with him. Yet she felt wrong if she reacted to this, even if only by becoming silently upset. The main emphasis was on the problem of feeling wrong uncontrollably, even when she thought she had some just cause for distress. The therapist then suggested that she could act to resolve this problem of feeling wrong, if she seriously wanted to, by following a simple instruction. After a pause, she agreed. The therapist's instruction was that, during the following week, she should deliberately do something that she considered wrong. The only conditions imposed were that the wrong was not to be a really serious one and was to involve some other family member in some way; other than that she should choose the action. During the next session, she revealed that the daring deed she had committed was subscribing to a book club.

The members of the research group laughed as they heard this section on the tape, thinking how constricted she was to commit such a minor sort of sin. However, they had failed to appreciate the limitations placed on the range of action in this family, because the father, who in the session heard for the first time what she had done, angrily disapproved. Although his reasons were a bit obscure, they appeared to concern the expense involved. In fact, since this was not great, and money was used by the father as a means of control, the mother's independence seems more important. From this episode, the therapist and the group as a whole learned a little more about why this woman had to breathe her sick son's every breath. The fact that she was severely controlling did not mean that she was not similarly controlled by herself and her husband. And if control is this severe, then even the small change of behavior, change of evaluation, and change in relationship with her husband that this act represented, though initiated by the therapist's instruction, may be correspondingly significant.

FAMILY PATHOLOGY AND THERAPY:
A THEORETICAL SUMMARY

Perhaps we can now utilize the preceding material to attempt a more condensed and general statement of our ideas on the pathology of these families and its treatment. Even though such a theoretical statement is bound to be oversimplified and incomplete at this stage of our knowledge, it will provide a basis for some comparison between our theoretical and therapeutic slants and those of other workers.

Summing up very broadly then, it appears that these families of schizophrenics are enmeshed in a pathological but very strong homeostatic system of family interaction. That is, regardless of their past history--although that might be enlightening--they are at present interacting in ways that are unsatisfying and painful to all, provocative of gross symptomatology in at least one, and yet powerfully self-reinforcing. Their overt behavior may appear varied or even chaotic, but beneath this a pervasive and persistent pattern can be discerned, and one that is quite resistant even to outside therapeutic efforts at change.

How and why is this so? On what basis may such homeostasis be clarified and understood? We may at least begin to do so by using further our basic concepts of the double bind and the still broader concept of the necessary multiplicity of messages, of different levels, in all communication. These ideas, which were helpful in understanding the occurrence of schizophrenic behavior, are also helpful in attacking the more fundamental problem level: Why does pathological behavior or organization persist, even under pressure to change? We have not solved this problem, but we can state a few leading ideas. First, the double bind pattern itself tends to be circular and interactive in a self-perpetuating way, even though we may speak of it carelessly as if it were a one-way matter, with a "binder" acting on a "victim." Actually, if A sends incongruent messages to B, B is very likely to respond with a correspondingly incongruent set of messages in reply. The one main difference likely to exist between their communications only serves to intensify the vicious circularity: If the incongruence between A's messages is concealed and B falls in with this, then the incongruence in B's reply is apt to be correspondingly exaggerated, the typical case for schizophrenic utterance. This in turn influences A toward further incongruence, even more concealed or denied, and so on. In three-party situations, [6] essentially the same process may occur. If A and B are parents giving incongruent messages to C, their child, C is likely to respond in a disturbed way with markedly incongruent messages and ones likely to have some reference to the family relationships; at this A and B are very likely to insist more strongly that there are no differences in what they think and say, rather than admitting differences, as we have described earlier.

_____

[6]Discussed in Weakland, footnote 3.

Second, the existence of a multiplicity of messages obviously offers great possibilities for interaction among family members in which nothing is ever clarified because both agreement and disagreement can be avoided. It is possible, with incongruent messages, to agree with another person, yet not agree, by agreeing at one level of message yet disagreeing at another or indicating that it is not really the speaker who is agreeing. And similarly with disagreement; this also can be no-yet-yes. We find that members of families in which there is a schizophrenic are likely to communicate largely by remarks we may call "disqualifying"-- that is, they effectively negate what someone else has said, only in an indirect way, so that statements are not really met. This sort of communication and its paralyzing effects have been particularly striking in some standard interviews that we have given experimentally, since these interviews focused on family organization, leadership, and planning, first by asking the family members to plan something they would like to do together, and then by inquiring who was in charge of the family.

This sort of problem may be seen from a somewhat different angle by considering the two sorts of families of schizophrenics discriminated by Lidz:[7] One ("skew" families) in which harmony is conveyed overtly, but with covert persistent disagreement; the other ("schism" families), in which there is constant overt scrapping yet the family members somehow remain together for many years. Both may be seen as types of pathological organization whose stability is related to the existence of such incongruent double messages about family relationships plus the avoidance of recognition and acknowledgment of such incongruence by family members.

Any move toward change or therapy, finally, immediately encounters difficulties similar to those just mentioned. The members of these families have long been adept at using incongruent messages. Thus, if some change in behavior or family organization is proposed, what is more likely than that it will be met with agreement that is not agreement; with disagreement that is not disagreement; with agreement from one member and disagreement from another, while they insist they are together on the matter,

---

[7] Theodore Lidz and Stephen Fleck. Schizophrenia, human integration, and the role of family. In The Etiology of Schizophrenia, pp. 323-345 (see footnote 3). For other references and more extensive discussion, see Weakland, footnote 3; pp. 380-382.

and so on? If a specific change can be brought about in the behavior of some member, it is likely to be negated by a shifting of the general context, by the same person or another: "Yes, my husband is behaving better to me now; but of course that's just because you told him to, not that he cares any more about me." Or a more general shift may be negated by a specific change; or the two parents may both change at once so that they remain on opposite sides of whatever fence divided them, even if reversed from their original stands. All this also throws light on why description or labeling of family behavior is usually ineffective, even where the members themselves appear to grasp it; thus we are more concerned with altering interaction than with "insight."

In other words, these families have a tremendous aptitude for "plus ça change, plus c'est la même chose." It appears increasingly clear to us as we work with them that to be effective we must meet them on their own ground, though with different orientation--toward positive change instead of defensive maintenance of a sick system. That is, the therapist must himself employ dual or multiple messages involving such incongruences as will serve to come to grips with the whole complexity of the messages of the family members he must deal with. A reconsideration of the techniques we have mentioned earlier shows readily enough that for many this is already explicitly so, and it is implicit for most of the others. That is, we have been concerned with using explicit statements that convey concealed and unexpected implicit meanings as well; with using content messages joined with framing statements; with giving instructions whose carrying-out will constitute a further message. We have spoken of this elsewhere, perhaps too narrowly, as the "therapeutic double bind"; the broad principle described here, of using multiple--and often incongruent--messages therapeutically, is what needs recognition, and then further investigation.

OURSELVES AND OTHERS: FAMILY THERAPY AS A
COMMUNICABLE DISEASE
Except for political rallies, baseball games, and burlesque shows, it is difficult to imagine a situation more capable of arousing enthusiasm among therapists than conjoint family therapy. It is not completely clear to us why this should be, but it does make us cautious about accepting new adherents and we do attempt to review our work with the limited objectivity available to us.

There is little question that exposure to conjoint family therapy alters the psychotherapeutic approach of the exposed, both in his private and research work. Most of those engaged in our family therapy research project have private practices on a part-time basis. It is fascinating and predictable to note that their psychotherapeutic approach undergoes at least the following changes:

1) The therapist will become more 'active' in individual therapy, especially in suggesting the meaning of other people's behavior vis-a-vis the patient.

(2) The therapist will be less interested in diagnosis or the accepted dynamic formulations; he will tend, rather, to describe his patients in terms of an interlocking milieu, consisting mainly of the immediate family situation, but drawing also upon the wider family context and sometimes including ethnic or subcultural factors.

(3) The therapist will greatly increase the number of couples he treats, mostly in the conjoint situation. We believe it is rare for our therapists not to have met the spouses of all their patients.

These tendencies, in other words, parallel several distinctive emphases in the orientation of our family therapy: activity of the therapist rather than passive listening; more concern for alteration of behavior than for 'insight'; more intense focus on the present than on the past; and more attention to interaction than to intrapersonal experience.

Perhaps two brief examples will illustrate how the family therapy bug affects its victim:

Example A. A catatonic young woman was discharged from a Midwestern state hospital because her parents were moving to California. She was referred to one of us for recommendations as to local hospital care. Although the patient was mute and stiff, she appeared evanescently pleased by the suggestion that if she and her parents were willing to start family therapy, we could see how it would work out to have her live at home, with a practical nurse assisting the mother during the daytime. She has remained out of the hospital now for two years and appears to be functioning fairly adequately. Previous to our family work, it would have been unthinkable that such a catatonic patient who did not appear to be in good contact would not be hospitalized.

Example B. On an emergency home visit, one of us met a 60-year-old woman who had made a mild suicidal gesture. She appeared to be in a typical agitated depression, and the question seemed to be where to hospitalize her and whether it should be in an institution where she would receive electroshock therapy. After speaking to her for a few minutes, the psychiatrist asked her daughter with whom she was living to join them; and he noted that, despite a smiling cooperative kindliness, not all was well between daughter and mother. When this was touched on, the daughter mentioned that she had her husband and her own 17-year-old daughter to worry about and perhaps her mother's attitude was a little bit too much. The mother sparked noticeably at this and implied that the daughter didn't have a complete romance with her husband and had in fact invited the mother to live with her partially on this account. The patient was not sent to a hospital but was seen in conjoint therapy with her daughter, son-in-law, and granddaughter. After a very brief time, the blocked communication in the family had noticeably improved and the mother decided she would like to live by herself. In retrospect, it seemed fairly certain that getting the patient's daughter involved after a few minutes of the initial visit, and the orientation of the therapist, altered what would have been fairly standard psychiatric disposition.

TRANSFERENCE, COUNTERTRANSFERENCE, AND INTERACTION

Many analysts have had strong doubts about the idea of family therapy, which are often put on transference and countertransference grounds. Thus the terms "transference and countertransference" are troublesome unless it is kept in mind that they refer strictly to aspects of a very special situation--psychoanalysis. We have no doubt that our therapists have feelings about the family members and vice versa; on the other hand, no clarity is achieved if we label such states of mind transference and countertransference. There are several reasons for this:

Transference is a manifestation related to the inactivity prescribed for standard psychoanalytic treatment. The patient, on the basis of minimal cues, creates a framework and embroiders it with past personal references. In conjoint psychotherapy, there is a good deal of activity, even if the therapist is only acting as a traffic cop. If skillfully managed, the interaction is largely among family members and not with the therapist. Thus we would consider the proper intervention when a wife is chopping her husband to ribbons, not to be "Look what you're doing

to the poor man, " but to ask _him_ if she always shows her attachment to him in this way. The wife will be fascinated awaiting his
reply and will be busy with her rebuttal.

That is, with so much interaction among the family members,
and active therapeutic focus on this, there is no emergence of
standard transference phenomena. What we do see can better be
labeled parataxic distortions, since the data consist of discrete
examples of expectations on the part of a family member that the
therapist does or does not fulfill. Some of these instances even
seem to be a combination of ignorance and misinformation as to
what one can legitimately expect of a therapist, while others
appear to result from explanatory concepts that the person
brought with him into therapy, such as, "All men are..."

It is difficult to explain the difference between these phenomena in individual and family therapy unless one has observed or
participated in both forms of psychotherapy. A statement by a
family member, which if it occurred in an individual psychotherapeutic session may be labeled evidence of transference, can have
a very different meaning in family therapy. Thus, a comment by
the wife that the therapist is the only one who has ever understood her is apt to be an expression of dissatisfaction with her
husband, a pointing out of a direction he should take; and before
the therapist can label this himself as father transference, the
husband's reaction will have to be dealt with, plus one of the
children, plus the wife's reaction to her husband's reaction, and
so on.

The same difficulties apply to countertransference. If the
therapist is active, he becomes aware of his feelings partially
through the kind of action he takes, and often not until a supervisory session. An experienced, fairly secure therapist may
change the direction of a beginning feeling in himself by taking
an action opposite to the feeling. For example, if he finds himself irritated by the mother's quietly nagging, martyred tone, he
may turn to the father and ask what he experienced in himself
during the time when the wife was speaking. On the surface, it
would appear that the therapist simply passes the buck to the
father and that this technique might be a fairly destructive one.
On the other hand, if it is kept in mind that the father has been
having thoughts for years about his wife's attitude, and that now
is his chance to express them with the support of another male
present, a different face is put on the situation. By the time the
husband has made his comments, the therapist may then be in a

mood to reaccept the wife and to help find out what she has to complain about. Such interlocking transactions are part of the ordinary family life and have been referred to in papers on everything from pecking order to role playing.

RESULTS

We are not yet in a position to support any claim that family therapy is better or worse than the more usual methods of treating schizophrenics. Insufficient time has elapsed, and unusual and difficult problems of evaluation are posed by our interest not only in the identified patient, but in the parents and siblings and especially in the functioning of the family as a whole, while means for evaluation at this level are largely lacking in psychiatry at present. Thus it is appropriate that the emphasis in this paper has been on our ideas and methods; we have pointed out that family therapy differs from individual therapy, in ways we have tried to outline, and that this difference helps to shape a new orientation in the therapist. We may, however, end by discussing briefly the inconclusive yet promising results of our therapeutic efforts so far.

Various studies have shown that prognosis for recovery from schizophrenia is importantly related to the history of the illness --that is, its duration, amount of hospitalization and other treatment without success, and so on. Therefore, our evaluative scheme for family therapy, with reference to the identified patients, is based on comparing the level of their social adaptation before family therapy and currently, against the background of information on the prior history of their illness. On this basis, our cases can hardly be considered other than difficult ones. We have worked with eighteen families so far. Of the identified schizophrenic patients in these families, eleven were males ranging in age from 13 to 41, and seven were females ranging in age from 14 to 34. Of these eighteen, six had been originally diagnosed as schizophrenic between 10 and 16 years ago, four between 5 and 10 years ago, and eight less than 5 years ago. Perhaps four of these eight were first seen by us as fairly new or acute cases, but fourteen of our eighteen patients could be labeled as already chronic cases when we first saw them. Some had been diagnosed in early childhood, as young as 3 years; the maximum age at first diagnosis was 25. Eleven of these patients had been hospitalized at some time, from a minimum of 2 months up to 6 years maximum, the average being 3 to 4 years. Of the seven patients never hospitalized, probably three or four were clinically sick enough to justify hospitalization and had avoided it only because they were so young or had such passive-with-drawing symptomatology that their behavior could still be tolerated or handled within the home.

Information on prior treatment other than hospitalization, although it is certainly not complete, shows that at least seven patients had received EST, one insulin shock, eight had had tranquilizing drugs, and twelve had received individual psychotherapy ranging from a minimum of 3 sessions to a maximum of 9 years of intermittent examination and treatment. In several cases family members--usually the mother--had also had some individual psychotherapy. In only four instances, all young persons and fresh cases, had there been no therapy before family treatment was started.

At the time of writing, our families had been seen, usually on a once-weekly basis for an hour or an hour and a half, from a minimum of 3 months up to 41 months in one case, the average being about 12 months. Most of our families are still in treatment, although four terminated therapy against our advice.

There were seven patients hospitalized at the outset of family therapy. Of these, one is still in the hospital, three are living at home and able to go out unaccompanied, one is living at home but working, one is living alone and caring for her child though still financially dependent on the parents, and one is living alone, working part-time but financially dependent on her parents. Thus, six of these seven have shown a noticeable improvement in terms of social adaptation and independence. Of the remaining patients, nine were young persons, mostly never hospitalized, who were living with parents and restricted to the home or, if going out, not productive--that is, not working or doing badly in school. All but two of these improved in such degree as starting to school again, changing from failure to passing, starting to work, or at least starting to go out unaccompanied, as did the two remaining patients who had previously been confined to their homes after release from hospitalization.

It is still more difficult to characterize results with the parents and siblings, and with the family as a whole. But, very broadly, it can be said that the other family members generally have improved, though less noticeably than the identified patients. More than half of the fathers were judged improved by their therapists, with the rest showing no distinct change. The picture for the mothers was similar except for two cases where it was judged that the mother was worse. And limited data on siblings showed about evenly divided improvement and no change, excepting again one sibling judged worse.

Finally, though it often appeared a severe course of treatment, all of our therapists seem to have been helped, without exception.

A REVIEW OF PSYCHIATRIC DEVELOPMENTS IN
FAMILY DIAGNOSIS AND
FAMILY THERAPY

Don D. Jackson
and Virginia M. Satir

We are presenting our brief observations on the history of family diagnosis and therapy, we trust, more in the spirit of Toynbee than in the style of the Encyclopaedia Britannica.

We must begin by defining what we are including under the rubric "family diagnosis and therapy" because the designation of "family" as a treatment unit, in contrast to a uniform understanding of the individual as the treatment unit, means different things to different people. A family approach, we believe, requires an orientation stressing sociocultural forces and explicitly acknowledging more diagnostic and prognostic implications of the "here and now" situation than might be subscribed to any clinical therapists generally.

Technically, using the family as a treatment unit has been interpreted differently by different clinicians. The different approaches seem to fall into the following general categories:

1. The members of a biological or nuclear family are treated conjointly, which means that all family members are seen together at the same time by the same therapist. The members of the family include parents, children, other significant relatives such as grandparents and aunts or uncles, and other significant non-relative people, with the selection dependent on relationships and not neces-

Reprinted from EXPLORING THE BASE FOR FAMILY THERAPY, (Nathan W. Ackerman, M. D. , Frances L. Beatman, and Sanford N. Sherman, eds.) pages 29-51, 1961. Copyright, Family Service Association of America, New York; reproduced by permission.

sarily on blood ties. This is our approach at the Mental Research Institute.

2. The members of a family are seen conjointly for diagnostic purposes, and family members are then assigned on an individual basis to different therapists who will work collaboratively. Another variation is to select one member for individual psychotherapy after a family diagnosis has been made. It is our impression that this latter practice is generally used when geographical circumstances, such as the patient's being in a hospital some distance from his home, necessitate it.

3. Family members are seen individually from the outset by a single therapist who then pieces together the picture of family interaction and continues to treat the family members individually. Family members may also be seen individually from the outset, each by a different therapist. The therapists then sit down together to pool their findings to try to arrive at a picture of family interaction--perhaps in much the same spirit as the family itself might do--with subsequent individual treatment. The family interaction is observed primarily at the level of collaboration.

All the above approaches are predicated on the necessity for viewing the symptoms of the identified patient or patients within the total family interaction, with the explicit theoretical belief that there is a relationship between the symptom of the identified patient and the total family interaction. The extent to which the therapist "believes" in family therapy will determine his emphasis on techniques that convey this orientation to the patient.

4. In another form of working with the family, the identified patient is seen in individual psychotherapy and family members are seen occasionally to determine how best to elicit their aid, or simply to urge them not to interfere with the patient's progress. We feel the utility of this method is limited. It is based on the theoretical concept that the patient alone is a sick unit, and that the other family members are well and capable of change in the interest of the patient. This approach emphasizes the existence of two units within the family--the identified patient as the sick unit and the other family members as the well unit.

It seems to us that, for clarity's sake, "family" should refer to parents and children (or other persons who are a part of the immediate social family), and the terms "diagnosis" and "therapy,"

and "concurrent," "conjoint," or "collaborative" should be employed to designate the exact nature of the technique being used.

A search of the <u>Cumulus Medicus</u> for the past thirty years for
papers in which the noun "family" appears, reveals that this designation relates to methods of study or treatment that can be considered "family oriented." We believe the terms "family diagnosis" and "therapy" should be restricted to those systems of
study where the therapist's impression of state X in subject A
carries probability statements about subject B; if B is in the
same nuclear family and at a different level, A's inferences
about B change A's probable state (behavior, motivation, and
so on) from X to X_1, X_2, and so on. In individual therapy,
the focus tends to be on how A feels about B or about himself,
without shifting levels.

One final point in connection with terminology. Although it is
possible to label what is meant by "the family," and to label the
approaches used to the family as a unit, the language used in
theoretical descriptions about family interaction reveals the need
to find new and more appropriate terminology that may correctly
define the concepts. Writers attempting to explain concepts of
family interaction seem to be struggling to apply to family interaction terminology that is useful in describing individual therapy,
with resulting unclear conclusions. At the present time, if we
were able to find a common denominator in all the literature about
description and analysis of family interaction, we would have a
greater pool of common observations and probably greater agreement about their significance.

SOME INFLUENTIAL FACTORS
The following general factors seem to us crucial in contributing to the development of family-oriented rather than individually-
oriented psychological observation and treatment.

1. Psychiatry, since the late 19th century, has been gradually
losing its fraternal position to medicine and is becoming instead
a cousin who, though a blood relative, springs from a different
family. Psychology, sociology, and anthropology are increasingly influencing the kind of psychological data obtained and the nature of the interpretation given these data. For example, it has
been recently reported that eldest sons of Indian families living
in Singapore are many times more vulnerable to a schizophrenic
psychosis than any other member of the Indian family or any of the
members of the Chinese or Malayan families who constitute the

other two main ethnic groups (27). Such a finding surely must eventually influence the diagnostic and therapeutic approach to the patient who is an Indian eldest son. Thus, in this simple example, we see how anthropology and sociology may make direct contributions to the etiology of emotional illness and consequently influence psychiatric practice.

2. The child guidance movement, which was initially developed through efforts of the juvenile court to treat delinquent children specifically, rather naturally expanded to look for and include expeditious and economical means to diagnose and treat neurotic and psychotic children. Experience, especially on the part of social workers, has led to the conclusion that treating the child is not enough and, more recently, that treating the child and the mother may not be enough. In 1942, Mildred Burgum published a paper (9) in which she demonstrated by statistics from a child guidance clinic that the father's role was ignored in the early approach to the family and that this fact might account for a high drop-out rate. Such findings have gradually become incorporated in child guidance practices. If the clinic is to keep the father involved, however, it means further manpower problems for the clinic and thus a push in the direction of family therapy. Our own group has discovered that the child who is labeled by the family as the patient is not necessarily the "sickest" in the family. Such datum casts doubt on the wisdom of seeing only the identified patient and the mother. A family approach thus comes to offer increased data that were not always available under the older methods, as well as possibilities for increased economy and research.

3. The psychoanalytic movement, which has been so largely responsible for loosening the ties between classical medicine and psychiatry, has been a prime influence in family diagnosis. Flugel, in The Psycho-Analytic Study of the Family, the first book of its kind, states, "It is probably that the chief practical gain that may result from the study of the psychology of the family will ensue more or less directly from the mere increase in understanding the nature of, and interactions between, the mental processes that are involved in family relationships." (11)

(a) Although psychoanalysis is a system that focuses on the individual, reference to the family has been appearing since Freud's case of little Hans. The classical Oedipus situation, originally an intrapsychic construct, has become increasingly interpersonal especially as the mother's pregenital influence has come to be recognized. The sociologist, Parsons, and others have expanded Freud's original notion into the broader framework of anthropology and sociology. The emphasis on ego psychology since the 1920's and the writings of the so-called neo-Freudian psychoanalysts have become increasingly interactive or transactional and thus have focused on the patient's significance to others, usually his family. Even the emphasis on intrapsychic objects by Klein, Fairbairn, Windicott, and others stirs a curiosity to discover these objects in the real world.

(b) Freud's extreme position in relation to the relatives of the patient has led to re-examination of his position and, on the part of some analysts, to a search for more workable arrangements. Freud issued an urgent warning against any attempt to engage the confidence or support of parents or relatives, confessing that he had little faith in any individual treatment of them. It was inevitable that individuals like Mittelman and Oberndorf would be challenged to test these dicta and thus lead to further developments toward a family concept.

(c) Another influence toward family studies, which has indirectly stemmed from the psychoanalytic movement, has to do with the disappointment in the results of this expensive and time-consuming technique and the possible relation of results to a change in the type of clinical material with which psychoanalysts deal. The shift in emphasis from symptom neuroses to character, marital, and child guidance problems has resulted in a broadening of analytic techniques with an emphasis on parameters and on psychoanalytically oriented psychotherapy.

(d) Child analysis failed to fulfill its initial promises as analysts discovered that even five one-hour sessions a week could not keep up, in most cases, with the influences of the remaining 163 hours at home. The number of child analysts who have stuck to their last is surprisingly small, and this fact must have had some influence in giving tacit approval for others to seek new techniques in treating children.

Thus, psychoanalysis has acted both in a positive and in a negative sense to expedite the family movement and it is obvious that many of the authorities on family diagnosis and therapy are psychoanalytically trained. This latter factor has contributed to a complication of which we shall speak later--the current lack of a language for family diagnosis and therapy.

4. Gradually an awareness has been developing of the existence of health within the same framework in which pathology exists, which has led to a beginning re-evaluation of the prognosis of emotional illness. The concept of "adaptation" has helped focus on the "why" of the illness rather than on fixed psychopathological symptoms. Jahoda's recent book on mental health and mental illness (18) introduces dimensions of health and emphasizes the needs to see the "sick person" or "sick family" in dimensions of health as well as illness. A diagnosis of a sick person described entirely in terms of pathology often presents a dreary, hopeless picture. None but the most brave, foolish, or dedicated would attempt the apparently hopeless. However, a visit to the home, a session with the whole family, can reveal to the therapist unsuspected pockets of ability of family members to relate, to share a joke, or even to be a little kind to each other.

5. Another important factor in the development of a family approach has emerged from the psychotherapy of schizophrenia which blossomed in the thirties and underwent an increased growth rate during the forties. Federn and others thought that the schizophrenic's irrepressible id created an atmosphere in which the therapist needed to focus on current situations and actual experience. Sullivan, from a somewhat different point of view, advised the same procedure and cautioned that reality factors existed as a kernel in all the patient's distorted productions. These points of view brought the therapist more in contact with the patient's real experience within his family, and this practice was strengthened by the eloquent writings of Fromm-Reichmann. In addition, the hospital management of schizophrenics involved visits from relatives and led to a suspicion that these relatives were difficult people to handle. It is interesting that a recent report by G. W. Brown of the Maudsley Hospital confirms the validity of this early suspicion (8). He demonstrated that the success or failure of chronic schizophrenic patients after leaving the hospital depended on whether they returned to their parents or spouse, or were able to live alone in a lodging or with siblings. The highest failure was in those returning to their parents and in those returning to a spouse and was not related to their diagnosis or to their prognosis on admission. On the other hand, if a married patient was able to return to his spouse and remain outside the hospital over three months, he achieved a higher level of social adjustment than any of the other schizophrenics studied. Other recent studies have revealed that the single most significant correlate of the patient's length of stay in the hospital was the number of visits he received during his first two months of hospitalization

(10, 37). In the face of such discoveries, it becomes increasingly difficult for the therapist of the schizophrenic to remain purely patient-oriented.

6. A final factor is an augmentation of point 1, concerning the growth of anthropology, psychology, and sociology and their increasing clinical orientation. A psychiatrist interested in the family would not think of ignoring the work of Parsons and Bales (28), any more than he would overlook Ackerman's recent book (1). Two of the most promising avenues of exploration of family interaction lie in the field of social psychology and its study of small groups and in the field of communication and information theory, largely peopled by experimental and clinical psychologists.

The factors that we have mentioned are not mutually exclusive and interdigitate in a way that makes it difficult to tease them apart. For example, the child mental health program was largely conducted in clinics where non-psychiatrists did the bulk of the work and where finances were of great moment. In the search for efficacious brief methods it was a recognized fact that a social worker could more properly interview parents than could a psychoanalyst since the latter would be uncomfortable in crossing tradition-bound lines that dedicated him to a single patient. On the other hand, the fact that a good deal of family work has evolved from interest in schizophrenia is due to slightly different combinations of circumstances. Schizophrenia, an increasingly important illness with no predictable means of cure, was psychologically everyone's baby but no one's baby, and therefore analysts, psychiatrists, and social scientists were free to contribute to and experiment in its treatment.

Whatever the various factors contributing to the evolution of family diagnosis and therapy, one thread runs rather clearly through the history of modern psychoanalytically-oriented psychiatry. This is the gradual development of concepts from a monadic viewpoint to dyadic and currently, triadic or larger. Even though Flugel saw the need of studying family members, he used his study of individual family members and of family systems in order to increase the knowledge of the individual. His approach, therefore, is essentially monadic. We have not come a great distance from his position, as witness the words of Spiegel and Bell:

> Practice may or may not follow theory faithfully. The dynamic theories of psychopathology and the findings de-

rived through their use have been largely individual-centered. However, these theories have been constructed in such a way that the individual is conceived as a self-contained system becoming relatively closed early in life. Even the social and cultural variance of these theories share this assumption. We do not find evidence that treatment procedures vary significantly from what one would expect on the basis of theory. In the context of the habitual lip-service paid to the family as a whole, isolated groups or individuals have attempted to maintain a focus on a family unit in diagnostic formulations and treatment procedures but attempts to bring the family to the forefront have not been established (39).

The one portion of this statement we wish to disagree with is the authors' claim that there are no treatment procedures that vary significantly. It seems to us that Nathan Ackerman's treatment of a family at the Family Mental Health Clinic and our own approach at the Mental Research Institute are significantly different from any recognized method of individual therapy. It is possible that some therapists would be shocked at what goes on in family therapy because the approach is so much a transactional one rather than a careful hovering attention to the individual's apparent thoughts and feelings.

The literature reveals relatively little that could be described as organized formulations that would set the theoretical base of those who diagnose and treat emotional illness of a labeled patient as a part of sick family interaction, apart from the theory underlying the treatment of an individual. The reason may be that concepts surrounding individual diagnoses and treatment are pretty universally accepted and form the primary content of respectable professional training. Much of the writing deals with the family in relation to schizophrenia, a disorder that is set apart from neuroses and has not had an important part in psychoanalytic theory. Any resemblance between interaction in families where schizophrenia exists and interaction in families where other forms of emotional illness exist is difficult for some individuals to accept. In the same vein, these same individuals make a sharp distinction between the techniques of treating schizophrenic patients and non-psychotic patients.

EVENTS LEADING TO ACCEPTANCE OF CONJOINT TREATMENT

After some soul-searching and much library searching we would like to present some of the events that we believe have played an important part in the relatively new idea of conjoint family diagnosis and therapy. We use schizophrenia as a model for simplicity's sake and because of our greater familiarity with this subject.

The following events are some of the high spots in the approach to conjoint work with the families of schizophrenics--a type of treatment that is apparently less than ten years of age.

1911: Freud wrote his famous Schreber case (13). The dynamics of paranoia were discussed and were seen to have defensive aspects and underlying dynamics which made schizophrenia more than a cerebral defect. Incidentally, in the description of this case are allusions to "wife" and "mother" which are of interest to students of schizophrenia.

1916: Rudin's monograph on the genetics of schizophrenia appeared (34). Patients' families were interviewed and a connection was made between their difficulties and the patients'. During the twenties and thirties some of Rudin's students published further studies of the families of schizophrenic index cases. Especially important were those studies in which the children of schizophrenic parents were examined and found to evince many mental disorders including neuroses and manic-depressive disorder. Although the approach was biological, the schizophrenic and his family were nevertheless brought together for study and the lack of nice. Mendelian findings raised the question of social forces.

1920: Moreno and others began group psychotherapy with hospitalized patients (26). The whole group therapy movement has had a definite, if not obvious, effect on family theory and therapy, since it pointed up the value of analyzing interaction as it occurred between individuals. Through witnessing interaction, the group therapist was able to improve his diagnosis. Identifying interaction and interpreting this interaction in terms of motivation were means by which psychological growth was enhanced.

1927: Sullivan reported on his spectacular work with schizophrenics at the Sheppard and Enoch Pratt Hospital (41), where the transactions that went on between the hospital personnel and the patients were seen to lead to behavioral changes when the response on the part of the staff member was changed so that it did not meet the patient's usual expectations as he had come to experience this in his own family. Sullivan saw that, in the patient's mind, the staff was an extension of his family and that he responded and dealt with them in the same way. Thus, Sullivan emphasized the importance of the hospital family, that is the physician, nurses and aides, in contributing to the patient's recovery.

<u>1934</u>: Kasinin and his colleagues described the parent-child relationship of some schizophrenics and implied that this relationship was an important and specific etiological factor (20). Later Kasinin described a pair of identical twins discordant for schizophrenia and described differences in their relationship vis-a-vis the family.

<u>1934</u>: Hallowell published an article on culture and mental disorder (14), one of the early attempts to demonstrate the importance of social factors in psychoses.

<u>1938</u>: Ackerman wrote on "The Unity of the Family" (2), conceptualizing a clinical purpose in viewing the family as an entity when dealing with individual disturbance.

<u>1939</u>: Beaglehole published a ten-year study of schizophrenia in New Zealand (5) comparing the incidence in the white and native Maori populations. The difference was great enough to invite the citing of family and culture as possible causative factors.

<u>1939</u>: Pollock and others published <u>Heredity and Environmental Factors in the Causation of Manic-Depressive Psychoses and Dementia Praecox</u> (31). Among other things, this volume indicated that schizophrenic patients might have a special position in the family, for example, being the more financially dependent.

<u>1939</u>: Abram Kardiner's book, <u>The Individual and His Society</u>, appeared (19).

<u>1943</u>: Sherman and Kraines published an article entitled "Environmental and Personality Factors in Psychoses" (36).

<u>1944</u>: L.S. Penrose described mental illness in husband and wife as a contribution to the study of associative mating, where essentially it was postulated that mate selection might be a means of groping for health (29).

<u>1945</u>: Richardson brought forth his book, <u>Patients Have Families</u> (33). This was in part an attempt to formulate some family diagnoses rather than treating the individual vis-a-vis his family group.

1950: Reichard and Tillman published an article entitled "Patterns of Parent-Child Relationships in Schizophrenia" (32).

1950: Ackerman and Sobel wrote "Family Diagnosis: An Approach to the Pre-School Child" (3), which inverted the typical child guidance approach and highlighted the understanding of family processes as a means of understanding the young child.

1951: Ruesch and Bateson published their famous book, Communication, the Social Matrix of Psychiatry (35). Many of their contributions foreshadowed the current interest in communication, information theory, and feedback mechanisms.

1954: Stanton and Schwartz published The Mental Hospital (40). Among other important contributions was their discovery that acute upsets in schizophrenic patients' therapy coincided with a covert disagreement between the administrator and the therapist. A similar phenomenon in the family context was discussed recently in a paper by Weakland and Jackson (43).

1954: Wahl described antecedent factors in the histories of 392 schizophrenics (42). The importance of psychological and family events stood out clearly in this group of young males hospitalized while in the military service.

1954: John Spiegel published a paper, "New Perspectives in the Study of the Family" (38). A later report of the Committee on the Family of the Group for the Advancement of Psychiatry, prepared by Kluckhohn and Spiegel (21), has become a classic in this field.

1954: Jackson presented a paper to the American Psychiatric Association entitled "The Question of Family Homeostasis" (17), in which he described some psychological upsets occurring in family members in relation to improvement on the part of the identified patient. Parental interaction patterns were tentatively related to specific symptoms in the patient and the concept "schizophrenogenic mother" was rejected as being incomplete and misleading.

1956: Bateson and others presented some ideas on a communication theory of schizophrenia which were based, in part, on conjoint therapy with schizophrenic patients and their families (4).

1957: Bowen presented a paper at the American Orthopsychiatric Association entitled "Study and Treatment of Five Hospitalized

Family Groups Each with a Psychotic Member" (7). His findings, based on the most intensive family study ever undertaken, supported the findings of Lidz and others who had observed the fluctuating nature of symptoms from one family member to another as changes within the family interaction were taking place. Further, there was the observation that the nature and kind of symptom bore a strong resemblance to the content and nature of the total family interaction.

1957: Midelfort published The Family and Psychotherapy (25). Working in a small Wisconsin community, he capitalized on the hospital's traditional use of relatives to assist in the care of the patients, by involving families of schizophrenics and depressed patients in brief therapy.

1957: Lidz and his co-workers published "The Intra-familial Environment of the Schizophrenic Patient" (24). They have subsequently published a number of outstanding papers in this area.

1958: Wynne and others described "Pseudo-Mutuality in the Family Relationships of Schizophrenics" (45) in which they stressed the discrepancy between a superficial and a deeper look at these families.

The way in which ideas about family therapy and diagnosis have come about is clearly evolutionary rather than revolutionary. The impetus was provided by the continuing search for further knowledge about the causes of mental and emotional illness and a more effective means of treatment.

As one looks over the literature of the last fifty years, one notes the patchwork pattern, in a chronological sense, of reports of successful treatment results that came about through a new method of treatment or new knowledge about the causes of illness. When one assembles and analyzes these reports, the direction toward our present concepts about treating illness as an integral part of the total family interaction can be seen as slowly evolving and inevitable.

At the present time there is not yet a well-defined, total, conceptual framework for diagnosis and treatment of the family, but some isolated brave souls have provided us with important experiences and research findings which, if integrated, may well be the beginning of a validatable conceptual framework.

SPECIAL CONTRIBUTIONS

Since 1958, the number of contributions that could be listed would more than equal the brief and incomplete list already given. From the above chronological list we have omitted several names only to offer them special mention. They are Eugen Bleuler, Adolph Meyer, and Manfred Bleuler. Among them, they have exerted tremendous influence in bridging the vast gulf in conceptualizing relative influences on human behavior from neurone to family. Bleuler devoted more of his famous book (6) to the so-called secondary symptoms of schizophrenia than to the primary ones, and laid the basis for psychological therapy in this disorder, particularly by his humanitarian approach and his observations on the patients' response to human contact. Adolph Meyer, originally a neuropathologist, stressed the individual's experiences, present and past, and helped bring schizophrenia out from under the microscope. The life history form that Meyer evolved must have brought parental characteristics to the attention of his students even though the parents were not present in the flesh. Many American psychiatrists have stressed their debt to Meyer, including Sullivan and two of his students, Leo Kanner and Theodore Lidz, and have contributed much to our understanding of family interaction in the schizophrenic disorders. Finally, to Manfred Bleuler goes the credit for synthesizing the methods of population genetics, and he and Book have removed the focus of the schizophrenic genetic study from the index case to the epidemiology of local populations. Bleuler's interest is indicated by the fact that when one of his associates discovered eight of the families of fifty schizophrenic index cases were reported in the hospital chart as normal, he went to visit them in their homes and made his own observations. He was, needless to say, disillusioned about the good impression they had made at the hospital.

The early association of the schizophrenic family, via the suggestion of poor protoplasm, with mental illness, mental deficiency, criminality, epilepsy, and tuberculosis has undergone sweeping changes, and yet these very studies unwittingly helped us focus on the "family" as an object of study. As evidence for the hereditary or infectious etiology of mental and social disorders waned, it was a natural step to ask, "All right, but why do they appear to be familial?" Perhaps the familial incidence of pellagra and the subsequent discovery of its relation to family eating habits played a part in this shift of emphasis.

It is obvious then that the family approach owes much to many and that these contributors have been from both the biological and the psychological sides of the fence. We realize that it is not considered good form to dichotomize; yet such dichotomy does very strongly exist in our science. Using the family as a treatment unit seems to us to be a recognition that the patient does not get sick alone, nor does he get well alone. Furthermore, it is consistent with a common observation: that people direct love, hate, fear, and destructiveness toward someone, which implies interaction; done by oneself, such action does not count for much.

Conjoint family therapy validates the widely accepted personality theory that the learning about handling love, hate, anger, and fear takes place in the nuclear family. In our opinion this learning then becomes the basis upon which any family interaction is shaped. By the nature of things, it influences the development of individual self-esteem and consequently the individual's behavior.

PREDICTIONS AND PORTENTS

Since no red-blooded historian these days is content merely to report, we shall take the liberty of naming current trends and possible future trends that we feel will be important in shaping the development and outcome of family diagnosis and therapy. These trends will be listed under certain topics for the sake of convenience.

1. Psychoanalysis

We feel that just as events point to increasing union between psychiatry, the family, and social science, there will be no such union in the main current of psychoanalysis for some time to come. Although there is a small group of psychoanalysts who are interested in participating in family studies and research, there is a much larger group who do not consider this work immediately relevant to their own interests, and even a rather hard-bitten group who feel that current family approaches are superficial and tangential and can in no way be compared scientifically with the depth analysis of psychoanalytic therapy. There is also a group of well meaning psychoanalysts who are attempting to correlate and collate family data with their own observations as individuals, but who unwittingly do the family movement a disservice. This is because some of them feel that knowledge about family individuals is old stuff and is now merely being refurbished. Their descriptions of family work are largely couched in the monadic framework of psychoanalytic terminology and are still essentially individual. They have not yet become convinced that the parts are greater than the whole; their main tenet is that the treatment of a family is theoretically impractical because of the difficulty the therapist has in handling more than one transference at the same time. This latter observation is part of the reason why family diagnosis and therapy needs a new terminology since the concept of transference cannot be carried over in its entirety from monadic encounters on the couch to experiences a single therapist has with multiple family members.

We feel that the concept of family diagnosis and therapy owes much of its current position to psychoanalysis. We predict that there will be an increasing divergence between the two groups. The divergence is due partly to the inapplicability of psychoanalytic terminology to family work, and partly to the fact that the majority of analysts will probably remain interested in their own line of endeavor and find the shift to a family orientation rather difficult to make. This situation has not been unknown to science previously. Witness the findings in electromagnetics of Clark and Maxwell, and the change in concepts following Einstein's contributions. The observations of the electromagnetic theorists were not rejected because a broader conceptualization made its appearance. The current scene reveals evidence of friction and we hope the struggle will not produce a generation of fence-sitters who are waiting to see how the whole business comes out, but will instead serve to stimulate all clinicians to look at all new data rationally and objectively.

2. The Social Sciences

In contrast to its relationship with psychoanalysis, the future of the diagnosis and therapy of the family through its linkage with the social sciences appears very promising. Several recent and current efforts point up possible avenues for exploration.

a. The family is seen as the unit of health, both physical and psychological, a concept crystallized by the publication of Richardson's book, Patients Have Families (33). We all have experienced or have been aware of episodic outbreaks of various illnesses in families. Even such an obvious factor as contagion does not always explain these outbreaks and many times there appear to be inexplicable combinations of infections, psychosomatic disorders, and "accidents." Just as we know little about the siblings of the identified patient, we know next to nothing about family disease patterns.

b. Foote and Cottrell in Identity and Interpersonal Competence (12), and Parson and Bales in their volume on family interaction (28) have pioneered efforts to devise operational definitions and measurements describing families.

c. Spiegel and Kluckhohn have focused on family cultural patterns and taught us not to mix our observations indiscriminately. It appears that the family researcher has to be pro-segregation or his generalizations will not hold up.

d. Similarly in the socioeconomic arena, Kohn and Clausen (22), Hollingshead and Redlich (16), and others have indicated important differences in families as far as their socioeconomic level and their beliefs, values, and child-rearing practices are concerned. Kohn has found in his Washington studies that the mother is the accepted head of the household in most of his lower-class material. [1] What adjustments, then, must one make in using the term "Oedipus complex" if he would generalize from lower- to middle-class families?

e. Pollak, in his work at the Jewish Board of Guardians, has demonstrated how invaluable the efforts of a sociologist may be in shaping psychopathological concepts (30). His approach escapes from the closed system of psychiatric nosology and his concepts lend themselves to further expansion by other workers.

f. Westley and Epstein at McGill University are demonstrating the importance of choosing a healthy index case rather than the traditional sick one (44). If their conclusions are verified--for example, that some of their healthy subjects come from homes wherein the parents maintain an atrocious sex life--then some of the basic concepts we have borrowed from psychoanalysis and indiscriminately used in studying the family need careful scrutiny.

g. Finally, I want to mention one of the outstanding and certainly most indefatigable workers in the family area, Reuben Hill (15). He and his associates at the University of Minnesota are assaying the entire literature of marriage and the family with the idea of organizing concepts, pointing up promising leads, and outlining areas of conflicting data.

CONCLUSION

None of us knows what system or systems will be worked out in the area of family diagnosis and therapy, but without doubt they will differ greatly from anything that currently appears in psychiatric textbooks. The possibilities are legion, but the current emphasis on data-processing via machines will probably influence the development of family description.

---

[1] Melvin L. Kohn, personal communication.

The importance of social sciences in this area probably means a greater focus on systems of health, rather than disease, which has been the traditional occupation of psychiatrists. Current promising concepts include family homeostasis, coalitions within the family and their stability, role-playing, acquisition of family models, three-generation theory, the theoretical applications of the game theory, decision-making, recognition of resemblance, and so on.

In our work at the Mental Research Institute, we have been tremendously impressed with such a simple matter as the difference in goal-directedness of healthy versus psychologically sick families. During a structured interview, the family is asked to plan something together—a trip, a vacation, an acquisition, anything. The healthier family seems to operate on the premise that the good of the individual rests in the greatest good for all. Even lively sparks of sibling rivalry fail to get the family machinery off its course; the operation seems unequivocally focused on the goal, rather than on the relationships between the family members who are trying to achieve that goal. The sicker families have difficulty even in fantasying that they might plan something as a group; should they attempt a plan, one member is apt to comment at a meta level about another's suggestion. That is, it becomes not a question of whether A prefers the beach. There is great harkening back to the past and even jumping to the future with the implication that it doesn't make any difference since it will not work out anyhow. Such processes as co-operation, collaboration, and compromise can be studied microscopically in small sections of recorded interviews and related to the enormous literature in social psychology on the nature of small group process. Family movies help us discover learned mannerisms, disqualifications, via nonverbal behavior, and so on.

Another way of studying family interaction is to adumbrate a set of explicit and implicit rules under which the family appears to be operating, which can be observed clinically in terms of what family members may or may not overtly expect of each other. If this notion has any value, we eventually hope to find differences in rules, and rules about rules, in psychologically healthy versus psychologically ill families. For example, it is our impression that the family of the chronic schizophrenic is guided by a rigid set of rules which are largely covert. These families do not like to think of themselves as being rigid and they do not explicitly acknowledge what the rules are. When a rule is made more explicit, it automatically is called into question and this produces family anxiety.

Rules may be called into question if they are stated too overtly. A may challenge a particular rule and B will then point out how this particular rule does not fit in this particular instance. Rules may be called into question if a member threatens withdrawal from the group. It may be one of the covert rules not to acknowledge the possibility of independence. Withdrawal may be interpreted as rebellion against certain rules. The particular rule that A is alleged to be rebelling against may be revealed by the kind of implication the other family members attribute to his reason for withdrawal. Rules are called into question if they are exposed to an outsider's opinion; for example, the opinion of the therapist. This may mean some tricky foot work for the therapist if he is to keep the show on the road.

On the other hand, if rules are too closely followed, then a skew will result because the enforcement of each rule becomes a caricature of previous rules and a model for future ones. This was observed during the 1930's by Lasswell in his work with large companies (23). He noted that if the boss was a short man with a bow tie and a cigar, the assistant boss would be even shorter with an even bigger cigar. Similarly, the schizophrenic patient is apt to caricature the rules in his family. It is this behavior that becomes labeled as "sick" by the family and may provoke both laughter and anger on their part. Generally, the sick family will attribute the greatest evil possible to the breaking of a rule, but at the same time they may excuse it. This contradictory behavior is not unknown in government. If a citizen complains, he may be labeled as unpatriotic and a scoundrel; if he does not complain he may suffer from gross inequities. Rationalizations are invaluable in handling such situations whether they are claims that the opposition is trying to cause trouble or, as in a family, the parents claim that the school system is outmoded and additionally that their child happened to get the worst teacher in school. All these maneuvers result in denying and obscuring the facts. A family governed by a rigid set of covert rules finds itself unable to deal with the vicissitudes of life, whether pleasurable or painful, and yet the family pact to hold to the rules may give to outsiders the illusion of strength. The inadequacy of the rules is shown by their not being discussed or debated and by the family's rationalizing each unfortunate happening as a separate chance matter. This concept of rules can be very directly translated into the therapeutic effort. For example, one family had a rule that the mother treasured loyalty above all else and had a right to feel hurt if a family member were critical of her, especially if this should happen within earshot of an outsider. A therapist was able to convince the husband that <u>true</u> loyalty demanded that he be able to be critical of his wife (if only via thought), since true loyalty consists in relating to the total person including both his assets and liabilities. To relate only to the assumed assets would be merely blind following.

When communication within the family is studied, data about health and pathology become available. The social scientist, lacking the bias toward disease that is part of medical training, is in a better position than the psychiatrist to do research in this area.

SUMMARY

In general, it is our impression that family diagnosis and therapy have come a long way from the classic monadic description of early psychoanalysis. The trend, influenced by many contributions from many fields, has been toward a horizontal and vertical expansion. Horizontally, more members have been included, more cultures and more socioeconomic data. Vertically, levels of interaction, communication, and information have been taken into consideration to replace a simple stimulus-response description, or more colloquially, a "who did <u>what</u> to whom" orientation.

Currently, the crying need seems to be for a useful language to describe multilevel interaction. Even a single message is multileveled, and the response is multileveled and related in a complex way to the first message. The context adds at least another level.

With regard to therapy specifically, we feel that all psychotherapists are related to change and growth and that conjoint family therapy offers one of the most impressive laboratories for studying growth and change available to the researcher. In only the last few years, many aspects of the individual's emotional growth or lack of it that would previously have been labeled "constitutional" have been interpreted as part of the matrix of family interaction.

REFERENCES

1. Ackerman, N. W. <u>The Psychodynamics of Family Life</u>, Basic Books, New York, 1958.
2. Ackerman, N. W. The unity of the family. <u>Archives of Pediatrics</u>, 55, No. 1:51-62, 1938.
3. Ackerman, N. W, and Sobel, R. Family diagnosis: an approach to the pre-school child. <u>Am. J. Orthopsychiatry</u>, 20, No. 4:744-753, 1950.

4. Bateson, G., Jackson, D. D., Haley, J., and Weakland, J. H. Toward a theory of schizophrenia. Behavioral Sci., 1, No. 4:251-264, 1956. Reprinted in Don D. Jackson (Ed.), Communication, Family, and Marriage (Vol. 1, Human Communication Series), Science and Behavior Books, Palo Alto, California, 1968.

5. Beaglehole, E. Social Change in the South Pacific, Macmillan Co., New York, 1958.

6. Bleuler, E. Dementia Praecox, or the Group of Schizophrenias, International Universities Press, New York, 1952.

7. Bowen, M., Dysinger, R. H., Brodey, W. M., and Basamania, B. Study and treatment of five hospitalized family groups each with a psychotic member. Read at the Annual Meeting of the American Orthopsychiatric Association, Chicago, Ill., March 8, 1957.

8. Brown, G. W. Experiences of discharged chronic schizophrenic patients in various types of living group. Milbank Memorial Fund Quarterly, 37, No. 2:105-131, 1959.

9. Burgum, M. The father gets worse: a child guidance problem. Am. J. Orthopsychiatry, 12, No. 3:474-485, 1942.

10. Carstairs, G. M., and Brown, G. W. (Maudsley Hosp., London, England). A census of psychiatric cases in two contrasting communities. J. Ment. Sci., 104, No. 434:72-81, 1958.

11. Flugel, J. C. The Psycho-Analytic Study of the Family, Hogarth Press, London, p. 217, 1921.

12. Foote, N., and Cottrell, L. S., Jr. Identity and Interpersonal Competence, Univ. of Chicago Press, Chicago, 1955.

13. Freud, S. Psycho-analytic notes upon an autobiographical account of a case of paranoia. Vol. 3. Collected Papers, Basic Books, New York, 1959, pp. 387-416.

14. Hallowell, A. I. Culture and mental disorder. J. Abnorm. & Soc. Psychiatry, 29, No. 1:1-9, 1934.

15. Hill, R. A critique of contemporary marriage and family research. Social Forces, 33, No. 3:268-277, 1955.

16. Hollingshead, A. B., and Redlich, F. C. Social Class and Mental Illness, John Wiley and Sons, New York, 1958.

17. Jackson, D. D. The question of family homeostasis. Psychiat. Quart. Suppl., 31, No. 1:79-90, 1957. Reprinted in Don D. Jackson (Ed.), Communication, Family, and Marriage (Vol. 1, Human Communication Series), Science and Behavior Books, Palo Alto, California, 1968.

18. Jahoda, M. Current Concepts of Positive Mental Health, Basic Books, New York, 1958.

19. Kardiner, A. The Individual and His Society, Columbia Univ. Press, New York, 1939.

20. Kasanin, J., Knight, E., and Sage, P. The parent-child relationship in schizophrenia. J. Nerv. and Ment. Dis., 79, No. 3:249-263, 1934.

21. Kluckhohn, F. R., and Spiegel, J. P. Integration and conflict in family behavior. Report No. 27, Group for the Advancement of Psychiatry, Topeka, Kansas, 1954.

22. Kohn, M. L. and Clausen, J. A. Social isolation and schizophrenia. Am. Sociol. Rev., 20, No. 3:265-273, 1955.

23. Lasswell, H. D., The Psychopathology of Politics, Univ. of Chicago Press, Chicago, 1930.

24. Lidz, T. et al. The intrafamilial environment of the schizophrenic patient, I. the father. Psychiatry, 20, No. 4:329-342, 1957.

25. Midelfort, C. F. The Family in Psychotherapy, McGraw-Hill, New York, 1957.

26. Moreno, J. L. The First Book on Group Psychotherapy, 5th ed., Beacon House, New York, 1957.

27. Murphy, H. B. M. Culture and mental disorder in Singapore. Culture and Mental Health, Marvin K. Opler (Ed.), Macmillan Co., New York, 1959, pp. 291-316.

28. Parsons, T., and Bales, R. F. Family Socialization and Interaction Process, Free Press, Glencoe, Ill., 1955.

29. Penrose, L. S. Mental illness in husband and wife: a contribution to the study of associative mating. Psychiat. Quart. Suppl., 18, No. 2:161-166, 1944.

30. Pollak, O. Integrative Sociological and Psychoanalytic Concepts, Russell Sage Foundation, New York, 1956.

31. Pollock, H. M., et al. Heredity and Environmental Factors in the Causation of Manic-Depressive Psychoses and Dementia Praecox. State Hospitals Press, Utica, N. Y., 1939.

32. Reichard, S., and Tillman, C. Patterns of parent-child relationships in schizophrenia. Psychiatry, 13, No. 2:247-257, 1950.

33. Richardson, H. B. Patients Have Families, Commonwealth Fund, New York, 1945.

34. Rudin, E. Vererbung und Enstehung geistiger Storungen, I. Zur Vererbung und Neuentstehung der Dementia Praecox. Monographien aus dem Gesamt-Gebiete der Neurologie und Psychiatrie, 12, Springer, Berlin, 1916.

35. Ruesch, J., and Bateson, G. Communication, the Social Matrix of Psychiatry, Norton, New York, 1951.

36. Sherman, I. C., and Kraines, S. S. Environmental and personality factors in psychoses. J. Nerv. and Ment. Dis., 97, No. 6:676-691, 1943.

37. Sommer, R.   Visitors to mental hospitals. Mental Hygiene, 40, No. 1:8-15, 1959.
38. Spiegel, J. P.   New perspectives in the study of the family. Marriage and Family Living, 16, No. 1:4-12, 1954.
39. Spiegel, J. P., and Bell, N. W.   The family of the psychiatric patient. American Handbook of Psychiatry, 1, Basic Books, New York, 1959, p. 134.
40. Stanton, A. H., and Schwartz, M. S.   The Mental Hospital, Basic Books, New York, 1954.
41. Sullivan, H. S.   The onset of schizophrenia. Am. J. Psychiatry, 7:105-134, 1927.
42. Wahl, C. W.   Some antecedent factors in the family histories of 392 schizophrenics. Am. J. Psychiatry, 110, No. 9: 668-676, 1954.
43. Weakland, J. H., and Jackson, D. D.   Patient and therapist observations on the circumstances of a schizophrenic episode. Am. Med. Assn. Arch. Neurol. & Psychiat., 79, No. 4: 554-574, 1954. Reprinted in Don D. Jackson (Ed.), Communication, Family, and Marriage (Vol. 1, Human Communication Series), Science and Behavior Books, Palo Alto, California, 1968.
44. Westley, W. A.   Emotionally healthy adolescents and their family backgrounds. The Family in Contemporary Society, Iago Galdston (Ed.), International Universities Press, New Yori, 1958, pp. 131-147.
45. Wynne, L. C. et al.   Psuedo-mutuality in the family relationships of schizophrenics. Psychiatry, 21, No. 2:205-220, 1958.

FAMILY THERAPY AS A RESEARCH ARENA

John H. Weakland

No one who has attempted or even observed family therapy--
meaning conjoint treatment of a family group--would think it in-
apt to call the family treatment situation an arena. There, with
a therapist as actual observer, and also as representing a wider
audience, the members present family dramas, spectacles, and
often contests. But this as a research arena? Can it be, and
should it be even if it can be?

My own answer is "yes" to both questions, and I would like here
to discuss 1) how the family therapy situation offers some special potentialities for important research and 2) why, at least at
this stage of our knowledge, grasping these research opportunities
seems quite consonant with holding basic therapeutic aims in interviewing family groups.

This second point had best be dealt with first. Otherwise,
doubts about the propriety of any deliberate mixing of research
into therapy might block free and unbiased considerations of the
research potentials of the family treatment situation. I see two
main reasons why research and therapy are compatible in work
with families. The first, to speak plainly, is that at present we
know so little about family therapy, both theoretically and practically, that whatever we essay in treatment is bound in large
measure to be only tentative and hopeful. We simply have not yet
developed a well-defined concept and technique of treatment with
certain known powers and limits, nor can this be approximated
by relying on principles taken from the practice of psychotherapy

Reprinted from FAMILY PROCESS, 1, No. 1:63-68 (March 1962).
Copyright, The Mental Research Institute of the Palo Alto Medical
Research Foundation and The Family Institute; reproduced by per-
mission.

with individual patients. Even if much more were known and agreed on in that field than is now the case, family therapy is too different from individual psychotherapy for any simple transfer of rules to be reliable. Thus, there is in this area no standard of "conservative treatment" from which exploratory operations would be a clear departure, properly requiring certain decisions and safeguards because extra risks would knowingly be run. Therefore, in practicing family treatment at present one has only the choice between being cautious in overall attitude--without having adequate guides to what appropriate caution specifically would be--or being more frankly exploratory.

But to be exploratory is not necessarily to be irresponsible, and indeed the reverse may be the case here, as is true in many critical human and medical situations. Probably the most important fact we do know about families in treatment--at any rate the families of schizophrenics, my primary focus here--is that they are exceedingly resistant to any change in their basic patterns of interaction. This is true in spite of their sad condition as families and as individual family members, and in spite of the particular or recurrent family upheavals or frantic behavior they may often exhibit. The real problem in therapy is not that too much is likely to occur, but too little. Therefore, not only do we need research to improve and extend our knowledge, but we need to explore, with these families, for means of promoting enough real change to give alternative forms of family behavior and interaction a chance to exist; almost any change might be an improvement on the schizophrenic systematization. This is not to deny all need for caution, or all need to avoid provoking any really destructive behavior, but we should not absorb the families' own attitudes that any real changes or freedom of action would lead to catastrophes. Their operational, if not verbal, position is "For God's sake don't rock the boat, "--or more accurately, "Don't change the way it's rocking now, "--but why should we adopt the premises of confused and troubled families that come to us as authorities for help?

We may now consider broadly what possibilities for exploratory research the family therapy arena offers by its very nature.

The nature and results of such a consideration necessarily depend considerably on one's basic premises and conceptions about the nature of "psychopathology" or "mental illness" and its understanding. In my view, these terms themselves reflect a traditional emphasis on the individual in psychiatry and psychology. This individual-oriented point of view in our efforts to understand and deal with strange or pathological behavior had led to much concern with childhood and the remote past, with particular dramatic events, with fantasies, and with concepts of internal psychic organization. These concerns, however, mainly involve reports and inferences rather than observable events; they are not very helpful in relating behavior and interpersonal transactions--either symptoms and interpersonal influences, or therapeutic changes and patient-therapist interchanges.

Accordingly, there has been a growing trend in psychiatry toward a more interpersonal approach, and family therapy represents a further development along this line. Family therapy, in fact, implies a point of view which may be explicitly stated here: That which is most important for our understanding and handling of pathological or symptomatic behavior is the nature of actual current interaction between real individuals, especially family members. Such behavior and communicative interaction can be observed and studied directly, and should be the primary focus of scientific attention, with the past, subjective experience, and concepts of internal psychic mechanisms left in a secondary place.

An important corollary of this point of view is that ordinary human communication and its influence must be examined and considered seriously, in terms adequate to its complexity and importance. In particular, communication always and necessarily involves interrelated multiple messages by every participant, which are at different levels of communication. This may be obvious, as when one message is conveyed by words and the other by tone, movement, or by symptomatic behavior, but it is equally true when the words of a verbal message carry two meanings, at different levels, in relation to different possible contexts of reference. For example, a wife may tell her husband, "I want you to dominate me." Specifically, she says he should be in charge of their relationship; but at another level, by directing how he should behave, she is proposing that she be in charge. Since such related multiple messages are at different levels, there cannot be identity, nor direct contradiction; yet the nature of the relationship between them, and thus the influences exerted and effects produced by them jointly, is open to wide variation. There may be similarity and reinforcement, as when a mother says "Come here, dear" to her child in a warm voice, or with a beckoning movement. Or there may be incongruence and conflicting influence in many ways. Mother may say "Come here, dear" in an angry voice; she may say "Come here, dear" and look off to the side; she may ignore the child until he turns his attention and interest elsewhere, and then say "Come here, dear." These are only a few suggestive examples of kinds of incongruence; there are many others, some playing a quite positive part in the richness and subtlety of human communication.

On this view, then, one first tries to relate confused or disturbed behavior to such conflicts among influential messages, and we note in practice that the husband whose wife says "I want you to dominate me" is likely to act confused, angry, or both, especially if he fails to notice and comment on this incongruency. In contrast, orthodox psychology and psychiatry has seemed based on an implicit model only slightly caricatured as "Messages are plain and simple, but some people receiving them are internally confused or divided." The difference in viewpoint is simple, and not absolute, but it makes a profound difference in one's whole approach to both individual and family problems.

Given the general viewpoint just outlined, it is clear that as an arena for research the family therapy situation fits its basic requirements as to the relevant data and conditions for collecting them. It is a situation in which individual communicative behavior, communicative reactions to this, and ultimately overall patterns of communication, influence, and interaction, are directly observable by the therapist. He does not have to rely only on reports of past events. Another way of viewing this is to point out that the therapist directly receives data on actual current family interaction that immediately includes more than one level of communication--that is, as a simple but basic example, he sees how the family members interact while also hearing what they say about their interaction. In particular, this situation, continuing over a period of time, provides opportunities for repeated observation, and for the detection of repetitive patterns of interaction typical of certain families or kinds of families, despite differences in context or detail, in a way difficult to match.

This special observation situation is particularly suited for investigations in three areas, which include some problems hard to investigate otherwise. First, in the course of family therapy it reasonably often occurs that the identified patient will start to behave in a noticeably more symptomatic way, briefly or for some while, than is usual in the sessions. Conceivably this might be avoidable if our therapeutic knowledge and skill were great enough, but as things stand, such behavioral changes do occur and provide an opportunity for direct investigation of any interpersonal causes and circumstances of schizophrenic behavior, especially if the preceding interaction is available on tape or film records. For example, in one family session a schizophrenic son, supported by the therapist, managed to say openly that he had meant a message to be critical of his mother. The father meanwhile kept denying that this was so, and the mother told the patient "I'll take all the hurt in the world if it will help you"; the patient then became confused, tearful, concretistic, paranoid, and claimed amnesia. Such incidents provide opportunities to investigate the contribution of all family members, and their system of interaction, to the occurrence of schizophrenic behavior, rather than focusing on the patient's "sickness" alone, or focusing on some one family member in a "Who is to blame?" fashion.

It is obvious that there are many specific problems connected with such inquiries--for example, how far back in the session record should the investigation start? And there are larger questions about the extent to which such occurrence of symptomatic behavior is similar or comparable to the schizophrenic break situation, or relevant for any ultimate etiology of schizophrenia. But any other inquiries into the etiology of schizophrenia or the psychotic break also involve similarly serious research problems. In particular, the lack of immediate data because the relevant events occurred in the past and were not directly observed by the investigator makes it seem appropriate first to investigate any observable onsets of symptomatic behavior as such, and to defer until later, when these are better understood, questions of possible wider or deeper relevance.

One can not only examine such symptomatic outbreaks as responses to preceding family interaction, but also, viewing such behavior as itself communicative, one can observe its consequences for succeeding family behavior and interaction. Thus, shortly after the criticism-parental reactions-symptomatic behavior sequence described above occurred, it was observable that the family had returned to its usual state, with mother mainly in charge, the father weakly platitudinous, and the son withdrawn.

Combining these two approaches to symptomatic behavior thus leads towards the development of a circular view of family behavior. This begins the second type of inquiry for which the family therapy situation is adapted, the investigation of family homeostasis; that is, how the patterns of interaction in such families--including the patient's schizophrenic behavior, but by no means limited to this--operate to maintain the existing family system.

This increasingly appears as the most important question in family therapy, or even for schizophrenia or psychopathology quite generally. Unless one is to fall back on some idea that people by fundamental nature are oriented toward disease, so that pathology is inherently self-sustaining, rather than "normality is normal, " the central issue is not the question of the original root causes of schizophrenia. It is not even the question of what sort of present family interaction leads to schizophrenic symptoms in one member. Instead, the central issue concerns the nature of the maintenance of family systems involving a case of schizophrenia. What in the family interaction makes for the fundamental stability and persistence of these family systems that is so striking in the face of the general dissatisfaction and unhappiness of the members, their stated desires for change, and often the best efforts of a therapist? Here is something worth investigating, which in the family therapy situation can be inquired into directly and repeatedly--even if still not readily understood.

The third area for investigation obviously consists in the opportunity to observe directly what immediate or longer-term results in family behavior are produced by any given moves on the part of the therapist. Many important specific problems relate closely to this: how are moves of therapists countered by family behavior serving to maintain homeostasis? What upsets may occur in other family members if one improves? This is a question that also raises very serious technical and ethical problems about the uncontrolled effects, on related individuals not seen, of changes made by individual treatment. What sort of therapeutic moves are really effective? Here again, important practical difficulties and basic questions about interpretation and significance of any observed results are involved in such investigation: perhaps a significant change is initiated by some therapeutic move, but one cannot see the change clearly until later, so the connection is not noticed or uncertain; or if an immediate reaction is observable, is this of any real or permanent significance? Such questions cannot be answered in general now. But similar ones--and others more difficult--also occur in any investigation into the nature or effects of therapy. In the family treatment situation, as regards therapeutic moves just as for the etiology and the maintenance of schizophrenia, at least we do have an arena where some pertinent direct observations can be made and followed up for some distance before it is necessary to plunge deeply into the realm of unobservables and into scientific-philosophical questions too broad to be resolved at present.